WORKING THE W[illegible]ESS

early leaders for wild lands

JOHN McCARTHY

Caxton Press

For Betty Jane McCarthy, who introduced all her sons to the wonders of nature.

Working the Wilderness
ISBN# 978-087004-625-4

First Edition

LC record available
Library of Congress Control Number:

Cover and book design by Jocelyn Robertson

Printed in the United States of America
CAXTON PRESS
Caldwell, Idaho
204827

WORKING THE WILDERNESS

early leaders for wild lands

for the Kids

JOHN McCARTHY

Caxton Press

Table of Contents

INTO THE WILDERNESS

Preface

People and land tell the American story.

WHEN AMERICAN SOCIETY and politics recognized the value of retaining unspoiled wilderness, a few old-timers remained on the land to show how to be in and how to treat the wild lands. The long first sentence of the Wilderness Act of 1964 concludes its purpose with, "to secure for the American people of present and future generations the benefits of an enduring resource of wilderness." A set of strong-willed and strong-backed individuals secured the benefits of wilderness on the ground and passed it on to future generations. Here is a story about some of those wilderness leaders.

The people who adapted the old ways to fit the new needs of official, designated wilderness have much to tell us today. Some of what can be applied from the past focuses on skills—with tools, animals, topography and weather. A lot of what we can carry forward from the elders is about attitudes. A spirit of self-reliance and independence runs through people who are linked to wilderness. A sense of humility in the face of the powers of nature is also timeless wisdom to pass on.

My experiences in the wilderness began in 1977 in the Selway-Bitterroot Wilderness of northern Idaho, working for the U.S. Forest Service. Stints in Hells Canyon of the Snake River and the Salmon River country followed, working on ranches and again for the Forest Service. Meeting some of the great old-timers in the 1970s and 1980s enriched my experiences and taught me much about these lands. Where there were gaps, to old-timers and the old ways, was also telling: of time marching on, of the ties to the past being frayed and severed. A primary motivation to recount stories of wilderness in transition came from seeing what was slipping away, being lost and often unrecognized in its passing.

The core of these stories started in interviews when I was a reporter in the 1980s at the *Lewiston Morning Tribune*. One summer, taking leave from the paper, I recorded extended interviews and explorations inside and at the edge of wilderness, back in the Selway-Bitterroot. A cassette tape recorder in my backpack became a different tool to carry. And through the years I've collected more stories about people and places.

The original intention was to describe all the work done in the wilderness by people of the U.S. Forest Service as the land managers and caretakers. Jobs that began in the days of the first forest rangers were reshaped to fit in the new ideas of wilderness, with backpack trail crews, the new wilderness rangers, a few fire lookouts, fire fighters, and then also fire managers, along with packers, river rangers and pilots, all carrying on in modified roles linked to the past.

My plan was to explain what wilderness workers did, mixing how-to with stories about who they were and what motivated them. And I wanted also to coax, rally, and inspire both the Forest Service and the public into action to preserve the critical roles of well-trained and well-supported workers in the wilderness. As the gaps of continuity to the old-timers began to show holes across the wilderness system, the lack of a skilled work force in the field threatened to unravel a system of land care. I wanted to alert people who cared about wilderness to a looming tragedy.

Thankfully, the tragedy did not fully come to pass. Intentional efforts to train and retain field staff in wilderness were initiated into the 1990s, although much more needed to be done and still needs to be done. Some new non-profit groups were formed as friends of wilderness, fielding volunteers and providing support to agencies. Studies of and teaching about wilderness expanded in universities across a recreational, social and ecological focus. Outdoor recreation equipment and marketing grew into big business, to outfit many different interests for an active segment of travelers.

At the same time, the full connections of a skilled, professional, field-based workforce to maintain the limited infrastructure on a landscape designed to show few signs of people diminished. The agency capacity and public involvement struggled over the years.

Into the 21st Century: Many conservation organizers and advocates like myself were too busy haggling over the unprotected lands, especially roadless forests, to make stewardship a priority. My capability to draw attention to the lands already in wilderness and to champion historical wilderness linkages was diverted into other issues. The wilderness worker stories I collected did not get shared. And some parts of the story slipped away.

Today we have great opportunities to renew alliances for wilderness and to bring in new people to be captivated by the wonders of the lands. Now, in recasting some of the stories I gathered, my primary intention is to celebrate teachers of old and engage the next students of wilderness.

After speaking in recent years at memorials for two of these wilderness heroes, people told me they wanted to know more about these protectors of the land. And so, here are their stories.

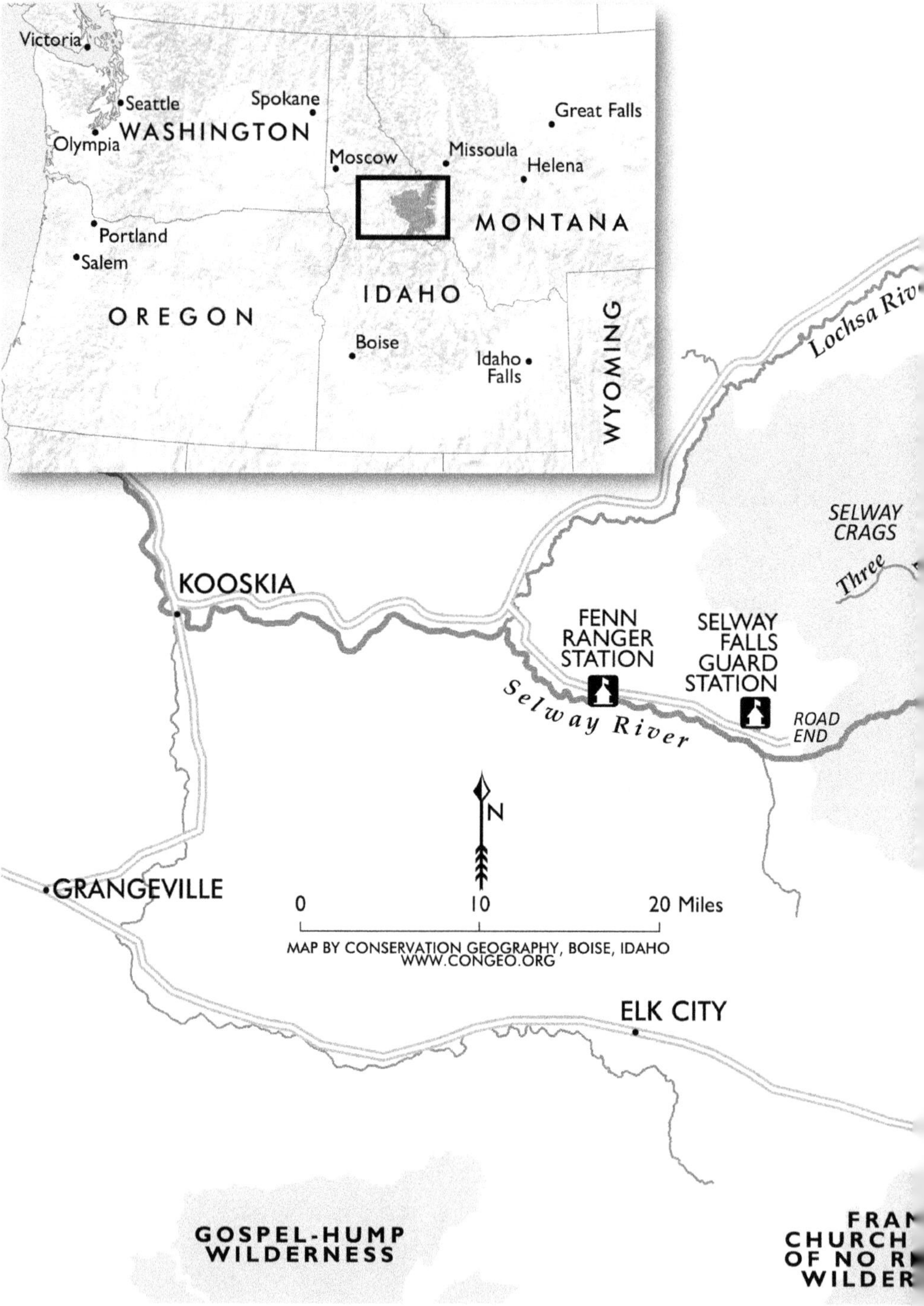
Victoria
Seattle
Spokane
Great Falls
Olympia
WASHINGTON
Moscow
Missoula
Helena
Portland
Salem
MONTANA
IDAHO
OREGON
Boise
Idaho Falls
WYOMING
Lochsa Riv
SELWAY CRAGS
Three
KOOSKIA
FENN RANGER STATION
SELWAY FALLS GUARD STATION
Selway River
ROAD END
N
GRANGEVILLE
0
10
20 Miles
MAP BY CONSERVATION GEOGRAPHY, BOISE, IDAHO
WWW.CONGEO.ORG
ELK CITY
GOSPEL-HUMP WILDERNESS
FRAN
CHURCH
OF NO R
WILDER

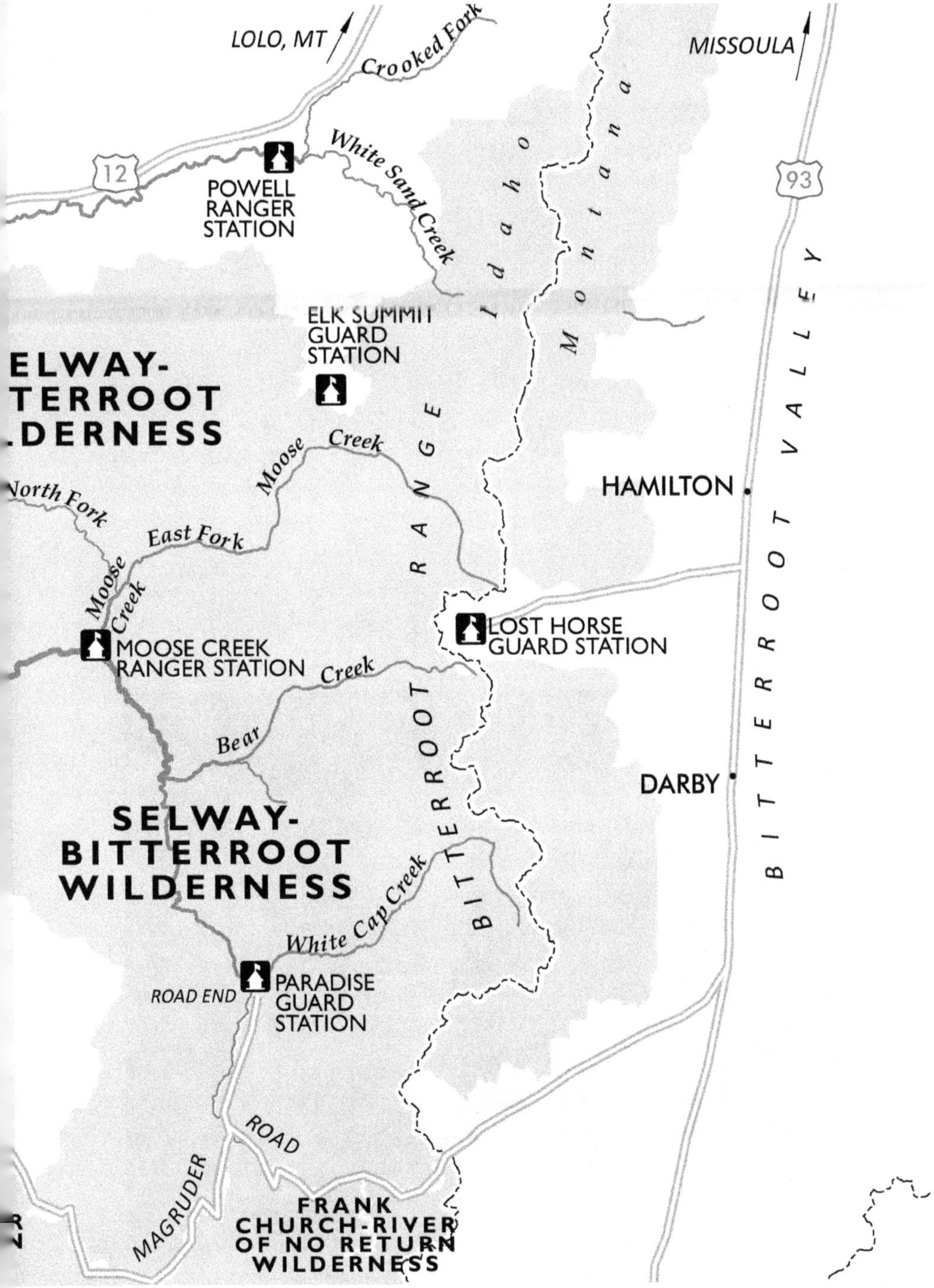

Conservation Geography

Emil and Penny Keck at Moose Creek Ranger Station, 1987 *John McCarthy*

END OF AN ERA

LAST GOODBYES CAN DRAG ON, but not when it's snowing. On a gray November morning, the day before Emil and Penny Keck left the Selway-Bitterroot Wilderness, snow descended in slow, fat flakes. The Kecks sat on their log cabin porch at the wilderness work place they called home for a combined 45 years between them. They looked much the same as always, in Sorrels and Bean boots, well-worn flannel, and wool shirts. Both wore stagged-off jeans, chopped at the boot tops to clear wet brush on the trail. Coatless and ignoring the chill of blowing snow, they tolerated one last photograph, half-looking away from the camera in bemusement and discomfort.

The remnants of the seasonal crew prepared to go out the 26-mile trail along the Selway River, ending their field year. The crew members stood and stomped their feet in the snow, made jokes about the ideal hiking weather, adjusted packs and readied to go.

The Kecks stayed behind for one final night in the middle of the wilderness of northern Idaho. Every other year when the crew pulled out before snow buried the Selway country, the couple settled in to take on winter construction and repair projects, often living out of tent camps. On November 23, 1987, after a quarter of a century tending the wilderness, the Kecks were forced to leave by their employer, the U.S. Forest Service. And so ended an era.

At a glance, nothing appeared much out of place. A couple of backpack frames, a shovel or two, and a half dozen Pulaskis and axes leaned against the wall of the porch. To the knowing eye, missing was the tangle of tools and equipment extending from the porch through the whole cabin. Gone were crosscut saws, winches, blocks and tackles, lengths of chain and cable, wooden and metal tool boxes, lanterns, hard hats, climbing gear, backpack frames, ropes, buckets, barrels, canteens, a first aid kit, and all manner of handle tools, from sledge hammers to log-rolling Peaveys. Inside, more camp gear, racks of running shoes and boots and odd, mismatched kitchen items were emptied from the cabin. Saddles, bridles, blankets, halters, and ropes were stored away in the tack shed again. Everything else was packed up and shipped to town.

The Kecks worked for the Forest Service, but they accumulated their own specialized tools to build bridges, to cut trails, to repair backcountry buildings. They grabbed the right tool from the porch to put on a mule or on their own backs, without going through government channels to get outfitted.

Emil and Penny Keck didn't file work plans or equipment requisitions—they went to work. Over time, government procedures required more and more planning and talking and meetings. Within the Forest Service, the can-do attitude of the early days in the organization was often supplanted by analysis, directed by accountants and desk-bound bureaucrats.

Emil said, "You can't really trust someone who can lay their hands flat on a table, with no bent fingers or any bumps from calluses—they can only do paperwork, not the work out here." When he stuck out an index finger to point with either hand it was difficult to track the line of direction, with his knuckles bent and swollen from years of grasping tools. Over time, it appeared many other people in the agency had gone soft and not only in their hands. In the end, it wasn't the rigors of physical labor, it was paperwork that finally caught up to the Kecks.

A four-page document, requiring "program management," was foisted on the Kecks the previous month. Their style of operations, crafted inside wilderness—based on skill, perseverance, and independence, refined over decades—was being undercut from requirements outside the wilderness. "Program management" meant paper tracking, not action on the ground. Instead of reordering their thinking and priorities, to write reports and attend more meetings, the Kecks packed up to leave.

Emil Keck with Sierra Club volunteers at Wahoo *Warren Q. Miller*

Emil and Penny, who mastered and taught the traditional skills from before the age of machines, prepared to leave a place that links Americans to our past. Through example, inspiration, blunt humor, finesse, and grit, they passed-on both their knowledge and ethics to many people who traveled through the wilderness. To be in wilderness defines self-sufficiency and individual ingenuity. The Kecks exemplified the epitome of wilderness values and value. All through the years, when they loaded mules with tools and camp gear, strapped on their own packs, and set out down the trail to another job site, people saw a couple who got things done in any weather and did it right.

The modern Forest Service did not account for people who, as Penny described it, "want to do the job the way we want to do it—not the way somebody else wants us to do it. We are the ones who are here, who know how to do the work and go out to do it. We ought to be able to make our own decisions, on our own time lines, just like we've always done."

Moose Creek Ranger Station was built on a bench between its namesake creek and the Selway River, in an opening cut-out of dense forest. The primary log buildings of the cookhouse, ranger cabin, fire cache, and warehouse were constructed in the 1920s and 1930s, from timbers felled by axe and crosscut saw, hauled by mule, scribed and notched by the early rangers. The ranger station was created as a work center, supply base, and training ground for fire and trail crews who traversed the wild lands. Tasks were basic and often backbreaking.

The landscape surrounding Moose Creek became classified as the Selway-Bitterroot Primitive Area in 1932, as an administrative category of the Forest Service to recognize its remote and unchanged nature. Three decades later, the Selway-Bitterroot Wilderness was one of the original nine wildernesses established by Congress in the Wilderness Act of 1964. The Selway-Bitterroot, with 1,338,000 acres in Idaho and Montana, was the largest wilderness declared at the time.

Emil and Penny Keck came to Moose Creek in the 1960s. Emil arrived one year before wilderness declaration and Penny arrived as a single woman, three years afterward. They worked to rebuild the trails, bridges, and structures that had suffered from years of neglect since World War II. They led trail crews and also worked in isolation as a two-person team. Their construction and maintenance work opened the way for visitors to see the wilderness, to experience the wilderness using a trail system maintained for adventurers, hunters, and anglers. For their efforts they received agency awards, local and national media attention, and appreciation from wilderness supporters. They did not get the chance to stay, on their terms, unimpeded by outside strictures. Before he left the ranger station after 25 years, Emil, then 75, said to the departing crew, "If they take people who have dedicated their lives to a place for a quarter of century, and can their asses—there's something wrong."

Penny, then 45, explained their situation as, "I don't think they like rabble-rousers anymore."

In her 20 years in the wilderness, Penny found satisfactions in physical labor and mental challenges, superseding any desires for comforts of the modern world. Before leaving her home, she said, "I feel a longing, a need for a connection with a piece of land—I enjoy feeling a connection with the motherlode. And you don't just tear that out of you without losing part of yourself."

Penny had not resigned herself to losing a connection to the wild land, where few people ever lived as she had, even as she prepared to go. She worried their imminent departure meant the wilderness would lose a rare skill-set and a continuity of purpose defined by protection of the land. Even facing personal loss, Penny acknowledged the big picture beyond their own lives. "No matter who comes and goes out here, the land will always sustain itself—as long as we human beings don't act all high and mighty to disturb it, to think we're in charge."

Emil, as always, was more blunt when he said, "The fucking land is going to last longer than these dumb assholes who are supposed to take care of it."

The crew members knew they had a long hike ahead, reaching the road beyond the wilderness boundary in the dark. Someone said, "Well, we'll be seeing you."

Emil replied, laughing, "Oh hell, yes, you'll be able to find me. Or I'll find you. You better look out wherever you are, because I might just sneak up behind you and you better see me first."

About four inches of slushy snow had accumulated. As the crew turned to head out, Emil said, "Hey, you be careful now."

Bruce Farling and Warren Q. Miller at Wahoo, 1980 *Richard Hildner*

Bruce Farling at Lost Horse Guard Station, 1984 *Warren Q. Miller*

GOING OUT

AFTER THE CREW MEMBERS said final goodbyes to the Kecks, they walked across the ranger station compound to the corrals to untie horses. Leading saddle and pack stock with light loads, they skirted the airstrip on a trail heading into the forest of pine and fir. They avoided the open airstrip with its broader views to not carve a line in the snowfall that could trip an aircraft on skis.

Within this wary band of four friends hiking toward the familiar Selway River trail walked a wilderness ranger, Bruce Farling, Warren Q. Miller, the Moose Creek station guard, Jim Torkelson, an assistant wilderness ranger, and myself, a newspaper reporter and ex-trail crew member who just turned 37.

I'd first come to the Selway country and Moose Creek ten years before, to work trails and to do repair and construction projects around the ranger stations. I traded Skil saws and nail guns from my house carpenter days for hand saws, hammers, and an axe. My first year began April 26, 1977, and ended December 20, flying out in a Cessna 206 on skis. My second year started in April but ended in October, when I took a job on a ranch in Hells Canyon. Emil Keck was my boss at Moose Creek and I learned more from him than anyone else, before or since. Life lessons from Emil went beyond how to use tools; he made me understand why it's important to believe in what you do and to care about your small place in the world.

We walked quick in the snow to get the blood flowing and warm up. Our last couple hours of the long day ahead would require reserves to power through in the dark and we paced ourselves steady yet sure to start. We turned to parallel the river on the main trail, pointing almost due west. High on the shoulder at the end of the airstrip, 150-feet above the river, we looked down at the Selway flowing dark green between white covered rocks with black, slick sides. A glimpse north, back up the long strip, showed heavy, low cloud cover, obscuring Bailey Mountain. Rushing riffles carried the comforting chatter of river song.

We knew the truth of what the Kecks said about the land outlasting any of us and the river always flowing. We also knew how fortunate we were to be some of the last people going out along the trail at the end of the year. Hunting season would close within the week. As the snow deepened and both soils and vegetation soaked up moisture, the wilderness would go quiet again without human interruption.

The challenge and reward of working in wilderness is to be out in all weather, early and late in the day and almost all year round. Long days and a long season means you get to see wonderful things, which rarely includes people, because the land is often empty of humans. Days in wilderness are heightened sensory journeys, sniffing pines and mud, hearing wind and creeks, seeing clouds and critters, blinking away rain and snow.

A pair of ravens taking flight from a bloated elk carcass in the river told us the story of a hunter's shot proving fatal too late to secure the quarry. Or, maybe it was a miscalculation of footing in the slippery, fast current leading to a broken leg. No one was wading out into the rush of water to look for a telltale bullet wound, to see if a hunter or harsh nature led to death. Either way, ravens tore at scraps between the ribs above the water.

A gray-feathered dipper bobbed on the river cobble, dunking into the cold water and popping up like a cork, skittering in flight and calling—*cheep, cheep, cheep*. Even in winter there was insect life, or maybe remains, to be found in the river.

Elk tracks in the snow indicated fresh movement from the morning, maybe before first light. Going down the trail in the wilderness is a threaded adventure, a recurring mystery story. The longer the trip and the time, the more to be seen, the more to be discovered, the more questions.

A side trail dropped down to the approach for the Tony Point Bridge. The popular camp site for river runners was now empty beneath a blanket of snow, with the boaters of summer in bright-colored kayaks and rafts long gone. The wooden tower and metal cable suspension bridge spanning the river was one of the pack bridges the Kecks maintained and then rebuilt when rot crept in. "Who is going to rebuild the bridges now?" I asked the other guys. "Who knows? It sure as hell isn't going to be the district ranger," replied Farling, who was finishing out his eighth year.

Farling was crisp. He'd already told the district ranger he was quitting. "I'm not burned out, I'm just burned," he said. A grim incident at the end of the previous year, with ten untagged deer carcasses and meat left to waste, never resulted in legal or administrative action. Farling had stepped-in to investigate a volatile situation with armed, agitated men who thought no one was looking. After months of submitting paperwork, he got no response from the upper Forest Service officials.

By the beginning of what proved to be his last season, he realized nothing would be done. "The people at the Regional Office and the Supervisor's Office are afraid they'll lose in court," Farling told me back at the ranger station. He'd followed procedures, collecting evidence, taking the cases to the district and Supervisors Office in Grangeville, and then pushing to the Regional Office in Missoula. "Here these guys are out in the wilderness breaking the law and they don't do a goddamned thing about it in town," he said.

After the situation simmered all year with no action, Farling threw in the towel. "Nobody gives a rats' ass about what's happening out on the ground," he summed it up.

"I don't really give a shit if our work is appreciated now," he continued. "I just hope we're appreciated in the future. Let's leave the option open for future generations to have something fairly pristine, where you can actually go to see someplace wild. So then maybe your kids, my kids if I ever have any, in 50 years will appreciate we left them the opportunity to enjoy a wilderness that's as wild as we had, instead of a

Selway River, 2015 *John McCarthy*

place that's less wild. But sometimes it's really hard to understand the whole picture when you spend your day picking up beer cans along the Selway River," Farling concluded with a laugh.

The Tony Point Bridge presented a glaring example of the contradictions between wild and settled. The wooden towers carry metal cables high above the river to hang decking eight feet wide for hikers and pack stock. The intricacy of metal and wood creates an engineering marvel many miles from a road. For all its intrusion, the bridge is beautiful and solid craftsmanship. It is also expensive, complicated, and a man-made contrivance to overcome the river current and cold water, especially in fall for hunters and in spring for hikers.

The Selway River was one of original designations in the Wild and Scenic Rivers Act of 1968, as a wild river—the most restrictive and pristine category. While bridges and trails are allowed, no roads can traverse wild river banks. The Selway was the only river included in both the original Wild and Scenic Rivers Act and the original Wilderness Act.

Selway River, 2015 *John McCarthy*

Two days before, Emil Keck was leading a young crew on reconstruction of the Selway Lodge Bridge, upstream about 14 miles from Moose Creek. One of six suspension bridges on the ranger district, the bridge next to the historic lodge of the same name spanned the Selway where the river was narrower than at Tony Point. It was the second time in more than 20 years Emil set out to rebuild the bridge towers. Emil told me earlier in the year he wouldn't be doing the dangerous, strenuous work of hoisting large timbers, except to help Penny.

Emil and Penny were a team. Once again, they planned to be in a tent camp for the winter and tear apart all the wooden pieces, reuse or replace metal parts, and replace the wooden towers, decking, running planks, and railings to reconnect the bridge. Then, before the busy summer season with visitors, they'd burn the old wood planks and timbers, restore the construction site to make it look like no one ever camped there. Unlike other years, they weren't planning to go it alone as a team of two; they had two additional young trainees, selected from the trail crews to learn the complexities of bridge work.

"We've just been following Emil around, trying to learn what we could," said Allison Zehner, then 28, who was in her fifth year as trail crew foreman at Moose Creek. "I wish we'd had more time, that was Penny's plan."

Their plans ended abruptly. Zehner flew to Moose Creek with Emil from Shearer Ranger Station two days before. Arthritis and age meant Emil wasn't hiking many miles any more. Even the one-mile distance from the bridge site to the small airstrip at Shearer was a painful chore for Emil. Knowing her season was over without Emil to lead the bridge crew, Zehner took a day to organize and store her gear at the ranger station. Then she walked out on the same day as us on the same trail but starting at 4 a.m. in the dark. She radioed that she made it to the road before 1 p.m., about nine hours to cover the 25 miles. Zehner never gave up on a job. She hiked out alone feeling defeated and cast off.

As we dropped down the slope to the next bridge, memories of better times came back to me. When traveling upstream along the river trail, the Moose Creek Bridge marked the return to home base. Steps quickened on the rise to the airstrip to swing legs in long full strides for the last stretch to the ranger station, where likely friends, food, a cool beer from the root cellar, a shower, and a softer bed awaited. Going downstream on the trail was always an adventure, carrying a full pack for another 10-day hitch. So many times, hundreds of times for work and for fun, I'd crossed the bridge and looked toward the point where Moose Creek meets the Selway. At the confluence, where a tongue of sandy beach lies exposed all year except at high water in late spring, I could imagine young Nez Perce Indians camped, fishing for fat cutthroat trout or hunting for white tail deer. The meeting of the waters surged in strength.

The trail runs close alongside the river, just above the granite gray streambank rocks. The froth at the confluence overcame the chance for talking and there wasn't much to say anyway. Melting snow dripped from over-hanging branches as we kept a steady pace. The river burble churned sounds and our thoughts, sometimes chattering, sometimes swirling, sometimes eddied out and stuck.

The river trail ran at an even grade, to allow smooth, strong steps for making good time. It's a mainline trail, always well maintained, wide with few rock obstructions. Hunters traverse the canyon bottom in the fall, when the trail sees the majority of its use for the year, to then seek side trails along creeks and ridges in their search for elk. Much of the work of wilderness in the northern Rocky Mountains is geared toward hunters, to keep travel routes functional and to provide guidance in a harsh environment.

Although we led riding stock from the wilderness rangers' fall field program, we kept walking to stay warm. We kept at a pace to match the speed of any horse. We tied slickers behind the saddle seats and hoped we wouldn't have to use them. We all wore lace boots. We wore wool. Synthetic fleece had been invented but our wool was not worn out. The dusky smell of wet lanolin was familiar and comforting reassurance against the cold.

Following the contour of the bend leading back to Jake Creek, Miller, the tall, often quiet man in a thick green shirt, pointed to a secret spot. One time, coming up river after a late start, when darkness and the night's chill settled in, he found shelter on a little flat just big enough to scrunch up his 6-foot-4 frame. He curled up in a sleeping bag under two big red fir trees, snug for the night with his dog. He made the last few miles to the ranger station in the morning at first light. "It wasn't too bad a spot, we were pretty cozy," he recalled.

When he did some talking, Miller had more stories than any of us, having been in the Selway country the longest. He was finishing his 17th season, 15 as wilderness ranger and the last two as station guard at Moose Creek. While his long legs served him well as a wilderness ranger, handling logistics at the ranger station tapped his precise skills in fabrication and organization. He'd always stayed late in the year and was one of the last of the seasonal crew to leave the wilderness. As the snow turned to a drizzle and threatened hard rain, Miller said, "You know, next year I might bag this wilderness hiking bullshit and just fly out."

Around another bend, Miller pointed to fog wisps floating up the canyon walls, drifting across the copper brown of dried bracken ferns and the dense dark green forest and said, "Isn't that just neat."

The first of many climbs took us up into open ponderosa pine forest, to side hill through widely spaced, old yellow-bellied pines. Grasses, tan and tawny, and a few shrubs, spread low underneath trees of all stages and sizes—some giants, some dead snags, some young and vigorous. The river quieted high up on the slope and the views along the canyon revealed its rocky sinews.

On the next drop to the river, we came to a three and a half foot thick Douglas fir log, cut at the butt end. Another year at season end Miller hiked out with Dick Kuhl, when they were both wilderness rangers, and they found the log in the early afternoon, straddling the trail. Kuhl carried a crosscut saw, as always, and the log took three cuts to slice two rounds to then roll each piece clear from the trail, after pulling the saw for hours. They got to the cabin at Selway Falls well after midnight. "That was one bugger of a tree," Miller said.

"Was the saw sharp?" I asked, tossing him an easy but loaded question.

"Of course it was sharp, Kuhl always took care of his saw," Miller replied, leaving it unsaid that the saw was sharp because he filed it. Miller was known to be the most accomplished crosscut saw filer in any wilderness and he didn't have to remind us—his saws were always sharp.

We hoped to avoid any major trail cutting in the lingering slush or any other obstacles that could slow us down. But things happen out in wilderness.

Wilderness rangers are eyes and ears on the ground. Equal parts protectors of wilderness character and leaders for visitors, they work for the land and for people. In the vast Selway-Bitterroot, they strived to put land protection first. Before any understanding took root that wild character needed and deserved protection, before the Wilderness Act, the backcountry was wide open for campers, mostly hunters, to operate on their own, with little oversight. The land showed intrusions from humans—some careless, some with the care of skilled woodsman adapting to the environment.

Now, wilderness rangers operated on the front line to discover and diminish the intrusions. They inform, they educate, they set an example. They often confront the contradictions of wilderness in the modern age where people are part of the landscape but sometimes leave scars on the land or just leave trash.

On the flats past Pinchot Creek we came to a camp where a sleek, young black horse stomped bare ground into a saucer shape at the base of the ponderosa pine it was tied to. Farling and Miller looked at each other as if to say, "Here we go again." Farling turned to the fourth and youngest member of our group, Torkelson, the assistant wilderness ranger in training, and said, "Tork, why don't you see if you can talk some sense into these guys."

Torkelson arrived at Moose Creek with six years' experience underground as an electrician in the Coeur d'Alene silver mining district near his home in Wallace, Idaho. When he got out to see the light of day in the wilderness on trail crew, he blossomed like a glacier lily. Then in his fourth season at Moose Creek, he'd spent the summer leading a trail reroute project at high elevation beyond Upper Bear Lake, where the air was thin and the lodgepole thick.

A guy in his early 30s, not much older than Torkelson, dressed in heavy wool and a slouch cowboy hat, rose from the campfire as we came up. He looked concerned about a crew descending on him with telltale signs of being Forest Service. Tork called out, "Hey, I remember you from last month up at Rhoda Creek. Did you get your elk?" An auspicious beginning to a conversation.

After the exchange of a classic hunter success story mixing skill, adversity and rotten weather, the guy followed our eyes to the offending horse and said, "Yeah, I know that young shit churned up some dirt, but I think he was a proud-cut gelding and he gets real nervous tied up with the other stock on a high line. Nothing but trouble in camp but he's strong on the trail and I'm working on him. Don't worry, I'll backfill in after him." He concluded with what may be the standard dodge, "Most of the damage was already done before we got here."

Torkelson suggested he tie the young horse with one of the seniors from his pack string, keeping them far apart to get him used to the idea of being on a line between two trees. Tork said throwing some extra dirt on the cavity under the tree and spreading the horse manure was a good idea. As we moved out from camp, Tork called out, "Hope to see you next year." The guy nodded and waved in agreement, saying, "You bet."

Given the guys' awareness of a problem and the willingness to do something about it, Torkelson found the encounter to be reasonably encouraging. No one knew how a gelding could be proud-cut. The next camp was a lot weirder.

We'd swung into the saddle to alternate riding with our miles of hiking until the cold creeped down the spine and we'd be on foot again. Near Ballinger Creek a young, roly-poly guy came up to us from a set of sagging tents and asked if we've seen three horses. They'd last been seen that morning heading downstream toward Selway Falls. How we might have seen them when we were coming from up the river was not clear, but the rangers professed concern. When Farling inquired if they'd be able to pack out without the three head of stock, the young guy sagged like the tents and said they'd be able to pack their gear on the remaining stock but would have to hike out, not ride. We sat comfortably on four horses.

Torkelson reminded the guy it wasn't very far to the road end, not much more than eight miles. They could make two trips if needed. The idea didn't seem to have much appeal. We wished him well.

We rode up to one of his campmates, a guy in his 60s, many days unshaven, with dirt caked pants, a revolver on his hip, an orange vest and a thick wool cap, sitting on a bolt of wood before a smoldering fire. A six-foot log stuck out from the coals and he held a joint of meat, likely an elk foreleg, carving steaks with a six-inch blade. An empty whiskey bottle and a bunch of beer cans were tossed to the side of the fire, maybe from the morning, maybe from the night before. The grizzled old guy in the cap looked up and said, "You hungry?" I expected a toothless grin, but he didn't smile.

We told him there were too many miles to go on the trail and we begged off from a barbecue. We departed with a quick exhortation to be sure to leave a clean camp. Going around the side of their last slumping tent we all spied used toilet paper strewn around, the all-too common, careless white flowers. Farling speculated, "They probably crap in a hole inside the tent, toss some dirt on it, and throw the shit paper outside under the flap."

I asked if it was possible there could be a woman in camp who went out at night to pee? The idea was hooted down. "Are you kidding me, there's a woman out here with those scum-balls? I don't think so," Farling summed up his assessment.

It was the end of the season, no one had the heart to go back to find out what their sanitation protocol was. Torkelson said he'd clean it up in the spring if need be. Farling said, "Be sure to carry a shovel." We kept riding.

To divert our dismay at crude campers, I asked Miller what happened with Bearwallow Lookout? The low elevation lookout, at 5,259 feet, hadn't been staffed since the early 1970s and rarely was used by trail or fire crews. I'd joined a heavy construction trail crew at the end of the 1977 season, where they'd worked for months on a major re-route up Sixty-two Ridge, and we'd go up the tower for spectacular orange sky, sunset viewing. Built in 1956, it used a 41-foot tower to put the standard 14-by-14-foot lookout cabin above the trees. It was a stroke of genius to get the cabin up in the air for a full view of the canyon and be able to look down into the river. I marveled that some construction wizard determined 41 feet would be just right.

Bearwallow Lookout, 1987 *Warren Q. Miller*

The building and tower were essentially kit construction common at the time, known as an L4 tower, with limited historic value. A couple of planks on the tower ladder had broken and there was potential risk to people or, even worse, risk of a potential lawsuit from any accidents. "Once the ranger and the SO (Supervisors Office) decided there was no unique historic values and there was no practical fire purpose anymore, they decided it should come down," Miller said.

When Penny Keck prepared to carry out destruction, Miller and Allison Zehner volunteered to help. "We knew it would be damn near impossible for her to do it alone," he said. With no extra funding for the project, they told her they'd go up the ridge on their days off.

They took out the windows, the Osborne fire finder used to line up smoke sightings on a map, kitchen gear, wood stove, stove pipe, and other metal. It took two days to strip the building and load a pack string to take out the materials that came in the same way, 40 years before. They torched it off at the end of the day when the wind was low and the dew point high. They took pictures of the tower in full flames at night, with orange and yellow blazing from the supports as a half-moon arced over the roof line.

A couple of weeks later Miller was at his bank and noticed an extra $200 in his account. A little later Zehner asked him if he had any unexplained money at his bank? A teller acknowledged deposit checks came in from one Penny Keck. They knew she'd never take the money back, so Miller and Zehner used it to buy a solar panel and battery to power a light at the Selway Falls guard station and limit fossil fuel use. No one filed paperwork.

Past Ballinger the trail climbs again into the pine with a wide tread and easy turns. At a level contour, clear of roots and rocks, the stretch of trail is a good place to ride, where the horses can see ahead and don't dodge rubble. The snow melted off the south facing slope. The horses knew we were not going somewhere to make camp. We were going out. And our horses were still fresh, making long, smooth strides.

By the time we got to Cupboard Creek, I'd dismounted and started to pull ahead from the rest of the crew. They'd stopped to retie some of the stocks' packs, indicating again that horses can slow down a fast hiker. Light almost faded by Renshaw Creek, with its long beach, a flat pool and a pair of giant pine and cedar trees leaning over the water.

Hiking in the dark presents an extrasensory experience. As you feel with your feet, you see with your feet. On parts of a trail with few obstacles of jutting rocks and roots, like along much of the Selway, you feel forward with low steps to follow the bends in the route. The river trail is well brushed out, unlike a lot of the wet Selway country, and the corridor is open. Creek crossings with only logs for foot travel and no bridges present the greatest challenge at night. But the lower Selway has span bridges across most of the creeks, designed to speed stock travel along the mainline trail.

Animals are well-attuned to darkness and many are most active at night. One spine-tingling experience is to encounter an elk on the trail at night and hear it crashing off into the brush without ever seeing it. Sometimes I'd worry about an animal charging toward me, but they never seem to get disoriented as they flee. Flashlights illuminate specific points but distract from the big picture and isolate vision, and thoughts, into a single line.

It was long after dark on the starless night when I got to the road end and waited for the guys to catch up, pacing to keep warm. Torkelson lagged behind to bag up some garbage, and so we three walked along the road leading the stock for the last mile to the guard station. Farling and Miller said they almost had a bad wreck earlier when they stopped to munch some cheese and the lead horse stepped over its line connected to the mule behind. The mule reared back and the line tightened up between the horses' legs, starting a kicking dance. Farling jumped clear and came back in with a knife to cut the pigging lead, the light line connecting the animals. Miller moved quicker to spring the mules' halter clip and avert a knife fight or worse.

At the end, as we walked side-by-side with stock trailing behind, we

Bearwallow Lookout burns, 1987 *Warren Q. Miller*

talked about our reflections from the last hours. Miller and Farling wondered if they'd been manipulated by the district ranger in his rush to purge the Kecks, playing unwitting roles. They saw Emil and Penny as anchors for the field program. They also saw the pair bucked authority and made trouble for chair pushing bureaucrats. They didn't see how the Kecks could fit in with the Forest Service anymore. They were uncertain about their own futures. They knew Moose Creek Ranger District would never be the same without the oldest and most knowledgeable people in the wilderness.

When we got to Selway Falls cabin, the mule Charlie Brown lurched on top of the loading dock, dragging the next mule in line, Lady, up with him. Falling on his side, smashing his pack and flailing his feet, the mule went berserk for no apparent reason. Both Miller and Farling waded in to grab the lead rope and drag him back to his feet. "Jesus, leave it to an end of the season stock wreck to almost get you killed," Farling said.

Patti Stigers, a new wilderness ranger who was finishing her first season already warmed the cabin with a fire and a lasagna from the oven. After a welcomed bite and a beer, I drove off downriver in the dark heading for home on the Palouse Prairie, to see the kids and to get back to my regular job at the newspaper, with a story to tell.

Builders of Bridges

Emil and Penny Keck

WHEN EMIL KECK went into the wilderness in 1963, he went to work. He didn't go to tame the land, like the pioneers and the homesteaders. He didn't go to extract riches, like miners and loggers. He went into the backcountry to keep the land wild and free, to provide all people the opportunity to experience their heritage of unfenced and untamed land.

Keck landed at the Moose Creek Ranger Station airstrip in the middle of the Selway River country of Idaho on August 23, 1963. At age 50, he took over the job of the fire control officer, the FCO. The previous FCO, Paul Wisdom, 36, was killed two weeks before by an aerial retardant drop on Elk Ridge.

Fifteen fires burned in the 550,000-acre Moose Creek Ranger District in the heat of summer. No rain was predicted and no FCO was on hand to lead the firefighting team.

Keck was in the woods logging at the time, near Moscow, Idaho, after quitting a different job as a U.S. Forest Service fire boss the year before. In the middle of the last fire season, he'd disagreed with the district ranger at neighboring Fenn Ranger Station about staying at the station to write reports and work the radio instead of being in the field taking action, leading the crews. He left without ceremony when the fires cooled but before the season closed out. He went back to his other line of regular woods work—cutting, skidding, and hauling logs. Word of the FCO fatality reached him soon after it occurred the next year and he called the Nez Perce National Forest supervisor, John Milodragovich, at his office in Grangeville.

"I hear you lost the FCO at Moose Creek," Keck said to Milodragovich. "I hate like hell to crawl over my bones from last year but if you need somebody to take over, I'll come up."

Milodragovich did need someone to take charge of a ranger district in flames, to protect the forest and the people fighting the fires. He knew Keck earned his reputation as a hard worker and leader the previous year and he took him up on his offer. Keck flew out of Grangeville to Moose Creek the next day and he didn't leave many times for the next 24 years.

Keck landed at the airstrip at Moose Creek, 25 miles from the closest road and a good 100 miles from Grangeville. "It was nothing but a dust strip when I came in here," Keck said later. Even facing a fire bust, he knew there was more to be done than just put out fires. Turning the bare dirt, he saw under foot into green grass would take many years and he was already thinking about how to spread seed nurtured by horse manure to regain growth and keep dirt from washing into the creek.

After being introduced to District Ranger John Hossack. Keck recalled his orders, "Before I got from the plane to the office it was all lined-out for what I was going to be doing—and it wasn't paperwork. The ranger said, 'I want you out with the crews on the fire line calling the shots. The only time I want to see you is to see your back when you leave the station heading down the trail.'"

Keck took him at his word. "I wanted to smell the pitch on my hands. I didn't want any ink on my hands. I like to be out in the sticks. I like to be out with the crews and work."

In 1963, wilderness did not have the official sanction of the United States people and their governing Congress. It wasn't wilderness with a capital W, until the presidential signature of Lyndon B. Johnson to the Wilderness Act, on September 3, 1964. The legislation established a national commitment for some public lands forever to be wilderness. As important as the Wilderness Act was, and remains today, it would be an empty gesture on paper without strong and strong-willed people who strive to see these lands remain wild, not cut up and sold off to special interests, and not neglected or abused.

Wilderness exists in America because people haven't been able to or seen fit to tame it—yet. Wilderness is what remains from our uncivilized and pre-industrial landscape, land without settlers, developers or hawkers. Wilderness is what is left of the raw, unfenced, rugged, ungentle, and empty wild land that was America. The Wilderness Act calls these lands untrammeled, meaning unrestricted, and shall remain unplowed, unpaved, and not stomped to dust. The Wilderness Act declares these lands are where people visit but do not remain. Even the Native Americans, here in the Selway with the Nez Perce Indians or Nee-Me-Poo, would only travel through these lands to hunt and fish and only overwinter in a few places in small groups on occasional years.

The mass of forest and mountains stretching beyond the eye's grasp where Emil Keck landed is now known as the Selway-Bitterroot Wilderness. The fast, cold, clean, dark green Selway River gives more than half the surrounding country its name. The river funnels the wooded drainages of ponderosa pine, grand fir, and Douglas fir toward the Clearwater, the Snake, and on to the Columbia rivers. The Selway River itself is drinkable, swimmable, fishable, floatable, and just beautiful to watch swirl and ripple.

The Bitterroot Mountains on the east side of the wilderness rise-up from a broad glacial valley of the same name, thrust upward from 4,000 feet at valley bottom to more than 10,000 feet at the highest peaks. Long canyons carved by creeks flow from the mountains, with exposed rock walls running east and west from the crest. This mountain crest forms a divide for the irregular line of the Montana-Idaho state border. From the mountain tops the views stretch out to grasses and gray-green sagebrush in the Bitterroot Valley, on to the blue-green Sapphire Mountains to the east and back westward into the emerald depths of the tree covered Selway country.

Even at 1.3 million acres, as the largest wilderness designated by the Wilderness Act in 1964, the Selway-Bitterroot Wilderness could have been much bigger. Many people continue to hope adjoining lands in Meadow Creek on the west side, the land around Elk Summit to the north, and the upper North Fork Clearwater country of Mallard-Larkins and the Great Burn will be added to designated Wilderness.

The Selway-Bitterroot remains as it always was—the same jumble of wooded ridges, steep creek bottoms and bare granite peaks—because of the Wilderness Act and because of Emil Keck, and a couple handfuls of other people who established how people interacted with wilderness. Even in these wildest lands people can and do leave a mark. Keeping signs of people from becoming scars on the land became the charge of the few early people who were protecting wilderness, not taking from it.

Declaration of land as wilderness kept the loggers at bay. Loggers moved elsewhere, sometimes deep into the backcountry in states like Idaho and Montana, punching in roads to reach over the next hill to get to the uncut old-growth timber. Wilderness was spared the saw and left to nature's forces.

Keck, himself a gyppo, or independent logger, for many years, might have remained aligned with the rough and tumble crews building roads, felling and hauling timber. Instead, he stayed in the wilderness after the fire season to be in a wild land and to keep it wild and open for visitors.

Keck didn't formulate policy for Forest Service wilderness management. He didn't write management plans or visitor use criteria. He left almost no paper trail. Keck's work was done with his hands and feet on the real trails, the pack bridges, the lookout towers, and the Forest Service cabins scattered around the Selway wilderness.

All those man-made constructions made the land accessible for visitors and established a staging ground for the Forest Service operations. The trails and work stations originated to gain access to fight fire. As FCO, it became Keck's charge to maintain it. By the time he took over, the purpose extended to a greater emphasis on visitor access.

Keck brought skills honed from decades of being in forests, laboring with tools and crews in camps where self-sufficiency and safety were requirements for survival. He not only possessed expertise, he brought attitude and determination, starting with a classic Keck motto: "You've got to walk this world with practical feet."

As the oldest of nine children, born October 20, 1912, work came early to Emil Keck. His first seven years were spent in a windswept soddy on the North Dakota prairie, near the town of Washburn in the middle of the state. He told of winters when the low house would be drifted over, indistinguishable from the sweep of snow. As blizzards blew away all visibility, a lifeline rope from the house led to chores in the barn. Young Emil would carry a bucket of melted snow in one hand, hold the rope with his other hand, and trudge with head down from the house to the barn to water the farm animals. Learning to clear and stay on a trail was life or death.

When he was seven, the family moved to a stump farm cut out the forest at Startup, Washington, east of Puget Sound. His parents were of German descent but both sides of the family already tried to make new lives as homesteaders in the Russian Ukraine. His mother and father met in Russia and soon afterwards struck out for America to find better land. Cutting out a farm from the tall Washington woods proved to be their last stop.

Keck described his father as, "hard-headed, my God he was hard-headed." He remembered his father's philosophy as simple. "If he raised a kid, he raised him to work and that was it." Both a commitment to labor and hard-headedness rubbed off on the first-born Keck in the new land.

Keck grew up at the tail end of the crosscut saw era of the great Pacific Northwest woods. Men balanced on spring boards driven into the butt end of tree trunks, to swing long-handled axes, chopping out slices of trees in preparation for the whistling teeth of eight-foot felling saws. He lived at the end of the time Darius Kinsey immortalized with photographs of men lying full length in the notch of a giant Douglas fir before they toppled the wooden spires. Now these behemoth trees are almost all gone, along with the lumberjacks who took them down. He rode the bus to Saltan High School, after walking to grade school in Startup. By high school, Keck earned good money cutting cord wood with a crosscut, for $1.50 a cord cut in four-foot lengths or $2.50 bucked up and split, delivered in the family farm truck. The forest suited him better than the farm, with its constricted spaces and animals always in need. He'd cut a cord of wood, four feet by four feet and eight feet long, in a day. After graduation he spent a year at Bellingham Normal School and another year at the University of Washington in Seattle, intending to be a football and baseball coach. Impatient from confinement in classrooms, before his third year of studies he struck out for the logging camps on the west side of the Cascade Mountains. Knocking over towering old growth trees and setting chokers for log skidders fit his interest in finding challenges in the forest.

Barely 20 years-old, his capacity to lead and motivate people moved him from being a sawyer to a crew boss for white pine blister rust control in the forests of northern Idaho in the early 1930s. Blister rust originated in Asia but came to the United States at the turn of the 20th Century via infected tree seedlings from Europe. The fungus devastated the tall, straight, clear white pines, the climax species in the north and the most valuable tree of Idaho. Control efforts concentrated on limbing infected trees and cutting the alternate hosts of berries low on the ground. Control efforts were labor intensive with mounds of material piled high to be put to the torch. The efforts of crews climbing trees to trim limbs, bending over to cut brush, and burning the cuttings, while living out at remote camps, all proved futile for the North American trees with no genetic resistance. The struggle to contain the spread of the destructive spores proved impossible, resulting in more tall trees dying and rotting.

Keck then began fighting fires at age 22 in 1935 with the Forest Service starting at the logging town of Plains in northwest Montana. Digging fire line to circle a fire and stop it's spread, cutting trees and brush to flatten fuels, tapped his physical strengths. Directing crews tapped his leadership capacities.

Fielding crews was part of the challenge and he later told the story of a big blow-up on the Henry's Fork, when he joined the District Ranger on a mission in town to draft a cook by the name of Jimmy Carter. Carter was found in the morning at Jig's Bar, drinking a pitcher of beer. Seeing the ranger, Carter blurted out, "You aren't getting me to cook on no goddamned fire so get the hell out of here," Keck recalled.

"Well, the ranger sat down and said real nice, 'Oh no, Jimmy, we just came in for a sip before we headed back up. OK if we join you?' And he ordered up a bottle of the best whiskey. He started pouring drinks and I don't know what the hell he did with his, poured on the sawdust or something, but he stayed steady and sober, while pretty quick old Jimmy Carter got smashed flatter than piss on a plate.

"We rolled him up in a manty, threw him in the back of the truck and drove 80 miles back up the dirt roads to get to the fire. Carter was a mess and didn't wake up until the next day. The ranger saved him a snort to get him going and pretty soon he started cooking breakfast. He worked between two banks of stoves to cook for 250 men, going through 25-pound sacks of flour for pancakes and then cutting up a quarter of beef, bags of potatoes, and onions to make stew.

"When we got the fire knocked down and were down to a crew of 40 men we were eating lemon meringue pie and every-fucking-thing else. He was a dirty son of a bitch but he was the best fire cook I've ever seen."

In 1938, Keck moved to Orofino, Idaho, to run slash disposal crews and to fight fire for two adjacent timber protection associations. Timber association fire crews in those days did all the work of maintaining a forest. Clearing trails and roads, repairing and constructing buildings, cruising timber, burning slash, and maintaining fire equipment were all parts of the job. When fires struck on either private lands or state lands, the fire crews mobilized to the front lines.

Being a fire warden for a small do-it-all outfit meant being with crews out in the forest. A photograph of the timber association's summer

Emil Keck on Bear Creek Bridge tower, 1969 *Richard I. Walker*

tour with state and local officials in the early 1940s, with 51 men lined up, most in clean white shirts and chino pants, shows Keck as one of four guys in suspenders and high boots —the ones who were ready to go out into the woods.

Timber ownership was not all in corporate hands in those days, with 65 to 70 landowners in a forest association block covering almost 500,000 acres. Working with many different people provided advantages for a young man. "The thing of it is, you learn to get along with people and you learn to build up credibility," Keck said.

In his stories he'd remember creek locations for slash disposal, the seller of a D6 Caterpillar tractor—Junior Church of Lewiston—the names and locations of fires in specific years and most of the names of the 54 people he supervised one year on his fire crew.

Keck left the North Fork of the Clearwater country to move up to the Palouse Prairie and take up logging on his own, working out of Moscow. His wife, Bernice, settled into keeping a home with three children in schools and Emil up early in the morning to head out for the forests. He went broke a couple times, then worked for other loggers to put together a stake to start again on his own with a couple saws, a truck, and a skidder.

His son, Arlen, joined him in the small gyppo logging crew after his high school graduation. Arlen learned the trade and learned from their missteps, to stay in the business as Keck Logging, out of Potlatch, Idaho, for more than 40 years, employing his own family and many other people in the community.

Loggers are often accused of cut and run, tearing up soils and vegetation in the rush to move big logs. Keck looked with concern at the effects of man and machines on the land, taking care to minimize his impact. "I always piled the slash, cut the stumps short and put brush or straw if there was any on the skid roads so it wouldn't wash out in the spring," he said.

With the kids grown and after some 16 years in the settled farm and forest lands around Moscow, firefighting and land protection out in the backcountry again took Keck away from timber harvesting. The fire boss job out of Fenn Ranger Station on the Selway Ranger District promised a new opportunity to use his skills in the forest and with crews. But after the one season and his abrupt departure, Keck expected to go back to logging and stay a logger. Then the wilder lands of the upper Selway, in the Moose Creek Ranger District, in what was then still called the Selway-Bitterroot Primitive Area, proved alluring for another adventure. In his first year back in the wildest forest, soon after he got control of the rash of fires, Keck determined to stay on at Moose Creek.

In those days a college education wasn't a standard requirement for permanent Forest Service employment. "If you could work harder and longer than anybody else, you could be top dog. So you became crew boss. And Emil could work the legs off anybody," said Dick Kuhl, a long-time wilderness ranger at Moose Creek.

With the three children out of school and on their own, Emil and Bernice stayed out at Moose Creek far beyond the nearest road. Although Bernice spent more time in town than Emil, they adapted to the isolated life far from comforts and close to nature. Simple living with wood stoves for heat, cooking, and water centered in their home base at a board and batten cabin at the edge of the ranger station.

Their settled routine was thrown into upheaval when Bernice was diagnosed with cancer and given six months to live. "By grit and guts she made it three and a half years," Emil recalled. But the cancer did not recede. In early 1967, they flew directly from Moose Creek to Seattle for another round of treatments, hoping to stem the creep, but she died in the hospital and Emil returned to Moose Creek on his own.

There were plenty of tasks to keep him occupied, but he admitted to being a little too friendly with Jim Beam whiskey in the time of emptiness. As summer came he regained his focus by being out in the forest for long hours, day after day, moving rock, cutting wood, digging dirt.

"When I first came up to this area you couldn't crawl through the goddamned woods or find your way around this country according to the maps," Keck said of the early days. "They had trails that were classified annual, biannual, and tri-annual maintenance and you couldn't tell the difference between them. Some trails were supposed to be worked every three years but that was a bunch of bullshit, they weren't worked at all and it was all growing back to brush. Slowly, with a lot of help from the fire crews when they weren't out on a fire, slowly, we started to get the trails back in shape."

The main trail system began along the Selway in 1907, when a crew that included 22 University of Idaho students started up the river from Selway Falls. Digging along the slope to craft a bench for tread and blasting rock through cliffs, the going was slow. The difficulty of travel during the massive burns of 1910, when fire crews could not reach many fires before the scale overwhelmed them, gave impetus for a major push for trail expansion.

Many trails were chopped out during the firefighting boom years of the 1920s and 1930s. A few trails followed ridges on routes trod by the Nez Perce Indians, but their primary tribal trails to the buffalo country of Montana ran farther north or south of the Selway country. Other trails originated from game tracks, without a lot of attention to slope and gradient on the secondary routes. Speed came first, and trails were often laid-out as the shortest distance between two points.

Trails have one purpose: to provide access for people to get around the backcountry. Trail work had two purposes: first, to open trails up for people, mostly firefighters and hunters in the early days, to get around safe and quick; and second, to keep trails from being silt channels running dirt into the creeks. In the vast landscape, the first job of clearing trails was often as far as it got.

"You'd get in a tunnel from a half mile past Bearwallow Lookout and you'd stay in a tunnel all the way up to High Springs when you couldn't hardly see the sky," Keck remembered. "The gullies were four and five feet deep and they went on mile after mile."

The Selway country gets upwards of 60 inches of rain a year on the ridges and 30 to 40 inches down along the canyon. Most of the moisture accumulates as snow, with spring runoff sending channels of waters down any steep trails. Trail erosion not only hinders travel for people and stock, it also runs dirt into pristine creeks.

Major debris flows and other erosive events are periodic in the Rocky Mountains, especially after fires remove vegetation and root structures. Scouring washes triggered by rain-cells from thunderheads carry vegetative matter, soils and rocks of all sizes. The deposit plumes from debris flows can clog and even dam creek flows when it reaches the canyon bottoms.

These events are singular and are flushed out by subsequent high flow years. In comparison, trails, similar to roads but to a much lesser extent, can provide chronic and persistent erosion sources to the creeks. Whenever it rains, erosion carries fine soils from poorly drained trails and roads. Fish and other aquatic organisms evolved to contend with pulses of vegetation and soils from debris flows, not with dirt fines choking spawning beds after steady infusions of mineral soils from exposed trails and roads.

The original Forest Service trails included excellent rock and wood craft, still seen today as intricate rock riprap walls undergirding trails and corduroy wood planking set above bogs. Early trails also included some steep climbs out of canyons without much planning or design. But the overall system hadn't seen major repairs since World War II. The road building boom of the post-war logging era captured the attention of engineers and crews, along with the biggest budgets. As haul roads and jammer roads extended far into parts of the backcountry to take out timber, trails languished in the wildest lands.

Keck did a full district trail inventory in late 1960s and into the early 1970s. To combat erosion and replace substandard trails, Keck flagged-in re-routes, plotted by eye at 5 to 6 percent average gradients , as an ideal goal, and up to 10 percent at the steepest when necessary. Wooden water bars cut from the forest and pinned across the trail at a 45-degree angle diverted flows from the trail channels. Elevated turnpikes with dirt pathways and corduroy puncheons with wooden slat surfaces were rebuilt or constructed to get trails out of bogs and wet meadows.

All the labor required being close to the ground. "If I had a raw piece of land, I'd get a raw son of a bitch to run it," Keck explained. "You can't run a place like this with a computer. All you have to do is put a silt counter down in the river at the edge of the district and see how much dirt passes through. That will tell you how well the trail system is being run."

Keck began rebuilding bridges in 1966, when he led a three-man crew to replace the timbers at Selway Lodge Bridge. At the same time another crew of nine, plus a camp cook, began replacing the wooden

Bear Creek Bridge camp, 1969 *Richard I. Walker*

parts of the Tony Point Bridge, downslope about a mile from Moose Creek Ranger Station. The big crew stayed at the ranger station. Keck camped on site with his small crew. When darkness fell on those long winter nights, Keck would often set up the next day's tasks by lantern—to maximize use of daylight hours—as his crew got some rest.

Both bridges were finished at about the same time in the spring. Keck's crew was not only competitive to keep pace with the other crew, they were more efficient. By running a small crew, his operation cost less than half of the big crew, even though the big crew could easily be resupplied at the ranger station.

A few years later, the Tony Point tower caps started to show rot. Wooden shims at the top cracked, opening the way for moisture and ants to eat into the caps. The tower strength was threatened and would only get worse.

At the time of initial reconstruction, Forest Service administrators said they had one of the best engineers in the business and he assured them the shim blocks would shore up the cables. Keck argued against the wooden blocks at the time but he was sent to Selway Lodge instead of putting in metal caps as he proposed. The outcome did not surprise him. He said, "I didn't give a shit if that son of a bitch engineer built the pearly gates in heaven, I told them it wasn't going to work and it didn't."

He replaced the towers the second time, using pressure-treated material flown in by helicopter. Again, he led a crew of three, including a smokejumper from Grangeville, Mike Uszuko, and a new person who would be on his crew for the rest of his life, Penny Kummrow.

The stories of how Emil and Penny got together in the Selway wilderness are as wild as the land they knew so well as home. Some stories are likely true.

Emil always said he could work with anyone who was willing pick up a tool and do his damnedest to get a job done. His willingness was limited to the male pronoun and did not extend to females.

Emil didn't get involved in the hiring process for summer crews and 1967 was no different. "I've got the philosophy that I'll work with anybody and I don't give a damn who they hire," he explained. On the list of new fire lookouts that year was one P.J. Kummrow. Emil didn't think anything about it, until he learned the P stood for Penny and Kummrow was a woman.

On his next trip to town, before the summer season started, Keck stomped into the district ranger's office and said, "now just a minute, I have some pride in what I do and working with gunny bags is not one of the things I do. A lot of guys I've been out in the woods with, if they found out I was going to be taking some girl out on the job—they'd look at me the way a bull looks at a bastard calf."

Penny Kummrow was already hired and ready for the wilderness. Raised on a small farm in Oregon, 15 miles from Portland, she began helping her father in the fields at 8 years-old, driving a tractor, discing and plowing. "I didn't like the house, I stayed out of the house whenever I could," Penny recalled.

Penny was an athlete who played basketball and field hockey in high school and at Portland State University, at a time when girls' sports barely drew relatives as spectators and news coverage was limited at best to box scores. Her shyness in talking to people or meeting people masked a different confidence and strength, both physical and mental.

She was the first woman hired in the post-war years at Moose Creek to be in the field as a fire lookout. Emil, as the fire control officer, was her boss. "From the start, I objected to her being hired," he said. "When did you ever figure a woman to be out in the goddamned sticks?"

Emil met Penny at the Grangeville airstrip at the beginning of the season. "Here was this quiet girl, skinny as a rail, waiting for me, standing there with a big grin, all happy to be going out into the wilderness."

Some 50-pound bags of oats for pack stock were stored in the airplane hangar and had been torn open by rats. Emil tossed Penny a burlap bag and barked at her to help pick up the spillage. Penny took the sack and rolled the edge back to make it easier to load. One simple act made a lasting impression. "Here was somebody who had at least scooped grain on a goddamned farm," Emil recalled. "And then she told me, 'this is old stuff to me because I helped my dad feed hogs on the farm.' So I knew then I had something else on my hands besides an ordinary chick. Plus, she didn't wear lipstick or nothing like that."

Penny was going through university at a slow pace, in her sixth year with maybe another year to go, taking semesters off to make money. She determined being a fire lookout would allow her to bank most of her earnings. She applied at many places and received offers from forests in Oregon, Montana, and Idaho. "I chose Moose Creek because it looked the most interesting, even though I didn't even know what wilderness was," she said.

Emil said he treated Penny the same as he would any other new employee. Anyone else would recognize the obvious truth, because she was a woman he rode her harder than other lookouts. He'd show up unannounced early in the morning, having walked up from Moose Creek to her tower at Shissler Peak before breakfast. Dishes might be sitting in a pan unwashed from the night before and Emil would pitch in with a harangue about her lack of housekeeping. Soon, Penny had his number. "Look," she'd say, "did you see the Pulaski leaning against railing on your way up here? I out-sloped the trail tread going down to the spring when I got water this morning. Should I be out doing trail work or washing dishes? The dishes aren't going anywhere and can wait."

Push back from a new, young employee didn't strike Emil as defiance, he viewed it as confidence from commitment. He always appreciated head strong individuals who spoke their mind and charted their path. As he began to see her dedication to be an astute fire spotter, while doing all the other tasks around the lookout tower, even if at her own schedule, Emil allowed maybe a woman could be as good a fire lookout as a man.

Penny shot back, "A woman can do anything as good as a man." Emil scoffed in disbelief and declared a fit man could outrun a woman any day. Penny came back, "I'll prove you wrong, mister, and do you want to make a small bet on it to make it interesting?" And Emil fired back, "How about a 100 bucks?" Penny was a poor college student and $100 was real money. "You bet, I'll bet you," she said.

Emil challenged her to a race from the lookout to the ranger station, about five miles down from 5,375 feet to 2,454 feet. They both started training, mornings and evenings. Penny did regular runs to the spring, hauling water back for the weight resistance. "I had so much water at the lookout I didn't know what to do with it," she said.

Emil took a different tact, training cross-country. "I knew she was faster than me. Oh Jesus, she was quick," Emil said. "But I was tougher and I'd just smash through the brush in a straight line, cutting off a mile from the trail."

Penny and Emil Keck at Moose Creek Ranger Station *Dolly Koons Carroll*

Legend has it on race day that Penny jogged across the airstrip to Moose Creek at a steady pace to finish far ahead, while Emil still crashed through the woods on the other side of the creek. But both Emil and Penny said it never happened. They both admitted to taking some tumbles in training, with Penny banged up on a fall onto a rock. They agreed to call it a draw before one of them really got hurt. Many years later, Emil admitted, "If I had made it uphill I might have had a chance. But down the hill? She would have beat me by a half mile, so I was damned glad we called it off."

In addition to relishing in the wide views of endless forested mountains from her lookout, Penny, then only 25, began to see other things beyond the blunt, brash, and confrontational exterior of Emil, a widower then 55. In talking with Penny, Emil's quick-witted irreverence and infectious peels of laughter recaptured some of his joy in life. Here was a man who could rail against the Forest Service in blasphemous terms as he walked along a trail and then go quiet to marvel at fluffy goslings swimming behind their mother. He found reasons to visit Shissler, even after the race was called off. Slowly, his time of solitude, constant activity, and shadows of gloom began to lift like the fog banks on the canyon sides.

"Before the summer was out things had changed," Penny recalled. "It wasn't an antagonistic thing any longer. He was looking at me differently and I was looking at him differently. You know he was still my boss. I've often joked, I couldn't get along with him as the boss—so I married him."

At the top of Goat Mountain, a couple miles from Shissler off the Jake Creek trail, they sealed their fates. Emil said to Penny, "I've got a different opinion of you than I had before. And if you're going to be back in this country anyway, if it's all right with you, I'll just propose marriage to you, right now, period."

Penny replied, "If I did marry you, and I'm not saying I will, if you think you can put me in one of those hovels down at the ranger station at Moose Creek and you go out in this beautiful land and leave me baking cookies at home—get lost buster. I'm not having that kind of a proposal."

"Oh no," Emil said, "all I wanted you to know is that the wife of the fire control officer on the Moose Creek District is a tough son of a bitching assignment. But beyond that, I don't have anything in mind that you would be left at the ranger station."

When Emil retold the story, he ended by saying, "Jesus Christ, she wasn't going to have any of that shit being left behind. And that's why I wanted her to be with me."

They married in October and became the team of Emil and Penny Keck. For the next 20 years they explored the wilderness together. Their base camp at Moose Creek, used mostly to store equipment, was a board shack and later a converted small, stout, log warehouse. They'd take off down the trail with a headlamp in the early morning hours, hiking with backpacks and leading a couple of loaded mules. In summer and fall they ran the trail crews, lined out fire crews, advised smokejumpers, toured the district to chart out trail projects, and did heavy trail maintenance with dynamite and rock drills. In winter and spring, they often camped at bridge sites, where uninterrupted months were spent alone as a couple, moving timbers and rock.

Winter is wet in the Selway country. Snow begins to pile up at higher elevations in October and creeps down into the canyons by November. Along the river bottom, snow lays heavy and storms blow in from the coast often warming to rain, often followed by another chill, leaving slush and crusted ice. Low clouds shroud the sun and trap dampness. The north facing slopes are a saturated, moss and tree-covered sponge. On rare clear days the sun peers into the canyons for a few hours of direct light at mid-day.

The Kecks spent two long winters and parts of two summers camped at their first major bridge reconstruction job spanning Bear Creek. As a large tributary originating up on the divide of the Bitterroots along the Montana border, Bear Creek was one of the first major stream crossings to be bridged along the Selway. The bridge linked the middle and upper Selway River trail, leading to Shearer Guard Station about two miles away and on to Paradise Guard Station another 14 miles upstream at the edge of the wilderness. The Bear Creek trail climbed almost 25 miles to the Montana state line before it dropped another couple miles over to Lost Horse Guard Station.

Across these distances, in this network of trails, visitors to the wilderness—both private individuals and Forest Service personnel—wanted to move safely without a lot of obstacles. The main Selway trail runs along the north side of the river for most of the canyon and requires no crossings to travel its length until upstream from Bear Creek. The major tributaries of Three Links Creek, Moose Creek, and Bear Creek come from the north and flush high during peak run-off, becoming impassible to horse or hiker in May and June, some years into July. By July the canyon would be heating up for a couple months and lightning strikes would regularly spark the first fires. To provide fire control access for people and stock requires crossing the major side creeks. Forest Service rangers were writing proposals for pack bridges as early as 1919, to get across Moose Creek and on over Bear Creek.

The first Bear Creek bridge was completed in 1927. It was rebuilt during World War II with Italian prisoners of war, who camped in wall tents. A captive bridge crew didn't have any choice on how long they stayed or how they did the job. In modern times, similar big crews in the wilderness proved cumbersome, expensive, and required a lot of logistical coordination to resupply and to move people in and out.

Starting in 1969, the Kecks set up their simple camp for two people and began to tear out the old wooden towers at Bear Creek. Emil's experience in moving timbers when logging was adapted to use pulleys, winches, and cables to deconstruct and reconstruct the bridge. The suspension cables were kept aloft with temporary gin poles secured by guy lines as they dropped the towers. They proceeded to replace all the wood parts and refurbish the metal cables and bolts, removing rust, and replacing anything weakened.

As a team of two, Emil and Penny provided their own basic support for supplies and kept their own pace. "Back in the wilderness, what's the big speed?" Emil said. "When the snow is piling down and you're sitting right there in camp, what's going to happen? We'd just wait it out, maybe cook a pot of beans, or cut some more wood. A big crew wouldn't want to stop and miss any pay. And then when it was the crews' four days off, they'd be waiting for an air-flight to get out. Penny and I, we just camped and lived right there. We didn't give a shit about going to town."

"We worked straight through, every day, from daylight until dark," Emil said. "We'd get up early in the morning to train, to run up the trail about three miles to shape up when we could. And we weren't so goddamned careful about getting back down by 8 o'clock because, fuck 'em, the government got the best of it anyway. What were we shaping up to do? To do the work. We'd read at night by lantern and that's it. We went to bed."

They'd slog back on snowshoes to the ranger station at Moose Creek a few times every winter, to shovel snow off the roofs. And they'd travel the length of the river to shovel off all the bridges to lighten loads, removing stress. During the winter Frank Hill of Grangeville Air Service would airdrop mail in plastic pouches about once a month for their only contact with people other than the radio.

"Sometimes the ranger would get smart," Emil said. "He'd send in something that needed an answer by, say, March 3. Who gives a fuck? We weren't going out to town, maybe for two or three months. What did we care? One time we were out there from Christmas to May before we saw the first human being. God, it was neat though, because nobody bothered you. And you knew what your job was and that was it."

In the fire control boom times of the 1920s and 1930s, small cabins with storage sheds and barns were built along the Selway for crews to work trails and fight fires. Both Bear Creek and Three Links had simple ranger stations at the confluence with the river. As the airstrip at Moose

Penny and Emil Keck skid bridge timber at Goat Creek, 1973 *Richard I. Walker*

Creek became the main supply route, the big ranger station became the storage center. The scattered cabins were burnt to the ground, moved or left to collapse rather than be maintained. When Emil and Penny worked at both the Three Links and Bear Creek bridge sites they set up a base camp to stay for months that led to years of living out of a 10 by 20-foot canvas wall tent, same as the first construction camps in the backcountry.

A scrap of plywood nailed to a stump made a table. Bolts of wood set on end made stools. Canvas mantees laid over the dirt formed a floor. Panniers and old powder boxes became shelves. Most food was freeze-dried, dry goods or canned, all cooked on a wood stove. A hole dug under the floor and lined with boughs created a root cellar with a plywood cap. The cool storage not only kept cans from freezing, they layered in fruits, cabbages and root vegetables. A Coleman lantern hung from the ridgepole for light on the long winter nights and early mornings. They packed in a metal bed frame to Three Links to sleep off the ground above the rattlesnakes. A crackly transistor radio to listen to baseball games with # 9 wire running up into the trees for an antenna offered the only thing in the tent that resembled a luxury and the only connection with the outside world.

The key to winter camp comfort was a Kimble wood stove, deceptive in its simplicity. The bottomless stove sat directly on sand with a space cut out from the canvas floor. A double layer of sheet plastic formed an envelope that encircled both the floor and over the peak of the roof. The plastic shed rain and slicked off snow from the roof, while trapping the warmth of the stove.

As Emil explained, the box stove warmed the sand floor "so pretty quick it gets so goddamned hot you could walk around barefoot when it's 40 below if you wanted to. That sure was a nice way to live. So when anyone felt sorry for us staying in a goddamn winter camp, we're warm as can be."

After two winters to rebuild Bear Creek, the Kecks moved operations upstream to Goat Creek. They reconfigured the girder span to reduce it from 72 feet to 32 feet by shortening the wooden approach ramps, which instead required hauling in tons of dirt and rock by wheelbarrow. They felled three big Douglas firs up the creek for the girders the year before reconstruction, leaving the logs propped above the ground to cure and dry out. When the creek iced up in the winter, they slid the logs with cables and winches along the slick rocks without causing damage to soils or the wood.

A stretch of weather at 20 below zero slowed them down as Penny was laying out timbers to hew level and flat, requiring bare hands to work the axe with precision and to do the set up. She'd work for about an hour before retreating into the tent to warm up and regain movement in her fingers after clenched on the tool handle. Slow but sure, she made headway on the logs, not waiting for warmer temperatures. Every night at those winter bridge sites, they'd put away or secure all tools and equipment so it couldn't be lost under snow before the morning came. Every step required planning and careful execution.

After they completed reconstruction of the next bridge at Ditch Creek, they moved downstream from the upper Selway to take on their largest and most complicated bridge project—Three Links. The task was so extensive it dragged beyond winter into the hot summer months over two years. To avoid the baking sun of the canyon in the heat of summer days, they staged tasks on the shaded south side of the river under trees and extended their hours. Active hours began before early light and stretched into the long evenings, to take advantage of whatever coolness came with the day. In winter, they struggled to find enough daylight hours and they wore headlamps mornings and evenings to extend the short work days.

According to Emil, bridge building was easy. "The problem with working on a bridge is, once you've got it figured out then you've got it built—it just takes time and a lot of sweat. It's like the guy that invented the wheel. As soon as he thought of it, he had it made."

When explaining how to tear off the decking or how to cut out the needle beams, Emil would slip in lines like, "There's nothing to it," or

"That's no big deal." Packing out the heavy, dirt encrusted planks was the hard part, he said. "Then you've got 'er made." Flipping upright the 252-foot cross-hatched railing at Three Links in one piece was a trick, but "You just take the come-along and crowd it, taking it up a notch each step along the line and pulling it up real slow and steady all along the length."

Bridge reconstruction sites were a spider-web of cables leading up to the gin poles that carry the weight of the main cables when the towers were yanked out. The two main cables looping across the river never came down and a catwalk spanned the needle beams to cross the river throughout the operation.

The old railings were torn off first. Then the running planks were ripped up but not the needle beam decking. Each needle beam, which carried the decking between the main cables, was taken out in successive order from one side to the other. A hole was cut through the decking to grab each beam with a winch from a skyline, just off center. The drop cables coming down from the main cables were freed at the end of each 8 by 8-inch beam. The beam was pushed vertical with a peavey and pulled out the decking hole. The process was reversed to put in and to cinch up the new needle beams to the drop cables. Once all 17 needle beams were replaced at Three Links, then the old decking was stripped off with crow bars and a three-foot catwalk was set.

The towers were flipped into place in one piece with sets of cables to both lift and to guide each side. Emil and Penny had pre-assembled the Three Links towers at a pole yard in Oregon, using stout, westside Douglas fir logs. The seven tower components—cap, joist, sill, two upright posts, and two triangulated support beams on each side—were cut to specifications and pre-drilled for connecting bolts. The towers were then dismantled to be pressure-treated with wood preservative, to get deep penetration even into the drill holes.

The dissembled pieces were trucked to the road end beyond Selway Falls and flown by helicopter to the bridge site. After drying out, some pieces twisted a little out of alignment when reassembled. Emil and

Penny were forced to get underneath the giant timbers and beat on the foundation bolts to line up to the pier sills, while providing downward pressure through a winch.

Otherwise, as Emil said, it was all just sweat and labor. On the winches, volatile Emil and cool Penny were both the picture of calm, calling instructions and calculations back and forth in easy voices heard over the rushing river. "Take it up two notches," Emil would say. Penny would take in cable a couple clicks on the 20-inch-diameter wheel of a hand winch. "I'll go the same, now you take it up three clicks." And timbers 50-feet long, 18-inches at the top and wider than man's circled arms at the bottom, were hoisted into vertical position in increments of centimeters.

The 252-foot span suspension bridge the Kecks rebuilt at Three Links was at the time the largest bridge in Forest Service wilderness system, and therefore the largest human creation in all the wilderness. What most interested Emil wasn't the complexities of replacing each wooden stick or the physical challenges of hanging on ropes above the river to do it. What he pointed to with pride was no telltale marks of a construction site remained where he and Penny camped and labored for more than two years, burning piles of spent timbers and planks. The bridge constructed for horses and hikers linked the main trail on the north to the south side of the river, across a major structure of metal and milled timbers imposed on the landscape. Now, the construction site can only be detected in a grown-over ledge about 10 feet wide, where their tent provided sparse shelter as they labored through the seasons.

Emil's directive was simple: "Fill in your holes. Leave only the bridge, or the cleared trail—not signs you've been there."

Emil and Penny's work at Three Links saved the Forest Service more than $100,000 in 1970s dollars, or four times as much today with inflation, compared to hiring a big construction crew. They worked alone, as a team of two, and did everything themselves.

With Emil and Penny camped along the river during the summer, traveling trail crews could always count on a meal when they stopped by. A two burner, white gas Coleman stove fired their summer kitchen and they cranked it up for visitors. At first light before temperatures climbed, plates would be piled high with Krusteaz pancakes smothered in syrup and with fried freeze-dried sausages, shockingly close to real food. The all-consuming bridge job kept them off the trail for most of two years and people went to see them in the canyon when planning was needed. Afterwards, crews would take off along the trail, heading for higher ground, stuffed with carbs and ears ringing from instructions, advice, and stories.

Ten girder span bridges across the smaller creeks around the district were also rebuilt over time by the Kecks. In addition to the Goat Creek reconfiguration, they redesigned other bridges to lessen the scale and the visual impact of the horizontal intrusions.

At Cupboard Creek, Penny altered the standard design of planks across double girders, to sandwich two, half log planks between two, half log stringers, all 26-inches in diameter. One log was cut in half with a chain saw, for accuracy not ease, —to form the walking platform, while another halved log became the two stringers to both carry the weight and act as railings. The four pieces of cedar are bolted together in three places with one-inch threaded stock six feet long. The span of 24 feet rests on a cement abutment on one side, obscured by dirt except when seen from underneath, and on a wooden sill for the other side. The butt ends of the logs were used as guides, laid on the ground in an open 'V' shape to direct stock into the narrow bridge. They again skidded the logs in the winter, to protect vegetation and to slick the slide. Almost 50 years after the construction, the cedar bridge remains sound.

On bridge sites the Kecks used chain saws and a small gas generator to power drills. At Three Links the railing alone needed more than 1,000 holes for bolts and the needle beams all required 8-inch holes at both ends. The issues were efficiency and accuracy, not speed and ease. Only a fool would question their administrative exemption to the ban on motors in wilderness.

Penny also developed a couple fords for pack stock to eliminate bridges, and instead she set foot logs for hikers. She always looked for ways to get rid of bridges and believed both people and stock could be challenged with wet feet or finding a down log for a crossing. "Let people find their own way or let them get wet," she'd said.

Emil told the story of one time when they did get wet and almost swept away. They were headed up North Moose Creek early one spring to check out the season's potential trail project locations. The trail stays on the north side of the creek until the confluence with Rhoda Creek. Only an axe hewn abutment on the east side remains of old bridge after it washed out in a flood and never replaced. When the Kecks arrived at the crossing the creek ran high and fast, with no bridge.

Emil went first, wading out into current rushing to his waist, taking low steps to keep his feet skimming across the rocks and using a stout staff he'd cut as a brace. At the far side he dropped his pack and jumped around with arms swinging to keep circulation going and power some warmth. Penny pushed out into the creek with the same measured movements but slipped on the slick, smooth rocks half way across. Before she could brace herself, "she went down quick and got spun around by the current, going all the way underwater with her damn pack on," Emil recalled.

Thrashing through the current without a pack, Emil charged out to meet Penny as she surfaced, still hanging on to her pack. He helped muscle her upright as the flow churned and pushed them downstream. Arms locked together they slogged out onto the rocky bank.

"When we got to the shore the first thing she says is, 'Is the radio OK?'" Emil recalled. "I wasn't thinking about the goddamned radio, I was thinking about her going underwater and gone." They pulled out an axe to make a big fire to dry out and make hot tea.

As the Kecks redesigned bridges to shrink the structure's footprints, they also eliminated some of the buildings scattered through the new wilderness. The Wilderness Act specified no condemnation or emi-

Bill Holman, Penny and Emil Keck at Bear Creek Bridge, 1969 *Richard I. Walker*

nent domain proceedings were permitted. No private lands within or adjacent to wilderness could be forced to sell out to be included in the new land designation. But isolated lands from the homestead era in private inholdings could be acquired from willing sellers, with structures to be torn down or burned. Trapper cabins and hunting camps without title to lands were also targeted for removal.

These far-flung physical examples of human perseverance and ingenuity embodied the pioneer experience. But the structures conflicted with the law that declared wilderness retain "its primeval character and influence, without permanent improvements or human habitation." On lands in private hands, surrounded by wilderness, people operated dude ranches or kept personal lodges. On the lands already in or acquired for public hands, signs of human habitation and their history were to be eliminated.

One of the early intentional obliterations terminated the famed Moose Creek Ranches. North of Moose Creek Ranger Station about five miles, it was constructed at the site of the original Forest Service outpost dating to 1909. After the ranger station moved to the confluence with the Selway River in 1921, more than 700 acres were eventually secured into private hands on the flats between North Moose and East Moose creeks. The ponderosa pine forest was cut out, with stumps pulled and rocks piled, for an airstrip and pastures. A hunting and fishing lodge was constructed for an advertised "One of a Kind Sportsman's Paradise," with more than a dozen cabins, barns, and support buildings. Fishing on both East and North Moose could be excellent and the forests on Bailey Mountain and beyond held herds of elk to challenge hunters from all over the country.

The heyday for the remote lodge proved short lived. In the 1960s, the distance to reach any major airport and the interests in shorter, more accessible vacations by car slowed guests. In June 1966, the final owner sold it to the Forest Service for $209,000. After flying out the things with monetary value, in late August, Emil Keck led a crew to torch the log buildings and then bury the remains.

The stunning blaze and the controversy in the destructive action resulted in photographs taken by a passing-by pilot and a story on the front page of the Idaho County Free Press in Grangeville titled, "Moose Creek Ranch Now a Memory; Torch Is Set." Keck didn't give it much pause. "In wilderness there are no buildings allowed, except the ranger station and the lookouts we need—that's it," he said.

Ten years later, in the broad meadow where there'd been structures, fences and an airstrip, instead a herd of elk always fanned out from a natural mineral lick in the mornings and evenings. Later yet, when the wolves came back the elk no longer stood around unperturbed in the open, although prominent tracks showed regular, more furtive movements. Later again, the trees seen head high in the 1970s became a 40-foot tall forest reclaiming the bench, with only a few piles of rock standing out to mark the human endeavors. Except for three grave stones tucked into the trees, from a group of ill fated trappers led by Eddie A. Wheeler, who all died of scurvy in 1895, the meadow showed little sign of people ever being there.

Keck sometimes applied a wilderness standard in ways unanticipated by framers of the law. In the late 1960s, outfitter Jack Liecking kept a large cast iron cook stove at his extensive tent camp about a quarter mile up Cub Creek beyond its confluence with Bear Creek. Keck told him he had to get it out of the wilderness and to pack the stove out to the Shearer airstrip to fly it out if he wanted to keep it. Otherwise, Keck would get rid of it himself. After no action for several seasons, Keck lit several sticks of dynamite under the stove and blew it up.

Once Liecking saw the condition of his stove, Keck planned to bury the pieces. When Liecking saw the stove remains, he was spitting mad. He rode downstream to the ranger station at Moose Creek, about 17 miles, where he confronted Keck and the ranger. After a spirited discussion, including threats of a lawsuit, Keck got his personal check book and wrote out a check for $200, handing it to Liecking and saying, "Stick it where the sun doesn't shine." The check was never cashed.

Less than a mile upstream from the ranger station, on the west side of Moose Creek, sat the Seminole Ranch, re-named by owner Robert "Bud" Griffith after he purchased it in 1964. The old homestead was serviced by a suspension foot bridge and a utility cart strung from another cable across the creek. A 1950s vintage Willys Jeep was parked on the east side of the creek, to drive up to the ranger station to shuttle supplies and people flown into the airstrip. Griffith was a concrete contractor in California and took on a number of construction projects, ferrying material with the Jeep and a trailer. Although he got along well with Keck, after the designation of Wilderness he was told the Jeep could no longer be used on Forest Service land. In 1966, all motor vehicles were officially banned from the Wilderness, according to newly drafted regulations. Griffith did not comply.

One warm August day at the ranch when Griffith entertained a group of friends from California, and the creek ran low, Keck took action. The creek runs 75-foot wide in spring but drops to less than half its high water girth in late summer. Emil waited until late afternoon when the group congregated on the porch overlooking the creek with cold beverages in hand and he fired up the Jeep.

Grinding gears and hopping over rocks, Keck drove the Jeep through the creek, with pools still deep enough to run into the cab. Lurching up the steep embankment onto the grass in front of the porch, with water running through the floorboards and the engine hissing, he slammed on the brakes, jumped out and said. "Here's your goddamned Jeep; if you bring it back to our side I'll blow it up clean to hell with dynamite. Now, give me a whiskey."

Amidst the appalled stares from his guests, Griffith buckled with laughter and poured his friend a drink. They all enjoyed the evening light.

As the assistant ranger at the time, Richard I. Walker later said, "Emil would use any excuse to do anything he could to reduce damage to the resource. And there was a very short connection between perception and activity with Emil. Some other people do a lot of pondering."

To further diminish the scale of human intrusion, the Kecks also moved trail maintenance away from large crews supported by pack stock, which require large camps with meadows for grazing. Low impact backpack crews with two people were pioneered in the Selway as more light weight packs, sleeping bags, and tents were manufactured to meet the growing national interest in wilderness. By the late 1960s, with the support of then district ranger Bill Holman at Moose Creek, both the wilderness rangers and trail crews traveled with backpacks. Horse packers sometimes resupplied crews or carried heavy specialized tools and continued to pack out garbage accumulated from old camps.

A backpack crew could camp close to the work section, often rolling out tents on ledges and small flats. The Kecks and senior crew members knew where to find water from springs and how to stagger camps at short intervals to limit morning and evening hiking distances. Many a night, a pair of trail crews would be perched on a rock shelf, hauling a couple gallons of water from a spring unseen from some alders. Camping only a night or two in one spot with only two people and naturalizing any fires or other touches on the land, meant minimal impact to the site. The intentional light touch led to the Leave No Trace concepts, where campers strive to leave no signs of being there. No wood piles, no cut stumps, no hanging ropes, no fire pits and, of course, no trash is left behind.

In comparison, traditional pack stock-supported Forest Service crews traveled heavy, with slabs of bacon, bags of potatoes and flour, cast iron pots, buckets and grain for stock, canvas tents and lots of cans, maybe even beer. The ease and speed of traveling in the saddle was counterbalanced by necessary animal chores morning and night and by loading and unloading packs every day. Stock always leave a mark, even in the Selway country where vegetation quickly grows back and even among experienced packers. "You bring a horse in here and it does eight times as much damage as a man," Emil would say.

On December 9, 1970, Keck wrote a memo to Holman about the site damage he found from stock on an inspection trip to the mouth of Three Links Creek the previous day after the close of the hunting season. "I write this as a strong protest against the increasing number of horses being used both in commercial outfitting and in large private hunting and fishing groups."

Visitor use was increasing and the ratio of stock to visitors also was increasing, with people packing in more and more gear, Keck wrote. At the same time, the Forest Service crews were getting away from stock. "We are doing a better job of administering the land, with less animals, and I believe within 2 years at the most, can cut them out entirely."

He goes on to write if he was an old man in his 50's or 60's maybe he would change his mind, but "if I couldn't do my job without an animal, I'd have to look for easier work." He was 58 at the time.

In making his protest against stock damage, Keck knew strong social and political forces were at play. He wrote, "The land is more important than the man. The land is more important to me today than my career with the Forest Service."

Keck concluded his hand written, steady cursive, two-page memo, "People that cannot appreciate what damage horses can cause can be excused for not knowing better, but those of us that can see the problem, can never accept the present trend of increased horse use."

Backpack trail crews carried a crosscut saw bent into an inverted U over aluminum frame Kelty backpacks, along with wedges and oil to prevent saw binding, a Pulaski for grubbing, a shovel for tread work, and two axes to brush, limb, and chop smaller logs. In addition to a brick-sized Forest Service radio and light cook gear, a 10-day hitch required 25 to 30 pounds of food to fuel the physical labor. Some people went the minimalist route, gagging on oatmeal or rice for breakfast and dinner, maybe with some tinned fish. Others took advantage of Penny's wholesale account with Mountain House freeze-dried foods.

On one of their winter trips back home to Oregon, Penny convinced the Mountain House company in neighboring Albany, Oregon to give her the dealer rate for a large order in the spring. She'd send out forms to all the crew in the winter and people could select full boxes with six #10 cans of vegetables, meats, and fruits. A can of each would be transferred into a plastic bag to last a full hitch. Supplemented by crackers, pasta, rice, peanut butter, cheese, granola, and other standard backpack fare, freeze dried food centered in many pots of stew. People traded cans not to get stuck with only green beans or only corn for the season. A little variety went a long way during months on the trail. Cottage cheese was a surprise favorite, with the seemingly Styrofoam type white granules soaking up water to take on the approximate texture and taste of source material. All over the wilderness at noontime, you could imagine the sound of people stirring cheese with a spoon in a metal cup as moisture sucked into white bits.

Getting crews outfitted with food and equipment was only a mechanical step, compared to assuring they knew how to work in the wilderness.

When the Forest Service first ventured into the wilds of Idaho and Montana, men with backcountry skills forged from the land sought employment. Packers, trappers, sawyers, dynamiters, and masons opened up the West, built towns and outposts, carved out travel routes, dug mines. The tools, craftsmanship and capacity to settle farms and ranches were readily adapted in the National Forests. Men familiar with horses and mules on farms, where teams pulled plows and harvesters, could easily adjust to stringing them out in a line for a trail, hauling everything from groceries to lumber.

Then came a surge of inexperienced laborers with the Civilian Conservation Corps, from the 1930s to World War II, who were young, 17-28 years-old, and became strong on the job. They were led and taught by locals with technical expertise gained from the landscape. In those years hard work and manual labor defined American life.

By the time of the Wilderness Act and its intentional application of a wilderness ethic to the wildest remaining lands, much of the local workforce was headlong in the opposite direction, as loggers, heavy equipment operators and saw mill operators. The Forest Service administration had shifted to men with forestry and engineering degrees, with the permanent positions filled by graduates of a few universities, mostly state schools. Firefighting and timber sale preparation could be lucrative summer jobs for the forestry students, while also providing field experience. But the technical labor pool out in the field became more limited to short seasonal employment with few long-term options for promotion. As National Forest budgets centered on timber extraction, both seasonal and permanent employees followed the money, which wasn't in wilderness.

Meanwhile, from the 1960s onward, many young Americans sought challenge and adventure in contact with nature. In the American tradition, wilderness provided an opportunity for individual exploration. But by the late 20th century, even among wilderness adventurers, familiarity with a skill set appropriate to the forest often did not extend beyond camping. The Kecks took young, eager, inexperienced enthusiasts and set them up to be seasoned, toughened wilderness hands.

By the time I landed at Moose Creek in April of 1977, specialization already compartmentalized much of Forest Service operations. Overall, fire and timber dominated, while recreation, range, wildlife, and fish played minor, supporting roles. As the only all-wilderness ranger district in the National Forests at the time, Moose Creek had a different, outlier focus, and it had a unified mission.

"We bring the crews in here for training, to get their gear and also to develop a love and understanding of the wilderness, which is just as important as anything else," Penny Keck explained. "They become thoroughly ensconced in the wilderness, but it doesn't happen overnight."

The annual 10-day Moose Creek guard school was the introductory, Wilderness Operations 101 course. Most of the training was practical, not theoretical or procedural. "When young people come in here they don't see a lot of formulas on the blackboard; they see these guys who are actually living and working in the woods," explained Emil Keck.

"It's a great responsibility to train people to use tools, to work safely and to choose the right tool and then to respect the land," he continued. "That's the whole thing, anything else is just whistling in the wind. Because they have only one chance to learn."

Training began in mid-June on the first day the crew arrived at Moose

Creek. When I started, most people flew into the ranger station on a twin-engine DC-3 hauling about a dozen people and supplies on each flight. The speed and the capacity to carry multiple people, along with personal and ranger station gear all at once made the old aircraft a desirable option.

In 1979, the year after I left, the DC-3 crashed into the Selway River flying the new crew into the station after mechanical failure of both engines. The ace pilot, Marvin (Whitey) Hachmeister, who knew all the river bends, almost glided the powerless plane onto the spring run-off flushed river at a wide spot near Dry Bar. The year before I jumped on the DC-3 for a round trip supply run to Grangeville out of Moose Creek just to see the country and sit next to the cockpit to watch Whitey guide the big bird. I was awed by his skill as he eased the relic of World War II through the canyon without stress and dropped down fully-loaded to the long runway without a hop or side slide on landing.

On the fateful flight with one engine in flames and the other torn off from the wing when the retaining bolts failed and fell into the forest, a tall ponderosa pine clipped a wing as he swooped into the final glide. The old airplane hit hard into the rushing waters of the Selway River. The pilot, co-pilot, and eight others died. Only two people survived. From then on, travel went back to the old way—walking into the ranger station.

Tool training started with the double-bitted axe. The Government Service Administration packaged 12 axes into boxes and maybe one in three had an acceptable handle. Penny Keck would pull an axe out of the box at random, sight down the handle in both directions, and say either, "This one might be serviceable," or "You wouldn't want to be 50 miles out on the trail and have this baby split in your hands when you're pounding a wedge in."

To people's surprise, the first step was often to cut off the handles with weak points or bends and then learn how to select, shape, and set a new handle, using a rasp to slim down the handle and a hammer for wooden and metal wedges. The useless shoulder under the head would be rasped down to fit snug in an individual's hand. The length would be customized to the users' arm length, shortened for ease in the brush and on the pack, with a knob of electric tape at the end to secure a hold. A handles' strength centered in straight grain, no wows or bows, with the grain running at 45 degrees to the axe head.

Sharpening was another time-honored technique. With a two-sided or double-bitted axe it is simple to set the head deep in a log, to then file the exposed side. Taking one side of the axe to a fine, thin edge for chopping and filing the other side to a blunt face for low swings near and sometimes in dirt. Crew members learned how to put the edges to their own tools.

Everyone carried a flat bastard file of middle coarseness with a wooden handle and scrap of fire hose as a knuckle guard, along with a round sharpening stone to take off burrs for the final touch, as part of a personal tool kit. The training included elementary thinking. Keep the stone and file in your pocket or put tools on or in your pack or on the trail in plain view. Never set down tools in the brush, or you'll end up searching for them. Always wear gloves, leather palmed cotton or all leather was up to personal preference.

The crew learned how to sharpen, clean, carry, repair, and then use all their tools: shovels, Pulaskis, pick mattock, rock bar, loppers, and finally, crosscut saws with wedges. A tall, lanky wilderness ranger, Warren Q. Miller, joined the Kecks in explaining the care and use of saws. Miller became a master saw filer and restorer in the early 1970s, learning the craft out of necessity when old, little-used saws rusted and warped in most ranger stations across the country.

The Wilderness Act prohibition of motorized equipment and mechanical transport except "to meet minimum requirements for the administration of the area," brought the crosscut out of the dust bin. Tagged as "misery whips," no doubt by sawyers who worked 10-12 hours a day, six or seven days a week in remote logging camps, crosscut saws long had a mixed reputation. For trail crew and wilderness rangers who carried the old saws, it could be as the master filer Miller said, "A well-tuned saw can be a fine tool to use."

On trails, sawing out windfalls can be one of the extended moments of skilled and satisfying labor. One time I came around a bend up on Barren Ridge to find a grandfather red fir almost four-feet thick lying in the trail. Instead of a groan, I felt the lift of anticipation and challenge, not any sink of disappointment. Here was our work for the afternoon, real work.

My partner, Alan Carroll, and I spent some time looking it over, determining where to make cuts, at what angle, planning how to protect the saw, and, most difficult, how to roll the behemoth log lengths once we cut it up. We swamped out brush to clear paths for our feet and the saw. We trimmed back the bark for a clean bite into the log. Then we set to work, making the rakers whistle and the teeth sing. The whistle and song of a saw is no cliché when you hear it, smell it, feel it, and see it slice downward, stroke by stroke, into a giant log.

We used all the wedges we had to keep the saw from binding and we poured on the lubricating oil, a mix of diesel fuel and motor oil at the time. We made three cuts for two rollable pieces each about four feet long, the width and lengths were about equal. Cuts turned at angles to both drop downward and then roll away from the remaining log lengths. Using pole pry bars to lift the almost chest-high tree rounds out of the tread dip, pushing with our legs and setting pole ramps to clear rocks, we inched the pieces out of the trail, leaving one parallel to the tread as a railing and pushing the other into the brush. Then we restrung the tools on our packs and hiked up the ridge for a late camp by a spring, on a knob, with a big open view of Bailey Mountain to the east, too exhausted to do any exploring.

Similar puzzles awaited all the young crews when they ventured out. They practiced during guard school by cutting firewood for the ranger station's cooking and heating stoves. Learning to find a shared rhythm in saw pairs took time. The pull is the power stroke and the push is a light touch for guidance. Once people found the right pace with the least pressure, saws bit into logs at a steady rate.

One year, a new young crew member questioned the long-term supply

Emil and Penny Keck's cabin at Moose Creek Ranger Station, 1969
Richard I. Walker

of trees for firewood at the ranger station. And Emil Keck responded, "Jesus Christ could come back from the dead 50 times before we run out of wood around here."

Emil and Penny Keck had a standard that they never asked anyone to do a job they couldn't do or wouldn't do. They were masters of all the tools used on the trail and around the ranger station. They did the specialized work of rock blasting and bridge building but never dodged any job as beneath them.

One year, the septic tank at the ranger's cabin clogged and had to be drained. The young resource assistant and Fire Management Officer, Barry Hicks, lived with his family in the cabin and had to fix the plumbing. As Hicks told the story, "I couldn't ask anybody to do it with me and nobody else but Emil would have done it." Keck and Hicks spent a very unpleasant day shoveling out buckets of feces to clear the tank. That night they washed off filth and finished off a fifth of MacNaughtons to wash away memories. At the end of the evening, Emil headed up the small rise to his cabin with a head lamp and Hicks said, "I could see the light going up the little hill, and then go backwards 10-15 feet, and then go up again and backwards again, I was laughing so hard I almost pissed my pants."

Guard school implanted a work ethic along with skills. "Work ethic is determined quite a bit by what you see the boss do; and what your opinion is of him and if you trust him," said Emil Keck. "Then it's easy to develop a work ethic. All it amounts to is you're looking at the job from the standpoint of something that has to be done. And you do the very best that you can. That I think is a good work ethic."

Decades later, people who learned these lessons of dedication and determination from the Kecks applied the same standards towards all kinds of careers. The simplicity of labor in the wilderness led to lifelong guidance, balancing safety and risk, grit and finesse, perseverance and pacing.

Everyone at guard school did two days of tool training and two days of fire training, including helicopter safety and a practice fire. A fish and game conservation officer came in to talk about state regulations and procedures for us on the ground. The understanding was the field staff would contact law enforcement specialists with any observations of game wasting or excessive kills, but not make any direct contact with violators and to avoid confrontations and disturbance of evidence. Additional time was devoted to general law enforcement and Forest Service regulations.

The packer did a short introduction to stock use, both for safety and to understand where and when pack string assistance was appropriate. A general understanding of everything on the district within a wilderness framework was outlined before crews broke into specialties of trail work or public contact as primary jobs.

After a day of falling dead trees and bucking up firewood, Penny surveyed the new crew members and said, "You can tell the ones that want to work and you can tell the ones who say in their minds, 'Well, it's a job—I'll work.' Then there are some others that don't know if this is what they want at all. The ones that want to work will be back next year."

Other labor-intensive tasks around the ranger station that needed to be done might also get guard school conscriptions, such as fence post replacing, painting or staining buildings, or cleanups. Later in the summer a scant cutting of hay off the airstrips would also require drafting all available hands to haul it to the barn for backup feed. The chores of maintaining the ranger station fell to everyone, with the station guard and the Kecks at the lead.

Along with maintaining the existing buildings at the ranger stations, new demands of government sometimes required new construction. The district ranger in the late 1970s, Art Seamans, was convinced by Forest Service specialists that compliance with federal drinking water regulations was required at Moose Creek. The spring box above the ranger station that supplied all water for upwards of 40 people for more than 50 years needed a chlorinator inserted into the main line.

Emil's reaction was, "Here we have the purest goddamned water in the country and they want to poison it with chemicals." When the chlorinator pump arrived, Emil buried it in the woods.

Later he dug it up under threats from the engineers. Then he built a tight 6-foot by 8-foot, board and batten shed with a peak roof and cement footings to house the pump and valves. Set at the northeast edge of the ranger station compound, it followed standard ranger station construction methods of the day. But when he hooked the pump into the main line, the chemical feed couldn't deal with the demands because the pipeline was constructed decades before as a buried cedar board box. The boards were rife with moss and algae that somehow never got anyone sick, same as a flowing clean stream, but retained more organisms than the chlorinator could overcome.

Another pump house had to be constructed in the woods closer to the spring box source. A new plastic pipeline to supply the ranger station would be laid in a shallow trench. I was assigned to build the new building and do the plumbing. The ranger and the forest engineers told me to get the job done according to their specifications or find other employment. I needed the job while waiting for the trail season to start.

I flew to Grangeville to pick up plumbing and building supplies and talk to the water engineers. Back at Moose Creek, I told Emil what my marching orders were. "You mean they're going to can your ass if you don't get that bastard chlorinator to work?" Emil questioned. "OK, Johnson, don't you worry," he continued, using one of his many nicknames. "The goddamned bridge at Three Links can wait. I'll just drop everything and we'll fix that fucking chlorinator so it spits out water as pure as the Virgin Mary's piss. Because if they're going to fire you, they're going to have to can me first."

Emil often walked as he talked, often in constant motion. When he hustled through the compound to get something, I'd tag along and ask questions. He explained what I needed to get from town for hardware, what boards and dimensional lumber could be selected from storage in the barn attic. Even as he prepared to load mules or gather equipment, he paced as he talked, stopping and starting. In between, he explained each step of construction to be sure I knew what tools and materials to use.

All construction and maintenance projects for the ranger station began at the Shake Shack, the tool shed. When I unlocked the door to the tool shed on the April day I arrived at Moose Creek it was like finding a golden treasure trove. More hand tools were concentrated in a smaller space than I'd ever seen before. It was the Woodcraft catalog come to life. Everything you'd need to rebuild after a nuclear holocaust and civilization dimmed could be found inside the 16 by 20-foot, pole and split shingle cabin.

A forge, anvil, and a full set of blacksmith tongs, with an acetylene torch, and a complete set of pipe fitting and threading tools for copper tubing and heavy galvanized pipe took care of anything that needed to be done with metal, along with a half dozen hack saws and a hand crank drill press. Shelves and racks held wood planes, chisels, screw-drivers, hammers, saws, brace and bits, and files, everything in multiple lengths and sizes, everything to cut and shape wood. A closed cabinet held paints, oils, solvents, glues and all kinds of brushes and scrappers. Another cabinet held a complete first aid kit, an emergency chemical wash station and protective gear for hands, eyes, and ears, and a fire extinguisher hanging on the outside. Racks held axes and Pulaskis, some to be re-handled or sharpened on the hand crank grinding stone fastened on the heavy work bench. Vices for pipe, wood, metal, and the drill press were also bolted solid to the bench. Clamps of all shapes and sizes were spread out on another shelf. Across the back wall was a chest-high hardware rack with bins for all manner of metal, wood, and plastic pipe, nails, screws, nuts, and bolts. You could cut anything and fasten it back together in whatever configuration you needed. Everything you could think of was there, except extension cords or anything with a motor.

A set of windows running along the length of the work bench on the long side of the building provided ample light. A small wood stove to burn scraps was rarely used. On warm days the wide swinging door could be propped open for more light and air flow.

Under Emil's instructions, I replicated the pump house shed. I poured footings mixing bags of concrete in a wheelbarrow with buckets of water from the spring. Cutting studs, rafters, and boards propped on saw horses and using a fine, wooden-handled saw, I framed and sheathed the walls and roof. I built a door with boards, using a classic Z-pattern backing for strength and hung it with strap hinges, using an egg beater drill for screw holes. I shingled the roof with milled cedar shakes, cut from the forest outside the wilderness.

My previous five years' experience as an itinerant house carpenter was put to good use. Hauling everything up on my back or in a wheelbarrow, which was allowed at a Forest Service administrative site, working with hand tools, listening to the occasional grouse drumming, and watching the spring flow pure and clean from the ground at its source, was peaceful and quiet. I wanted to split cedar shakes using a froe and peel poles using a draw knife. But the engineers wanted speed and demanded standardized materials flown in from town. No matter, I walked into the woods in the morning and down in the evening with a satisfied mind, making something simple and solid, even if silly in purpose.

Pleased with my construction, I began cutting and threading pipe to plumb the fool machine. Sending word over the radio that I was ready for the next steps, Emil came back from the Three Links bridge site to line me out. As I worked at the plumbing vise we'd set under a fir tree in the station yard, turning a hand crank ratchet threader for the galvanized pipe, Emil checked out the building. He came back fuming and got inches from my face.

"What kind of a dumb son-of-a-bitch are you?" he snarled. "When I said build it exactly like the one I built, I meant exactly—not like something else."

"I did it just like you showed me," I protested. "It's the same thing." Then he got really mad.

"You think those rafters are cut the same?" Emil said. "You think leaving the butt end square is the same as cutting it at a 45-degree angle? You're dumber than I thought."

I got the picture. I'd left the outside ends of the rafters uncut, perpendicular to the run, to save a cut and to keep a more useful piece of scrap. Emil had cut the end at a 45-degree angle, to have the butt end vertical and plumb to the wall, which could possibly aid water drainage off the roof and keep it away from the building. I soon learned his way was certain to put runoff away from the building foundation, as Emil told me in no uncertain terms.

As he reamed me out, I couldn't imagine why it was such a tragedy and how far he'd go to make his point on my failure. He was angry. I was scared. I had a two and a half foot pipe wrench in my hands. If things got really bad, I figured there was one chance to bash him in the head and run like hell. I was 26 years-old and Emil was 65. I was pretty sure I could outrun him. But I'd be a goner if he caught me.

Then, as fast and unexpected as the tsunami hit, the waters receded. "OK, even though you think you're so fucking smart Johnson, from now on you'll do it my way," Emil said. I agreed and I meant it.

"Now, what pipe have you got cut already and what do we have to do?" he said, and we got to work. I'd already laid out the long run of plastic pipe through the forest and would bury it later. Emil showed me how to do the plumbing with the least amount of cutting and threading and we hooked up the machine to pass a few test runs, making some of the finest water on earth reek like a swimming pool and taste worse.

The system needed constant attention to replenish the chlorine and set the proper drip delivery. It collapsed soon after the entire crew came in for the summer. Running up a half-mile into the woods every day to feed a machine bleach to poison your water wasn't on anyone's priority list. We kept the bureaucrats off our backs by putting a few drops of chlorine in the water test bottles before flying it out to town. When we got the mix too strong, we were caught spiking the test flasks. It became apparent the system and operators needed improvements. At one point there were little signs in the cook house and the bath house, that said don't drink the water, it must be boiled first. The signs were ignored and soon removed.

Eventually, years later, another spring was tapped at its source; a pipe was punched into the hillside with a gas-powered drill to create an enclosed system. Another pipeline was run to the station to carry clear, clean water never exposed to air. My little building up in the woods was torn down.

When Barry Hicks, the district resource assistant, interviewed me and the woman who I was married to at the time, Mary Butters, for our job applications in March 1977, he told us about these strange and wonderful and impossible people, Emil and Penny Keck. Hicks said if we worked on trails and as the station guard, the Kecks would both be our bosses, even though Penny was listed as a volunteer and Emil was the official boss. He explained the Kecks knew how to do everything. Hicks said, "I wish everyone could have the chance to work with Penny and Emil." He wasn't just talking about us, or about Forest Service people in general. He meant everyone.

At the Moose Creek office in town, above the Grangeville Post Office, there was a yellowed newspaper clipping framed on the wall. It showed a picture of Emil in Carhartts cut off at the calf, jungle boots, and a field coat as he was getting an award and shaking hands with then Secretary of Agriculture Earl Butz, in a three piece suit. Emil Keck was getting the Forest Service's highest award for meritorious service in 1975, at the Department of Agriculture headquarters in Washington, D.C. Emil was the only person to receive the award who wasn't a scientist or an administrator. And he was the only person who didn't wear a suit and tie.

Keck said he wanted to tell Butz a few things about how the outfit was being run and how it ought to be run. Butz made for the door before Emil could corner him. Keck did talk to Forest Service Chief John McQuire about getting people out of the office, on the ground, and making more decisions from the field. Keck never saw any indication of change from his suggestions.

A couple years later, I asked one of the wilderness rangers, Tim Rich, how Emil Keck ever got the recognition in Washington? "They either had to give him the top award for all his years of work, or fire him and get him the hell out of here," Rich said.

CHANGES

Emil and Penny Keck

WILDERNESS EMBODIES NATURE in the raw. Wilderness is also a construct of the human mind, filtered through politics in Congress and economics in budgets. We have wilderness in America because it fits an ideal, fills a need and citizens support it.

One time Emil Keck described true wilderness. "If we really had wilderness out here, we'd put up a 10-foot high fence all the way around it," he said. "Outside you could do anything you wanted. Inside it would be undisturbed nature - no trails, no buildings, no bridges, no nothing for people. I'd be the protector inside to make sure no one did anything to disturb old Mother Nature. And you'd have to sneak over or under the fence to get in. And if I found you, I'd chase you out or kill you. Or if you found me first, you could kill me and then you'd be the protector of the wilderness. That would be true wilderness—survival of the fittest."

His views never caught on. Keck planned to burn down all the buildings at Moose Creek Ranger Station, to eliminate the human compound. But other than the old board shack he lived in and later torched, he never followed through on the structure fires. He maintained the buildings, replaced and repaired plumbing, mowed the airstrip. And he continued to build and rebuild bridges. People continued to use the bridges and appreciated being dry.

Another time Penny and Emil Keck debated the existence of a small farm tractor at the ranger station, used to cut hay from the airstrip and haul supplies at the administrative site. "The ranger is really getting clobbered by the public, believe me, on misuse of the tractor," Penny said.

"Misuse of the tractor?," Emil snorted. "My god, it's the most serviceable piece of equipment we've got in here."

"You may think so,' Penny replied, "but you can't argue with the public. Besides, you make everybody else do everything by primitive means but you won't do it yourself. You just take the tractor wherever you please. You're guilty of a double standard."

"Double standard? You're damn right," Emil parried. "It's the Forest Service responsibility to manage the god-damned land and it's the public's responsibility to shut up."

When the Kecks burnt their shack at the ranger station, they naturalized the site by removing the footings, planting grass and a tree, and digging in a windblown stump covered with moss like it had been there for 20 years. They must have burnt it in winter or in a rainstorm, because none of the surrounding trees and vegetation were singed.

They moved into the nearby warehouse, punching a stove pipe through the roof for wood heat and cook stoves. They plumbed in an old toilet, a metal shower stall and a deep stainless steel, double sink, all scrounged from one of the dismantled dude ranches or overbuilt outfitter camps. Three, 60-pound Cobra drills, used to drill blast holes in rock, leaned against the bathroom wall. Nails pounded into walls and ceiling joists hung everything from tools to laundry. A butcher block table salvaged from another demolished cabin was used mostly as a magazine stand, for *Newsweek, Runners World, National Geographic, Readers Digest, Prevention, Sierra, Harpers* and the *Oregonian* newspaper from home.

The Kecks and the half dozen crew members with a long season working out of Moose Creek grew a rudimentary garden for some fresh vegetables. Penny's upbringing on a multi-crop farm lingered in her interest to taste a few fresh tomatoes, some potatoes and some greens. Most of their food was flown in or packed in. Their meals at the station were almost as basic as when on the trail.

The ranger station was a storehouse, to get resupplied, do gear repairs, clean up, check mail and eat a few special things, maybe break out cool beer from the root cellar if there were visitors. The Kecks rarely stayed at their cabin for more than a couple days.

Government nepotism regulations did not allow Emil to be Penny's boss once they were married. So, to be a team, Penny became a volunteer. After more than a dozen years, given Emil's age and their interest in keeping at the wilderness job, they decided to flip the job titles. But government regulations are not known for being malleable. For Penny to get credit for her years of field work, at the appropriate level to run the program, required recognition through the Regional Office in Missoula. Persistence from district ranger Art Seamans to push the regulations and the demonstrated reality of Penny's skill set eventually prevailed. Penny took over title of supervisor for the construction and maintenance program in 1980.

Emil Keck made his intentions clear. "I'm only working for the old lady," he said. "I'm not volunteering for the Forest Service at all."

Other than the names on pay stubs, not much changed. Barry Hicks returned to Moose Creek as district ranger later in 1980, after a stint as the Fire Management Officer in big timber country on a district of the Willamette National Forest in Oregon. "When I went back as ranger I didn't think it would be much different, and it wasn't. Penny and Emil still did everything together. When they left the station, they left as a pair, just like they always did."

Hicks was curious if there would be any strain, having left in 1977 as more a peer when he was the combination FMO/resource assistant, and now returned as Penny's boss. Both Emil and Penny made sure the adjustment was not a problem. "Emil was the one who made it work well, he made the change easy," Hicks said years later. Early on, Emil told Hicks to talk to Penny about decisions on the trail program, she was the one in charge, not him.

Penny was also willing to be more incorporated into the Forest Service system and procedures. "Penny would actually come to staff meetings. You couldn't drag Emil to a staff meeting," Hicks recalled.

When Hicks got cancer in 1981, he underwent chemotherapy for six months and was absent most of the time. "They really looked after stuff while I was gone, they were as good as gold," Hicks said of the Kecks. By the time he got back on his feet, working full time in 1982, the leadership of Penny on the district was solidified.

Penny took more direct interest in the hiring of her crews. "What we attempt to do when people come in here is to have someone who has done some work in the past," she said. "Not necessarily with a cross-cut saw, because you can learn that skill. But you have to have a work attitude and to have had your hands wrapped around a handle tool somewhere. If they haven't been sitting at a desk hitting a keyboard all their lives that's a plus."

In the 1970s, Moose Creek required a supplemental application form for everyone with essay questions. People were asked to explain, what does wilderness mean to you? And to describe, why do you want to work in the wilderness? Unusual questions for young people aspiring to do manual labor with limited public contact of any kind, or so it seemed. Sometime in the early 1980s, the essay questions were dropped. The physical labor experiences from growing up around farms, mines, and timber increased the proportion of young, local Idaho people on Penny's crews. As she learned from her own experiences in cultivating a wilderness ethic, she figured anyone who took to the tasks and the pace of trails would soon absorb an understanding of wilderness.

After Penny took charge another change became so standard the progression became taken for granted. When Penny started at Moose Creek she was the first woman in the field since World War II, some say the first woman ever in the field on the district. By the time she was running the field maintenance program typically half the young crew members were women.

Female pairs working together on trail crew started in the early 1970s at Moose Creek and elsewhere. Soon crews were mixed and reflected the societal opportunity for young women to seek the same jobs as young men, as much or more so than outside the wilderness. Penny tended to hire a larger percentage of women than was the norm in the Forest Service but she insisted she showed no favoritism.

Penny and Emil Keck with hay crew at Moose Creek Ranger Station airstrip, circa 1980 *USFS*

"All people are welcome here, if they can do the work reasonably well," she said. "All people are equal until they prove they are unable to do something. And we as humans have to realize what our limitations are. Not everyone is made out to be a backpack trail person on the Moose Creek district."

Emil changed as well. "I've made a complete reversal of the way I had been working and the way I had been taught," he said one day after Penny took the leadership. "It took a long time to change. Still, according to the old lady, I still have preconceived ideas on the value of women versus men. But that's not true, although from her standpoint I can understand and appreciate why she thinks that I'm still stuck in the old ways."

The expansion of gender roles was all positive. Emil continued: "the women on this district take no back seat from nothing. They know working on the trail system or on fire control for the old lady and me, they're going to get the same god-damned break right down the line

Three Links Bridge, 2015 *John McCarthy*

as the guy. They respect that and feel at ease, and then they aren't worried about kissing your ass; they're worried about learning the job and taking care of the land."

The unwanted change for the Kecks in the 1980s was the inevitability of time. Emil was growing old. Toward the end of the field season in 1983, I flew into to Moose Creek as a reporter for the *Lewiston Morning Tribune*, along with photographer Glenn Cruickshank. The *Tribune* is known as a photographer's paper and Cruickshank's keenness to spend most of a week capturing the infamous but illusive Kecks on film secured us approval from our editors.

We spent days following them around, me asking questions and Cruickshank grabbing shots out in the field and around the ranger station. Soon it became apparent Emil was spending more time at the ranger station than Penny and he was not going as far afield. They'd been doing some rock work and bog reconstruction up on Marten Creek, the same drainage where the first smokejumpers, Rufus Robinson and Earl Cooley, leaped out of a plane onto a fire on July 12, 1940.

Cupboard Creek Bridge, 2015 *John McCarthy*

The hike took it's toll on Emil and he didn't go every time. Penny, then 41, hiked the 25 miles in a day, going up to 7000 feet over Mink Peak from 2100 feet along the river. "If you really push it, you can make it in 10 or 11 hours to Marten Creek," she said. Emil, turning 71 in October, wasn't pushing it.

Earlier in the spring, as snow hung heavy in the high country, they hiked to Shearer Cabin, about 15 miles, cutting out a couple windfalls with axes along the way. They hiked back the next day. "We didn't get back very early," Penny said. "Emil had to stop every quarter mile because of his ankle. He said 'go on ahead,' but I said - no way."

Being on his feet carrying 90 pound packs, hiking thousands of miles over the years, often going 15 and even 25 miles a day, brought on arthritis and chronic pain in his ankles. Overall wear and tear on his body slowed him down and he struggled with the progression.

"I've had nothing but dangerous work all my life, like topping trees, setting choker cables, doing hazardous things all the time," Emil told

Emil Keck at Moose Creek, 1983 *Glenn Cruickshank*

me. "I don't like to do it anymore but I learned how to take chances and get the job done."

The footbridge across Moose Creek to Seminole Ranch was rotting out in the towers, creating a public hazard for the unofficial open walkway. Because the bridge led to private land, without a public easement, it could be required to be sealed off to the public. But to Emil, closure wouldn't follow a backcountry tradition of being a good neighbor and helping to keep a travel route across a creek open. "In my book you don't let equipment out here go to hell, no matter who owns it," he said.

The ranch owner, Bud Griffith, readily agreed to pay for materials when Emil offered to repair the bridge. And as an open bridge in the wilderness, Penny was responsible for it being safe. Emil had two reasons to do the work.

Since he was a volunteer already, for Penny, he saw no problem volunteering to repair the bridge. When I went to see him at the bridge site in late September, Emil insisted I go on ahead and not hike with him. It took him almost an hour to walk the mile to the bridge.

As he pushed a wheelbarrow with tools across the bridge, he cursed, "the god-damned ankle is really acting up today - it hurts like a son-of-a-bitch." Once he got going, moving tools into position to start freeing the needle beams, he resumed focus and was in his element. He described the set-up and procedures, and talked about yanking on the come-along, setting gin poles, hoisting cables and tearing off the deck. All the while, he carried on like it was nothing for a 70-year-old man to be rebuilding a bridge by himself. "You have to be patient out on a bridge, not go too fast and drop something or slip and fall. You just have to take your time."

Time was catching up to him and yet, he was also more willing to slow down and fully frame some of his thoughts. When I asked him about the importance of wilderness, he had a a lot to say.

Emil Keck at Moose Creek foot bridge, 1983 *Glenn Cruickshank*

"If you took a vote in the United States, for the people old enough to vote, they'd vote to keep wilderness. And I don't think they want it changed. They want it raw, but that's not the way it's going.

"The only enemy that the wilderness has, that's significant, is man. Winds won't hurt it. Rains won't hurt it. But human beings will kill it, absolutely. And that's what we have to guard against, human beings destroying the wilderness.

"All the people in the United States that will never see Moose Creek, they want to have a warm little place in their hearts to know it's there. Because I think innately, every person that is rational in their mind, that has ever read about history of this country, every person wants to know someplace in this god-damned United States is the same as when Daniel Boone walked across the country or when the pilgrims landed or when they dumped the tea into the ocean in that harbor back there, the fact they have something that ties them back to their history is much stronger than you can ever dream up.

"How would you like to know there is never going to be a piece of land that is the same as it always was? You wouldn't like it at all. Even if you never get into Moose Creek, it's nice to know it's there."

The story we did for the *Tribune*, starting on the front page and going to three full pages with lots of photographs on an inside section, including a double truck, where two pages open on the folded seam with fully connected content, was said to be the longest piece at the paper any one remembered. At first the managing editor, Paul Emerson, had balked at the length, and the many photographs. But after the city editor, Diane Pettit worked it over my copy, and the photo editor, Barry Kough, helped select images, Emerson relented and the stories went to print on Sunday, October 16, 1983, with a closeup portrait of Emil above the fold on 1A.

Within days many people throughout the Clearwater Valley commented on a clear portrayal of memorable people. Many people shared their own stories of Emil in his logger and fire fighting days or of meeting Emil and Penny at Moose Creek—never to be forgotten. After Emerson's barber, a regular guy in Lewiston Orchards, told him it was one of the best things the *Tribune* had ever done, he agreed.

Later that week, on the day of Emil Kecks' 71st birthday, October 20, 1983, Mary Butters gave birth to our son at Syringa Hospital in Grangeville. We named him, Emil James McCarthy, after our favorite boss for his first name and my father for his middle name. When I later told Keck we'd named our boy after him, he said, "why the hell did you name a cute little kid after an old bastard like me?"

Many times young Emil wondered the same thing, when his name pronunciation was butchered or he got asked what kind of name it was. Young Emil and I backpacked into Moose Creek when he was almost 12, in early October 1995. He walked across Three Links bridge and on up the river trail to the ranger station, across bridges built by the hands of Emil Keck. He knew then where he came from and understood the honor of his name.

By the mid-1980s, things continued to change for Emil and Penny. When I hiked out to see them at the beginning of the season in 1987, Penny said, "the thing that's changed in the last three years is that I'm out there alone now. There's not two of us any longer."

Penny talked about practical problems to single buck a windfall or to roll a large log out of the trail with only one person. The changes went far deeper than physical challenges on the trail.

As Emil approached his 75th birthday, he grudgingly acknowledged what anyone else would have realized years before. Years of labor wore his body out. His barrel-chested, short and stocky frame was always recognizable from a mile away. Seeing him hike up from the far end of the airstrip with his familiar waddling, bow-legged gait and boxy stature, he was unmistakable. But now he'd slumped and even gone soft in the belly, as he no longer kept moving from dawn to dark. His ankles tormented him and he sometimes used two cedar sticks cut as canes to get around.

Where someone else might have appreciated a rest, taking it easy was not his line. "I just poke around and help the old lady as best I can; it's the shits to not be able to be out on the trail all the time," he said from the porch that summer.

Directing a young crew for reconstruction of the Selway Lodge bridge fit both his interests in passing on practical skills and also in helping Penny. "If Penny has to inspect it, it's going to be a damn good bridge," he said. But it wasn't the same as before.

"I'm not as much help as she was for me," Emil said. "She went everywhere with me and did the work and that was it. Now, because of this fucking arthritis I can't get out on the trail anymore. No matter how much you try - to not be macho, macho—it's hard to turn the job over to the old lady and to not help her."

Penny compensated in part for his absence by leaning on other experienced hands. The guard school training included George Weldon, the resource assistant, Jim Savelund, the fire management officer, who were both smokejumpers with years spent using tools on fires, and Warren Miller, wilderness ranger and crosscut saw master. In the past, Emil and Penny did all the tool training, with Miller stepping in to help on saws. Now each of the younger men led sawyer teams into the woods, and the fire wood stacked up. An immeasurable quality, the connection to history, dimmed.

The obvious gap was the losing Emil's telling descriptions that enlivened the training. When explaining the value of packing in and setting up a Gorman-Rupp pump to draw water from a creek to stop a fire's spread, Emil said, "it's got enough pressure to knock Christ off the cross." And when he declared an outfitter could not use mechanized equipment around his camp, Emil said, "I don't care if he sleeps with the Virgin Mary, he's not hauling her in on a cart." Nothing replaced his wit, or him.

Beyond his outrageous sense of humor, Emil's wisdom in wilderness ideals, his courage in confronting challenges from man or nature, his knowledge of people and the land, and his conviction to stand with his people and for his beliefs, were no longer part of the regular training.

Emil's presence was still felt and heard around the ranger station. Always outspoken, never quiet and always friendly to everyone, he'd share his opinions with visitors and staff. While much of his holding forth from the porch flowed as great stories, some contradictions in his views and some differences with Forest Service policy created friction.

For 15 years the Selway-Bitterroot Wilderness led the progression toward ecologically based fire management in wilderness. Starting in the early 1970s at White Cap Creek in the upper Selway, wildfires could follow a natural role under a management plan. All fires were no longer always suppressed under an unwavering, national policy—to put all fires out as soon as possible. As a traditional fire fighter, and a former logger who valued timber even if he didn't want to see it harvested from wilderness, Emil never converted to support fire monitoring, instead of fire fighting. His original job as a Fire Control Officer,

FCO, became the Fire Management Officer, FMO. The one word and one letter difference in the title reflected a vast change, much of it he agreed to but with some sticking points.

Emil was vocal in objecting to changes from all-out fire suppression. He often used disparaging terms to question some fire managers physical and mental capacities. During fire seasons when wilderness lands were choked by smoke and resources were committed to track but not attack fires, Emil made his views known.

Pilots flying into Moose Creek often heard his criticisms when they landed. Flying over burning forests can heighten the drama of flames, exaggerate the apparent scale of fire perimeters and focus the eye on the devastation to vegetation. People's views are pulled toward flames and burnt-over areas, not toward the proportion of remaining live green growth. The remaining, resilient green growth in partial burns is more obvious when seen on the ground than from the air.

Emil and some of the pilots who flew into Moose Creek shared a position to oppose fires left unchecked. Just the smoke was bad enough for some pilots. The same pilots also flew out of the wilderness and declared their opposition to a natural fire program was backed by the most experienced person inside the wilderness—Emil Keck.

Keck said things like, "when I came into this area the water was clean and the air was clear. Now I spend about six weeks of the year arguing about the fire plan and breathing foul air. If it needs to be burned, let's burn it on our time, in the spring or the fall, and not burn the whole damn country up." As Keck bucked the future of fire management, he said, "I enjoy a good scrape."

An increased reliance on pack stock to supply the ranger station, decreasing the use of air craft, also distressed Emil. His intention to eliminate stock, except to supply lookouts and shuttle heavy equipment for trail and bridge crews, never came to full fruition. He thought the use of a team of horses and mules to pull an old style sickle-bar and rake to cut the airstrip was preposterous, when there was small farm tractor at

Emil Keck at Moose Creek Ranger Station, 1983 *Glenn Cruickshank*

the ranger station. "We have the equipment to farm exactly when we need to, not to wait for the packer to maybe get his ass in gear to do it with stock."

Emil's open mind toward people with different views and backgrounds did not apply to district rangers. Of the seven district rangers at Moose Creek during Emil's time, he often said complimentary things about them - before they came and after they left - but almost never while they were nominally in charge. "I think the rangers as a class should be eliminated from the face of the earth," he said one time. The conflict over stock use and the tractor with the district ranger did not bode well.

The expanding requirements of documentation and filling out forms for everything was met with derision by Emil, and by grudging dismay by Penny, who did all the paperwork. The Forest Service became more and more office oriented in the 1980s. Penny attempted to adapt to the new regime but was hindered by her remote location, her stand-offish temperament, her interest in being outside not inside and at least in part by her gender.

"As far as a woman in this position, the Forest Service is still male dominated and you have to tread lightly in some respects," she said. "They don't accept a woman saying a few choice words that you'd really appreciate saying to them, because they're idiots. Whereas a man can get away with that. That's the reality yet today."

"I do have as much say as I want if I pursue it in exhaustive detail," she continued. "I probably have to tell them eight to ten times—persistence is a value—because I'm not as dynamic and outgoing as some other people that might influence things. If you were much more dynamic and used the King's English much more vigorously maybe they'd stay tuned in. There is still a lot of old guard around. We say, 'hey, let's build a team and have a teamwork philosophy.' But in reality we do not have teamwork overall."

Two controversies within the construction and maintenance program also aggravated Penny and Emil. The use of wood preservatives came under additional scrutiny in society during the 1970s into the 1980s, for potential damage to the environment, especially to fish and water quality, and for detrimental human health effects. As the Kecks repaired bridges inflicted with insect damage and water rot, they sought out strong preservatives and sealants. The turpentinesque smell of Penta, or pentachlorophenol, and of fence post familiar creosote was prominent on bridge sites and often seemed ingrained into their clothes.

The application of one wood preservative, Osmoplastic, came into question over water, such as on bridges. Penny put it on bridge approaches to use it up and not store it at the ranger station. The line between a bridge approach over land above high water marks and where it goes over the stream itself became a point of contention between Keck and the ranger. Penny was adamant she followed safe procedures. It rankled to be questioned about her program and the actual technique of getting rid of a chemical no longer approved for all uses. She began a research project to update best practices for use, storage and removal of pesticides used in wood preservation. She planned to spend part of her winter on-leave studying the current research and applications at Oregon State University or University of Wisconsin, the leading wood products labs of the time. "I hoped this winter to find what types to use, when to use them and where," she said.

Another controversy simmered at Shearer Guard Station airstrip, upstream from Moose Creek about 15 miles. In the spring of 1983, someone put salt blocks out on the runway to attract deer and elk. The animals dug around the salt to get all the mineral deposits and dug holes in the airstrip. The holes led to some temporary closures.

The unknown opponents of the airstrip continued to throw out salt blocks every year until 1987, when they stepped up the sabotage by digging 21 holes laced with salt down into the airstrip. The hole pattern and depth was intended to make the airstrip unusable and the damage permanent. The efforts of Penny and others could not fix the unsafe conditions and the airstrip was closed.

As the controversy dragged on, aviation supporters went over the Forest Service control to enlist the help of Senator James McClure, R-Idaho. He secured funding through a Congressional earmark to fully excavate the holes, seal it off with wire mesh, cover it and then smooth over the airstrip, as well as engage greater law enforcement involvement.

Emil and Penny's potential knowledge of about the saboteurs came under questioning. The idea the Kecks would condone anything that could jeopardize pilot safety was offensive to them and their many friends in the backcountry pilot community. The idea they would risk injury to any pilot, when air support was often a lifeline in the wilderness, was out of the question. Emil was not graceful in dismissing the questions. Penny seethed at being questioned.

As Emil's presence on the porch increased friction and as Penny got questioned about her program, they bought a small house downstream on the road leading from Selway Falls to the outside world. The one-story house sat below the road, tucked into a clump of cedars, with grass leading to the river bank about 50 feet away. Penny bought it as a fall-back plan for Emil and his health issues. They paid cash. With the Selway River running clear and strong outside the south windows, it was only a half a world away from the wilderness - not completely in town. "At least we have a place to hang our hats, if nothing else," Penny said.

Then, on Oct. 1 1987, the district ranger, Dennis Dailey, dumped on Penny Keck a one and a half page memo titled, "Changes that must be made." The memo presented six subheads, followed by as many as eight bullet points.

Under the first subhead, "Acceptable Level of Program Management" were five points, all related to documentation and oversight by Dailey and other office staff.

Any review of project timing or design by Dailey was a waste of time for Penny. The Forest Service main office in Grangeville always assisted the Kecks on bridge material acquisitions and budgets. Additional review would be repetitive and a distraction. Tracking costs, budgets and accomplishments meant busy work to the Kecks and they kept it to the minimum. The actual accomplishments of the Kecks was continuously compared to a crew of six or more, because of their extra hours and days spent on the job and because of their advanced skills and pioneering techniques. And with the Kecks the Forest Service got two pros for the cost of one.

The next section "Visible Outyear Planning and Prioritization" was another demand for more paperwork tracking of items previously always in the Kecks' heads or pocket notebooks. The requirement was to maintain "trail logs," "condition surveys," and "transportation plans."

Emil Keck began trail condition surveys 24 years before and Penny Keck had been doing condition surveys for 20 years. An updated trail inventory was completed a couple years before, with a binder about two inches thick. The priorities for trail repair were determined every year by the trail crews in the field, with the Kecks making final determinations based on shared ideas and on anticipated budgets for the following year's crews. Every year trail crews and wilderness rangers cut out the main trails, with the majority opened up by July. Trail crews also took on critical drainage and tread work where needed, as they went. A simple ranger district map was posted on the cookhouse wall every year at Moose Creek, with trails marked off as each was cleared.

The map was a source of pride and competition between trail crews and wilderness rangers, with the secondary trails cut out before the end of summer. The thorny problems of rock work, reroutes, tread re-establishment, drainage or intensive brushing were tackled by trail crews on middle and later season hitches. The Kecks knew and remembered all 615 miles of primary and secondary trails on the district from having traveled everywhere. They provided advice, encouragement and technical expertise to trail crews as needed. Trail crew foremen took field notes, for future reference and for talks with the Kecks.

The third section was titled "Presence in Grangeville Office (Do not expect others to manage program for you.)" The points included "accessible during winter months to represent District in activities related to Trails, Facilities and Safety" and "Regularly scheduled office hours during field season..." The last point of the section was the demand for a "detailed itinerary of location and schedule when in the field."

The Kecks were the only year-round presence of the Forest Service in the 1.3 million acre Selway-Bitterroot Wilderness. They relied on the district ranger and the resource assistant to track the primary paperwork. Rangers and resource assistants spent three-quarters or more of their time in the office in Grangeville, at least since 1972 when Bill Holman left. He was the last district ranger operating from inside the wilderness at Moose Creek. The Kecks provided details on program needs for hiring and budgets and then managed their program from the middle of the wilderness. The Kecks never kept a set schedule. They operated according to weather conditions and project needs. Regularly scheduled office hours during the field season would mean less work got done in the field.

The Kecks often said if anyone needed critical assistance on the trail they'd drop what they were doing and be there - as quick as possible. In an emergency, everyone on the district knew the Kecks would hike through the night to help. A detailed itinerary of location and schedule in the field was superfluous for anyone in the field, with morning and evening radio check-ins. A detailed itinerary of the Kecks's location in the wilderness was like asking for a beat cop with 25 years in the neighborhood to describe what blocks he planned to patrol.

The next section headed "Move Out of Present House at Moose Creek" did not describe where they could move to, at the ranger station or anywhere else. The first point was "would like to be able to offer more suitable (housing) in event Resource Assistant has young family." The majority of this section covered what was headed by "Emil's presence at Moose Creek is creating unnecessary impacts."

The Kecks turned a dark log warehouse into their base camp at the ranger station, and it remained a warehouse for their tools and gear. While they used their base camp year-round, resource assistants typically spent a few weeks at the ranger station during the summer. Some years a resource assistant might spend most of three months at the station with frequent trips interspersed to the office in Grangeville. The Kecks were being forced out of their base at the ranger station, in case a resource assistant was hired with a young family and he or she would maybe spend a few weeks there in the summer.

Emil Keck told a lot of people a lot of things over the years. By the middle of the 1980s, he commanded attention while talking with anyone within earshot from his porch or as hobbled around the ranger station. His conversations and alliances with pilots, campers, and outfitters took different turns over the years, some times critical and in-their-face, sometimes complimentary and supportive of their special interests. The wilderness fire management program was dogged by many critics, especially among older Forest Service fire fighters who followed the absolutist credo of the 10 a.m. policy—to have every fire under control by 10 a.m. the next morning. Those critics often found ready allies with land owners, such as Everett Pierce at Selway Lodge, who saw the surrounding wilderness beset by flames. In arguments with Emil Keck about the fire program, fire managers found an intense, committed, if sometimes misinformed or misguided but worthy adversary.

The next section was headed by "Support Team goals—will need to cultivate a sense of District and Forest Service teamwork." The first point was, "operate programs in harmony with accepted policy and procedures (rather than in sprite of)."

Both Emil and Penny emphasized each individual should set his or her own goals for accomplishments, whether on trails, at lookouts or at the ranger stations. A certain skill level was required but actual output was based on an individual's physical capacity and experience. The crew was a conglomeration of often odd individuals with wide variations in backgrounds and relevant experiences—bound by an intention to honor wilderness. Anyone who made a personal commitment to do his or her best on the crew would be offered a job the next year, within budgets, and always were backed by the Kecks. No one did team building exercises - we worked together. The elusive quality termed esprit de corps thrived at Moose Creek, with the Kecks leading by example.

The last section was titled "Present Performance." The points included "reluctance to change and consider new or different ways of doing things (non motorized, non mechanical, wilderness sensitive trail standards..." and "preoccupation with production at the expense of personal freedoms (exploitive personnel practices) and the wilderness resource (osmoplastic, etc)." Other points included, "token support for District objectives, such as reducing flights (using personal flights to circumvent objective)", "practices that damage morale", "uniform misuse," and "routine fiscal abuse (maintenance of trails from fire funds)." Dailey appeared to not understand the Kecks established the wilderness trail standards, which defined how to limit mechanized and motorized equipment in trail operations. For a guy who never ran a Cobra drill, much less carried one on his back, never blasted rock, never rebuilt a bridge, never adapted sky-lines to move bridge timbers, never

Penny Keck at Moose Creek Ranger Station, 1987 *John McCarthy*

cut timbers, never set rock, never benched tread and never ran trail crews—Dailey didn't know shit about wilderness work on the ground.

To his credit, administrative air travel at Moose Creek decreased since Dailey arrived in 1986, with positive support from the whole crew including the Kecks. At the same time, stock travel to ferry supplies up the Selway trail increased to make up the difference, with concerns about associated impacts being voiced by many people including the Kecks.

Dailey was a stock man, using horses as his preferred means to travel the district. In the mid 1980s, flights to Moose Creek ran more than 900 a year for commercial, private and administrative uses. Dailey cut administrative flights from about 300 to less than 100 a year, not counting flights for fire management. The Kecks often paid for a personal flight or two in a year, to go out on their own schedule and to haul their own gear. With Emil not walking the 25 miles to the road anymore, they paid for a couple more flights to do personal as well as Forest Service business.

Penny Keck was known to sometimes wear a Forest Service shirt, over her stabbed off jeans, not following protocol to wear FS green pants. And often she didn't even wear the official shirt, preferring wool and flannel and not going in for badges. Wearing a uniform was a new requirement for technical staff and not something familiar to any one on trail crew.

The trail program had long cobbled together left overs from the much richer fire program, dating back at least to 1940 when the first smoke jumpers were stationed at Moose Creek. Districts got allocations for fire programs, including tools and equipment, and it was common for extra parts of the fire supplies to get handed down to trail programs. Fire fighters often worked trails during slow fire times. When the trail program was divorced from fire was not clear.

In an interview I did with Dailey in Grangeville in December 1987, he turned the tables on me to ask if the Kecks ever pressured me. He asked me if joining the airfield haying crew, without pay on my days off, was an example of the Kecks' preoccupation with production and an exploitive personnel practice. I told him, "no pressure, it was a honor to be part of the haying gang. The beers and steaks we all shared afterwards, at the Kecks' expense, were some of the richest payments I'd ever gotten for anything. It was fun, we knew how to work together and we ate great."

The contentions over fire management, pesticide use, tractor use, air travel, and stock use was effecting morale with the crew. People told me they found themselves caught, being forced to choose sides between the ranger and the Kecks, and it was tearing them apart.

Penny Keck did not see the memo as designed to make changes and improvements but as means to drive her out. The memo set the stage for termination. The memo contained so much misinformation, Penny was dumbfounded on where to begin a response. Emil Keck summed it up, "we're too god-damned hard to manage because we don't kiss his ass."

On October 18, less than three weeks after getting the "Changes that must be made" memo, the Kecks contracted a Vertol helicopter to bring in eight loads of timbers and gear for the Selway Lodge bridge reconstruction. The twin turbine, tandem rotor, cargo helicopter, known as a Chinook for the U.S. Army in Vietnam, did cable drops and landings with the timbers and hardware on both sides of the river at the Kecks' direction. Working with the engineers in the Supervisors Office, the Kecks did their part of the paperwork and administrative procedures for the contract to get all the material flown in to rebuild a suspension bridge in the wilderness. District Ranger Dailey was not at the bridge site to record if Penny Keck conducted an acceptable level of program management or determine if there was any uniform misuse.

The Kecks hoped to complete the primary bridge work in about two and a half months, depending on weather and any unforeseen difficulties in deconstruction. The team they assembled, two trail workers on extended seasons and the two of them, would continue until about Christmas. The Kecks would then go back to the ranger station for winter maintenance projects and return to the bridge in March on their own to finish off construction and do site rehabilitation.

Instead of initiating construction, the Kecks and their small crew did some organizing of the materials and then left. The young trail crew foreman being trained for bridges, Allison Zehner, then 27, said, "what really disturbs me is, the ranger has no way of knowing what the bridge status is. I don't know how he can make management decisions without seeing it."

Confronted by the memo from the district ranger, Penny Keck found her position untenable. Her conclusion was, "the job I've been doing no longer exists." And she did not want an office job, supervising crews but no longer in the field herself. Penny and Emil determined it might be time to leave.

The district ranger at the neighboring Selway District, Gloria Flora, who came on the same year as Dailey, got wind of the situation from her talks with Dailey and assessing the forest scuttlebutt. The Fire Management Officer on her district was retiring at the end of the season and Flora had an opening. While Flora was sympathetic to the Kecks, facing the loss of their wilderness home, she also viewed the situation as opportunistic.

Flora invited Penny Keck to lunch at the cafe in Syringa, for an informal, unofficial discussion. The two women leveled with each other. They both saw Dailey as intractable. Penny did not see how she could continue at Moose Creek, much less run her program the way she'd always done it. The FMO position did not match Keck's full skill set but it was a good job, with new challenges in the changing times of fire management and a lot of work in the field.

"In many ways it was serendipitous," Flora told me years later. "We had an opening. She had solid skills, knowledge of the area, and was a proven commodity. It was fast and easy with limited paperwork because she qualified for the job. And I liked Penny, we always got along well."

Flora saw the issues between the Kecks and Dailey as personality conflicts - not performance problems. "Penny and Emil really were icons, they deserved to stay at Moose Creek but if you looked hard enough at the situation - they weren't in a good position," Flora recalled.

Penny looked at Fenn Ranger Station, the Selway District headquarters, along the river road near their newly purchased but never lived in house, as a place to land. The district included a couple hundred thousand acres of roadless forest but no wilderness. As a timber harvesting district, there were broader fire management actions of prescribed fire, slash burning, thinning and planting, along with fire control. Penny saw opportunity and a future, as well as release. She took the job, starting with the assistant FMO title and soon getting promoted to FMO when she completed all the certifications.

When I heard they were packing up to leave Moose Creek, I hiked in to see them one last time at the ranger station. My disbelief turned to outrage when Penny showed me the "Changes that must be made" memo.

"If it were just one or two issues I could argue with them," Penny told me. "When it became all these issues I felt there was no sense in going forward."

When she asked Dailey why he was piling on all these perceived problems, without any systematic prior review or any procedure for resolutions, she said the response rankled even more. "He said, 'if you really want to stay, I would try to work with you.' And I thought, well if it's that much of a struggle—forget it buddy. Instead of saying, hey we can solve this and work together - he says he would maybe try to work with me. That statement has been my focal point for several weeks."

Being forced to manage her program from a desk in town made no sense to Keck. "Out here is where the work has to be done. You can manage the program from here 90 percent of the time," she said at the ranger station. "For the other 10 percent you have to be at the Supervisors Office but I'm already there that much of the time. He [Dailey] feels a manager should be sitting on his tail, a manager should not get his fingernails dirty," Penny concluded. "And I'd have to be holding his hand at least 60 percent of the time."

The problems between Emil Keck and Dailey were noticeable from the start and ran deep, Penny acknowledged. "There was animosity from the very beginning between Emil and Dennis, even more so than with other rangers. They've not said more than 10 sentences to each other all this year and that's only because they had to."

Several of the old hands at Moose Creek agreed with Penny's assessment that Dailey "came in scared of Emil." There was a big build-up about the cantankerous Emil Keck as the true commander in the wilderness. But the image did not match current reality. "Emil is not what he used to be, there's no question about it," Penny said. "He's lucky to work two-three hours a day at the max. Some days he hasn't worked at all."

For a man who lived by the credo—work is life and life is work—to not work took away much of the meaning of life.

Penny figured Dailey was mad at himself for taking Emil too serious. "Dennis now sees, hey old Emil isn't what they said. There are no gods at Moose Creek. And maybe he's taking a little heavier broomstick than he needed to clean it up."

"Emil made some broad statements about the Forest Service, as he normally does when he gets on his high horse, talking about fire and the airfields," Penny said. "It came back on Dennis and he couldn't control it."

Their cabin was in a central location within the ranger station and the forum from the porch proved irresistible for Emil to speak out. "So I either had to curtail Emil or leave," Penny continued. "What happened to free speech? And if somebody thinks I can control Emil they are out of their minds. Nobody controls that man."

Emil and Penny Keck at Tony Point Bridge, 1983 *Glenn Cruickshank*

From inside their makeshift kitchen and office, where the walls could fully be seen for the first time in the absence of tools and gear, Penny told me how she saw her options. "We were kicked out of this house no matter what we did, that's what really bugged me. Maybe we'd get a tent or something for the summer, he didn't offer anything else."

Speculation ran strong among the crew that Dailey was hired as district ranger to get Emil Keck out of Moose Creek. Wilderness ranger Bruce Farling explained it, "a lot of the people who want the Kecks gone are the same people that put them on a pedestal - to say here we have the Kecks doing all this wilderness work - we're Number One. They'd drag them out and show them off, in front of national media or the Forest Service brass. Then Emil gets old and gets even more mouthy being around the ranger station and they want to get rid of him."

A former wilderness ranger for more than a decade, Richard Kuhl of Kalispell, Montana, compared Emil to an aging fur trapper hanging around the fort telling tall tales or the shady gunslinger hired to clean up the town but then run off when not needed in polite company. The difference with Emil was, he kept the ranger station itself and the crews going for many years. "The Forest Service never considered the Kecks to be a detriment when the media was around or there was hard work to be done," Kuhl said.

"My final conclusion is, so what if Emil did make life more difficult for some people?," Kuhl continued. "Is the ranger's career more important than what I see was a handshake deal with Emil? They looked the other way from his opinions contrary to the company line when he worked 12 hours a day in the summer and built bridges in the middle of winter. They've put up with him for 20 years, I don't see what the problem is for the next five years. If he wants to die in there, if he wants to crawl into a snowbank and die, they ought to let him do it."
After I hiked out from Moose Creek, I spent an hour with Dailey in Grangeville at the district office. The key question I asked was if the Kecks made it easier or harder for the Forest Service achieve its management goals. Dailey said:

"I believe that they have made it harder to implement the law of the land and harder to accomplish the wilderness management job. And I don't believe that the violations were necessary. I think that Penny and Emil Keck have done quite a great service to the Selway and the maintenance of the trail system, the management of the trail system that they have done. They've done a good job of that. But they could have done the same job and conformed with the law. And they make the job of managing the wilderness for other people on the Moose Creek district more difficult."

I went back to Kuhl for his view. "They [Forest Service officials] knew what Emil and Penny were doing, whether it was pesticides or chain saws or whatever got anybody in a uproar, and they lived with it—when they both worked every day and they got two for the price of one."

Kuhl was part of the early wilderness ranger years, when their job was to get hunting and fishing outfitters to comply with the Forest Service new management plans for wilderness. Looking back, Kuhl said, "on the balance, the Kecks made it easier to implement the law of the land. Their dealings with the outfitters made it easier for us to come in and get them [outfitters] to clean up, both because of the Kecks' example and because the outfitters liked them and respected them. And their work ethic made it easier for us to deal with the public because when people went in there to Moose Creek they could see things were getting done."

"Go to any large wilderness on a par with Moose Creek and look at the outfitters' operations—I challenge anyone to find a better situation than Moose Creek. Same with the trails, I challenge anyone to find a better situation for trails anywhere," Kuhl said.

Brash talk and practical outcomes were connected, Kuhl continued. "Their spirit and thinking were part of the wilderness. Without that you have linear thinking, by the book, and that's worse."

Warren Miller, station guard and wilderness ranger, summed up the conflict between Dennis Dailey and Penny Keck as, "Dennis does things by the book and Penny threw out the book a long time ago."

While Penny laughed off the idea of "uniform misuse," Miller saw a deeper issue. "Dennis is always under control of the image he wants to present but I'm not so sure what's underneath the image. I tend to be a little suspicious of people who are always neat and clean."

Emil told me working without pay and training a young crew fit his plans. "It was going great until we got that memo from the ranger and then the old lady said button it up. I didn't give a fuck about the money, as long as they left me alone. It wasn't going to cost the Forest Service a thing to have me there. And we have the same regard for the land as we always have."

Given her limited options, to straddle a management chasm and to find new housing, Penny determined it was time to go. With winter coming on, she pulled together her plans to leave Moose Creek.

Flora at Fenn and her staff welcomed the Kecks. Going into the winter Penny operated from a desk in an office for the first time in her life. Come summer, she maintained a regular field presence to not be desk-bound. Field work included actual work alongside the crews, with Penny picking up tools, including chain saws now that she was outside the wilderness.

From the beginning, Flora said she had no complaints. "Penny learned the job in good time. She communicated well with the FMOs on the other districts. She got along well with the rank and file across the forest." Keck put to use her strong leadership capacity to direct people and her extensive on the ground knowledge, Flora said. She adapted these skills to oversee fire dispatch and management, deploying people and equipment all over the district.

The late 1980s and early 1990s were a time of great change in the Forest Service, as Flora recalled. The DG, or Data General, rose to prominence, with data and reports becoming all-important. Major social change also churned within the agency. "I was very interested in women moving up in leadership, to help them become more equal - not just in job titles - in trust and respect and pay," Flora said.

"I loved and prized employees that could think and observe for themselves and treat other people well," Flora continued. "They'd do well in tough situations and Penny did well. I found it possible to really excel with some renegade employees who had their own minds."

While Flora found Emil did not respect authority, she was not intimidated by his bluster. She remembered the first time they met, when Flora rafted the Selway River and hiked up to the Moose Creek station. She remembered Emil said to her, " 'let me take a look at you.' So I put my arms out and turned around in a circle. And he said, 'you're too little to be a ranger.' I just laughed and thought it was funny."

As tough, ornery and steadfast as he was, the move downriver to the little house along the road was difficult for Emil.

On my first visit to the Kecks at their house in late 1988, Emil said, "I'm just waiting here now to see what the old lady's going to do." He was more subdued than I'd ever seen him. In two hours I took a half page of notes when usually I'd fill half a notebook, writing as fast as I could to keep up with his stories. We talked about the weather. He had no plans. For long minutes he stared out the window without talking, watching the river go by. His blue-green eyes were clouded. "I'm not doing much around here but at least I haven't found Jesus," he said.

On a visit a year later, in late 1989, two years after he'd left Moose Creek, when I asked Emil how he was doing, the immediate response was—"I got canned." He then launched into an hour of non-stop stories. He talked fast and furious, like the old days, telling me about repairing airstrips, long ago trail inventories, ordering freeze dried food to lighten loads, being tight with money for materials to hire more people instead, and how sometimes when he got tired on the trail with a heavy pack he'd take a snort of whiskey to keep going. As he talked into the second hour, he dug out a bottle of Schnapps to share a snort and he kept going with his stories.

He spoke with bitterness and with joy about Moose Creek. In one thought line he went from "let me tell you about that son of a bitching whore the ranger," to say, "when you have a piece of land that is as beautiful as it was at Moose Creek and you have it under tight management and you are training your people, you just keep going steady and over the years you improve it. You repair the trails and the airstrips, you keep your fingers in everything. And that's all there is to it. And then this asshole comes in and doesn't have a fucking clue what he's doing and it all goes to hell."

Then he stopped his condemnation of the agency and pulled out a copy of Loggers World magazine to show me a story about his son and his grandson, Arlen and Charlie Keck. The story covered innovative uses of high line leads to move timbers without carving erosion ruts, same as Emil did with bridge timbers. "Isn't that neat, he learned it from me. They are good capable woods people," Emil said.

Emil and Penny had reconnected with Arlen and his family, making periodic visits to Potlatch, Idaho, home base for Keck Logging. Arlen proclaimed his religious values with a cross and the words Jesus Christ painted on all his log truck doors. Emil laughed when he explained Arlen would lead his crews in prayer at their home. When Emil visited, Arlen would say things like, "Lord, this broken down old bastard here is my father and he needs Your help to keep going, because he's beat up bad from being too damned stupid to take care of himself." Emil thought it was hilarious, saying, "Jesus Christ on the cross, Arlen prays to God like a god-damned logger."

I'd brought along my son, young Emil at 6-years-old. Old Emil took a shine to him as we watched the boy throwing sticks and rocks in the river. "He doesn't take any shit off anyone, isn't that great," old Emil said, laughing, "and he doesn't have to either."

Earlier in April, after a wet hike up the Selway, I stopped by for an hour to tell old Emil the boys' mother and I were getting divorced. Hiking in light rain, seeing first flowers of dogtooth violets and trilliums and watching spring flights of kingfishers and mergansers had rejuvenated my spirits. Emil always liked Mary Butters, who he referred to only by her last name, for her work ethic, willingness to learn new tasks and an ability to chart her own course. Emil talked to me about commitments and responsibilities. All sounds good until the rules change, I responded. We both struggled with change.

As I was leaving, Emil said he wanted to keep track of me because, "you're a person with ideas and you've got dreams and you've got guts."

In mid-January 1990, Emil got slammed by a stroke and was rushed to the hospital in Lewiston. When I went down the hill from Moscow to see him and asked how he was doing, he said in a creaky voice, "not too fucking good. They said I had the big one, but I don't fucking know." His had no strength in his arms.

A couple of days later when I stopped by the hospital again, Emil started off rasping, "I don't know what I'm fucking doing here, nobody tells me anything." A nurse encouraged him to sip juice and she said, "you want to get better and go home don't you?" Emil responded, quick as ever but slurring words without force, "no, who says I do."

Before I left, with Penny out of the room, Emil waved me over, barely able to move his good hand, and said, "Johnson, put a fucking pillow over my head and get it over with." His eyes locked on mine. He meant it. I said no, he'd bounce back. He snorted, groaned and said, "get the fuck out of here."

By the end of the month, Emil regained some mobility and was more talkative. He spoke in coherent phrases, almost every word understandable, still cursing. He talked about death coming soon, but not before he'd get a 20 gauge shotgun and take some people out. He stared with probing eyes, to see if I thought he was joking. Before he or I could say more, former Moose Creek district ranger Art Seamans and his wife, Joyce, came into the room.

Art was good at talking with Emil, sharing updates on people they'd both known and describing his own career opportunities with the Forest Service. Art chattered on and Emil just listened, a rare event. When they left, Art told Penny she was always welcomed at their house along the river. Just let herself in, the back door wasn't locked, don't worry about them. Penny was staying at a hotel but clearly appreciated the offer.

As I left, Penny said, if Emil did get the shotgun, "he'd leave no tracks. Reagan's got nothing on him for hiding the things he doesn't want people to see." She was joking.

Emil and Penny did go home, back along the Selway River, briefly, before going to Missoula for rehabilitation therapy.

In late-March, sitting over coffee at a cafe called the Shack in Missoula, on the return leg of a trip to the Utah Canyonlands, a soon to be abruptly ex-girlfriend looked at the local Sunday paper and blurted out, "Emil Keck?" I knew, without any consideration, it was his obituary.

Emil Keck died at Missoula Community Hospital the previous Friday, March 24, 1990, at age 77. Cause of death was pulmonary embolism, or a blood clot migrating to block an artery in his lung.

On the day of his death, I'd explored a wilderness canyon in southern Utah, slept on a sand wash with a sliver of stars bound by rock walls overhead. I learned how to be in the wilderness from Emil Keck, how to feel the wilderness for what it offered. He was a simple man in many ways, with a life pared to the essentials, without use for hobbies, or leisure, who saw pleasure as drinking a beer after a day of sweat and bullshitting with your buddies, or just sitting by a creek as it got dark. He was a man who knew how to do everything that needed to be done in the wilderness, and knew how to teach others—mostly by example.

On the drive back to Moscow, we stopped at a logger bar in St. Regis, Montana, where there was a sign on the door, "This business is supported by Timber dollars." I bought shots of Jim Beam for my two friends. They didn't know Emil, but figured anyone who brought out a tear in a Missoula cafe, and who I called the coolest guy I'd ever known, was worth toasting. Two old geezers nearby half-assed tried to pick a fight with each other. Everyone in the bar, except for the barmaid, seemed drunk at 5 p.m. Emil would have liked the place.

We stopped again, over the pass, at another bar, in Wallace, Idaho, for a round of Jameson. Somewhere I explained, Emil defined integrity and loyalty, he'd do anything to help one of his people. His skills are evident in the bridges standing in the wilderness. His legacy was in the people he taught how to work with conviction, honesty and intensity. The front page commemorative column I wrote about Emil for the *Lewiston Tribune* a week later got the headline, "He was a tough old guy, and I loved him." The schmaltzy inclusion of the "L" word ticked me off, dragging in some kind of touchy-feely emotional grabber, when I wanted it all tough and hard edged. Later, to further displeasure, I realized the headline writer got it right. It was true, he was tough and I did love him. And it's always unsettling to realize editors can be right.

The obit listed his son, two daughters, a brother, four sisters, 10 grandchildren, seven great-grandchildren and Penny, as survivors. At his request, no services were planned. But we defied him, and had a memorial anyway. Emil would have cursed us out and laughed.

Moose Creekers and Emil's family gathered at Johnson Bar, along the lower Selway River, in late spring. People set up tents and campers. We shared a pot luck supper. Into the night we told stories, told lies, drank whiskey, threw Selway country logs on the fire and remembered a great man, our leader without a title, or even a badge, much less a uniform, just a man of the wilderness.

Mountain Man and Pioneer

William R. "Bud" Moore

FEW PEOPLE WHO EXPERIENCED the true untamed American West, who knew firsthand the rough mountain men of this wild land, who then became a leader in understanding modern values of wilderness. Few people who saw the woodsmen of old—the trappers, packers, prospectors, hunters, and explorers out in their natural habitats—then carried their skills and traits to the wilderness of today. Few people who walked the halls of government offices in cities of the West and in Washington, D.C. as a top level, federal agency man, were also mountain men.

William R. Moore, known as Bud to everyone, lived as a mountain man in his youth, became a leader in understanding the land for the U.S. Forest Service, and lived out his days as modern homesteader. Bud Moore was a link to the old, wild West past. Bud Moore was also a bridge to the future, to a sustained appreciation of wild lands. Bud Moore understood what it took to survive and to thrive in wild lands and knew what it takes to keep those lands wild in America today. Bud Moore taught many people the ways of the West, by being in the wilderness, by taking other people along and by telling stories of a life lived in the wildest land.

"In the early days the forest rangers were highly respected people," Bud Moore said one chilly, early summer morning, while sitting by a barrel stove in a cabin whose logs he cut, skidded and notched to craft a combination office-warehouse-bunkhouse. "The Forest Service was then a young organization, unencumbered with a lot of bureaucracy. They were highly decentralized because they had no communication. They had to have men out there that knew how to get things done and who could do it on their own. These people were self-reliant. When they needed bridges built they built them, quickly and at low cost."

William R. "Bud" Moore with martin pelt, Bob Marshall Wilderness, Montana, 1986 *Richard I. Walker*

Moore paused to bring his story into the present times. "Emil and Penny (Keck) reflect this. They maybe don't build bridges only in the old ways, because they use some different tools and techniques, but they do it in the same spirit of independence and self-sufficiency. There is a tie here in how they live and work. What I see happening, and I'm not sure it's fully happened is: when we created the wilderness, what we really said was, when it comes to human occupancy we're going to stop the clock somewhere around the turn of the century, in the early 1900s, and live with these lands like we were living with them then. To do that we still need the skills that Bill Bell and Ed Mackay demonstrated back in the early days."

Bill Bell and Ed Mackay were legendary rangers of the old Selway National Forest. Mackay oversaw the forest along the Lochsa River, out of Powell Ranger Station, and Bell worked up slope out of Elk Summit Ranger Station, back in the early decades of the 20th Century. Norman Maclean wrote about Bill Bell as the lead character in his story, "USFS 1919: The Ranger, the Cook and a Hole in the Sky," recalling "a world of hoof and foot and the rest done by hand."

While Bud Moore was of the next generation, born in 1918, he not only grew up hearing stories of Bill Bell and Ed Mackay, he knew them personally and idolized them. Bud worked for Mackay as a teenager on his first Forest Service job and throughout his life he emulated the early rangers' capacity for hard work and commitment toward the forest. Moore later became friends with Norman Maclean when they both had cabins near Seeley Lake in Montana. Moore walked and talked as if he was a character out of a Maclean story from another time, and in many ways, he was.

Bud Moore was the oldest of nine children, whose family settled an 80-acre homestead on the Lolo Fork of the Bitterroot River downstream from Lolo Hot Springs. The Moore place was a stop-off for the mountain men coming and going through the Bitterroots into the Selway and Lochsa country. In summer, the mountain men would travel on horseback, pulling pack stock loaded with supplies going into the mountains and loaded with game meat coming out. In winter, he'd see the grizzled men come out on snow shoes loaded with pelts on their own backs.

"I thought in those days and still think the early mountain men of Bitterroots were some of the greatest people on earth," Moore said during a series of interviews we did in the 1980s. "My dad cranked out some pretty good moonshine liquor and they'd stop by for a jug."

The moonshine loosened their tongues and soon the often-solitary men would spin tales of their journeys in the wild lands. Their stories of animal encounters and unpopulated forests captivated the younger Moore. "I developed a great urge to go over into those mountains and it became kind of a mission with me. So, as soon as I grew up big enough to get over the windfalls and go, well, that's what I did. I took a bed roll and a rifle, some fishing line, and I went over into the Lochsa country."

The country calling to Bud had one road, up over Lolo Pass across the Idaho state line and downslope another 14 miles to Powell Ranger Station, where the Crooked Fork and White Sand Creek join to form the Lochsa River. When Bud struck out for the backcountry, the upper Lochsa canyon was impenetrable to any other roads. To the north and south stretched untouched wilderness, a heavily forested land rejuvenating from the multi-million-acre 1910 fire. "In those days the whole Lochsa, the whole Selway country, was wild. There were no roads or anything in there," Moore recalled.

The Lochsa country receives more moisture than its sister river basin of the Selway to the south, with 40 to 50 inches average annual precipitation—the majority as snow. The ridges can see upwards of 70 inches of precipitation, pushing the creeks high in snow-melt run-off and hydrating dense forests. Old-man's beard hangs from grand fir trees in long, light-green tangled tendrils and sphagnum moss spreads over the forest floor in a continuous cushion.

At age 13, Bud herded sheep for the summer, leading one of the first bands to graze in the grassy headwaters meadows of the Lochsa. After another herder and a camp tender quit, he traveled alone with his dogs and the sheep. "I was on a first name basis with the old grizzlies. And I got to know which lakes had fish in them and which didn't; important things like that."

Knowing his youngster was alone for months, his father came up from the valley in late summer to help finish out the season. Soon after the elder Moore's arrival, a grizzly bear tore into the band of sheep one night and killed 30 animals. They set out a leg hold trap to capture the bear. After six days of checking the trap they found a massive bear thrashing in the brush. Facing snarling muscle and fury, Bud passed-up taking the head shot and let his father fire his rifle to take down a grizzly in his prime. They estimated the bear to be 1,000 pounds and marveled at its power even when stilled.

At the time, the encounter pumped excitement and shaped an epic family story. Later, as bears continued to run into conflict from easy eating of sheep and hard impact of herders' bullets, Bud bemoaned the demise of grizzlies and the disappearance of iconic animals of wildness. "There ought to be a place for the great bear in our wilderness, they are part of the spirit of the place—even if they scare people," he said. Within 15 years of their fateful meeting with the sheep-eating bear, in 1946 the last of the Bitterroot grizzlies was shot. As a young sheep herder, Bud did not fully recognize his part in the ending of an era for wild nature at the hand of man, but as time went on he became a strong, public voice for restoring nature, advocating for reintroduction of grizzly bears to the Lochsa and Selway country.

In his early teens, Bud also began pulling a crosscut saw for timber and stove wood around the homestead and for hire. School interfered with his learning the ways of the forest and he stopped going after eighth grade. When ranger Ed Mackay offered Bud a job as a fire lookout on McConnell Mountain in 1935, the 17 year-old jumped at the opportunity for additional mountain lessons. He'd already hiked most of the ridges and canyons on both sides of the Bitterroot Crest and marveled at the view from McConnell across the vast landscape.

Later in that year, Bud bought out an old trapper's territory for $150. The ill-fated old timer accidentally burnt down his own cabin at Wendover Bar and, unwilling to face winter in a tent in the snow, was glad to unload his traplines on a youngster ready for adventure. Soon after Christmas, Bud bought new traps and supplies, loaded it all with his rifle onto an eight-foot toboggan and snowshoed up over Lolo Pass. Pulling the sled beyond Wendover, he searched and scratched through deep snow to find the other shacks along the trapline for shelters spaced a days' snowshoe hike apart.

"I'm probably the only person that essentially can say I grew up in the Lochsa from boyhood to manhood," Moore explained. "I went over there a lot from our stump farm we'd cleared from the forest. I was trapping fur in the winter and working for the Forest Service in the summer. I was in there year-round clear up to the time I was 39.

"So, I grew up there and there was nobody else that did. Everybody else was seasonal. But when everyone else was getting ready to leave as the snow flew, I was packing supplies to my trap cabins. The Forest Service would pull out and it would be just me and old Jay Turner. We were the only two trappers in the country then. I wasn't an in-and-outer. I was permanent. It was my home."

The next year he borrowed a mule from Ed Mackay to skid logs for a replacement cabin at Wendover, completing his base camp in the fall. He spent six winters, from his teens into his 20s, trapping alone, with only the one other solitary trapper, Jay Turner, as his remote neighbor.

"It was a dream come true. Here I was in the middle of the wilderness with a brand-new cabin and seven other line cabins, six to nine miles apart, running my traplines at least six times in a winter and making really good money." He covered 700 to 900 miles in a winter and made $1,100 to $1,600 in a season gross, during the Great Depression, at the time a forest ranger would be paid $1,500 a year.

In February, he'd hike out with a bale of furs on his back. "It looked like you're carrying a refrigerator, but it really wasn't that much weight. It was pretty exciting times for a teenager hooked on the mountains."

Gary Koehler and Bud Moore near Fish Lake, 1974 *Richard I. Walker*

Summers brought Bud back to the ranger station at Powell, to be part of a seasoned crew. When he walked into the bunkhouse at Powell for the first time on June 4, 1935, as "a pink-cheeked kid who wasn't hardly growing whiskers yet," he didn't find many young people like himself. The crews of the Forest Service in those days were mostly lumberjacks and in their 30s.

"They were the type of people that could do things. They were good sawyers and they could file crosscut saws. They knew how to fight fire. They could put up buildings and do all of the things you needed done because there was no reason to hire anybody that couldn't do it."

Bud was one of the few young people Ranger Mackay hired to spot fires and to fight fires near his mountain lookout. He was eager to learn everything about working in the forest. The lumberjacks of the crew disdained a lookout job that kept someone sitting on a mountaintop away from what they considered the real work of cutting trails and chasing smoke. The hard-bitten older hands also thought they could ride a soft youngster from the valley out of the woods.

"I survived by working the tails off the bastards. I could out-hike them all. And I could saw; I'd been a gyppo on my own sawing in the woods. When they were through with me some of them were a little leaner than when they started. So, I gradually earned their respect."

Ranger Mackay sent Bud up to McConnell, a bare mountaintop at 7,424 feet on the divide between the Lochsa and the Selway basins. Bud soaked in the empty expanse and sought an even better view. He built a 6-foot by 6-foot pole platform perched above the tree tops. He was uncertain what response he'd get from the ranger, without getting any instructions to build anything.

The next time Mackay rode up the ridge he took one look at the pole construction and grumbled. Bud kept quiet. The next time a packer came along he carried copper wire for lightning rods and nails to secure the platform with a railing, following Mackay's directions. Another new fire lookout was established, one of dozens going up on mountaintops of the Lochsa and the Selway in the 30s and 40s. And Bud started a career with the Forest Service, as one of the last people to rise to the upper agency ranks who started with practical, woods knowledge unencumbered by a college education.

To explain how the Forest Service operated in those early days, Bud described the beginning of the 1922 season—even before his time there. Bill Bell was ranger at Elk Summit, before merging with Powell in the late 1920s. The road had yet to be built and Bell determined a supply route over Lolo Pass could carry bigger loads and go faster than the more direct but steeper route up Blodgett Pass from Hamilton in the Bitterroot Valley.

Ed Mackay joined Bell for the June excursion to open their respective ranger stations. Mackay had three packers, each pulling a string of nine or ten mules, with his own gear packed on a couple head along with a saddle horse. Bill had two pack trains, along with his own short string. The crew of 25 men walked.

When they arrived at the confluence of streams that form the Lochsa

River, the Crooked Fork rushed in full flood but was possible to ford. All five pack trains and the men plunged in on foot, with water up to the men's chests. On the other side, White Sand Creek ran a raging torrent and was impossible to cross. The trail to Elk Summit took off from the far bank and it would likely be weeks before water levels dropped.

Bell anticipated flood conditions and strung a light cable between trees the previous fall, to carry a trolley for one man at a time to cross the creek. He also packed a heavier cable to line across the creek, to then guide and secure a ferry. The men felled cedar logs for a raft and ferried across the creek two fully-loaded pack strings. "And in two days Bill was on the other side and headed to Elk Summit," Bud explained.

Bell knew the log raft would prove too cumbersome, so he'd already hired a couple of carpenters to build a bridge. Powell provided food and a camp for the carpenters who traveled with a few pack animals to carry all their tools. Planks were split and Bell forged the metal hardware on site. They designed the bridge with one pier, set off-center in the creek to deflect flows and to reduce the span for log stringers from abutments on each side, anchored on cribs filled with rocks.

"By the end of the summer, two men with the help of a couple rangers had built a tremendous bridge. It was a big bridge. And then they went on to the next job. That's the kind of skills they had in opening the country."

Trail construction to service firefighters was the primary purpose of the Forest Service in the 1920s and 1930s. The Great Burn, Big Burn, or Big Blowup of 1910 torched three million acres across eastern Washington, northern Idaho, and western Montana. Exploding from hurricane force winds on a few hot August days, a collection of smaller fires joined together in a deadly and destructive conflagration. Small towns of Taft in Montana and Grand Forks over the line in Idaho were leveled to ash, never to be rebuilt. The major silver mining city of Wallace lost a third of its buildings and was considered saved, given the expected annihilation. Firefighters accounted for most of the 87 dead, many inexperienced and ill-equipped. The young Forest Service, officially formed and named in 1905, was shocked into action to do something about the scourge of summer flames.

"Fire was the big reason for being, for the Forest Service," explained Moore. "The Forest Service was geared to protect the forest for some future use, whatever that was to be. They didn't really know what use it was to be, but they did know they didn't want the forest to burn down again. Stopping the large fires, keeping those big sweeping burns down was an early-day, all-consuming mission of the Forest Service."

Although the remaining Selway and Lochsa forests stood far beyond the reach of settlement, and only a few scattered cabins required minimal timber harvest, logs from the forest were expected to go to sawmills someday. "The wilderness idea hadn't matured yet," Moore continued. "Most of the early day foresters weren't thinking about wilderness at all. They were in with Gifford Pinchot's philosophy that having commercial forests was first and foremost, and if there was anything else it was secondary."

As the first chief of the Forest Service, Pinchot dominated its foundational principles with an emphasis on active management of forests for production of timber. In declaring the greatest good for the greatest number to be the driver of National Forest policy, Pinchot adapted the European model of intensive private forest management to public land for a democracy. Pinchot recognized other resource values in the forests besides timber, particularly minerals, forage for livestock, and water for irrigation and municipal use. All his emphasis was on practical use, while eliminating corporate abuse and control, of the public lands.

Bud's action to build a lookout platform on McConnell fit within a pattern across the land. First a platform on a mountaintop, then a roof, followed by walls and soon a proper log cabin with a cupola on top for a man to scan for fires. Board cabins and towers on stilts started to be constructed in the late 1920s. At one time the Selway-Bitterroot was dotted with more than 75 lookouts on the peaks.

The fire spotters and the smoke chasers were connected through miles and miles of telephone wire, using 9-gauge galvanized wire, known throughout the forests as #9 wire. A system of long and short rings created a calling directory for the scattered lookouts to check in and to call in signs of smoke ignited by lightning. Splicing the breaks and rehanging wire strung through ceramic insulators in trees above trails, using climbing spurs to go up the trunks, was one of the first jobs of the spring. Today, a rare white or brown insulator can sometimes be seen high in a tree as final markers of a wired network later dismantled.

Along with trails, rough roads began to penetrate the wilderness of the Northern Rockies in the 1920s. The regional forester at Missoula, Major Evan Kelley, pushed for fire control access with so-called truck trails throughout the forests. When the Civilian Conservation Corps expanded the work force in the 1930s, more roads, bridges, ranger stations, and CCC camps reached into the backcountry.

Part of Major Kelley's plan was to punch a road up over Elk Summit and down along East Moose Creek to go to Moose Creek Ranger Station. The first 20 miles of road uphill from Powell Ranger Station and past Elk Summit Ranger Station were roughed-in when Bob Marshall, the first director of Recreation and Lands for the Forest Service in the Washington Office, heard about it.

Marshall adapted the land preservation ideas from the initiators in the Forest Service, Aldo Leopold and Arthur Carhart, to become the premier wilderness visionary of his time. Among the largest expanses of land within the agency's control that remained green blocks on maps without roads was the Lochsa and Selway country. As Moore described it: "Marshall worked on Major Kelley until he came around and became supportive of the wilderness movement. Kelley liked Marshall and his ideas and his energy. They stopped building roads in some places, damn near overnight."

The Elk Summit-Moose Creek truck road stopped its thrash through the forest in 1933, four miles beyond what would later become the Selway-Bitterroot Wilderness boundary. The land continues to heal, with remnants of the track visible today.

In 1936, with the driving force of Marshall, and the support of Kelley and a few others, the Selway-Bitterroot Primitive Area was established by the Secretary of Agriculture. Many people throughout the Forest Service continued to favor development and considered any lands not granted specific protection to be destined for roads and timber harvest. The reduction in timber values after the 1910, 1919, and 1934 big fire years in the Selway country did make preservation more palatable within Forest Service ranks, although many thought it was temporary until the forests grew back. "The Forest Service didn't want many constraints put on Gifford Pinchot's policies," Moore explained. People in the agency didn't want resources, timber in particular, tied up under law. With wilderness declared separate, Forest Service and local people also feared there could soon be additional protection areas, specific for wildlife or watersheds, further limiting operations.

Moore knew where he stood. "I was very supportive of the wilderness idea from the very beginning, being a trapper and a guy who loved the backcountry," he said. "I thought it was a hell of a good deal to keep some lands the same as always and not develop everything."

Regulations in the primitive areas banned roads but not motorized equipment. Soon, chainsaws replaced crosscut saws; motor scooters replaced pack animals, gas-powered drills replaced star bits to bore out blasting holes, Ford Tri-motors and other early aircraft buzzed into newly cleared airstrips, reducing pack animal reliance.

While policy, tools, and equipment were in transition, the people and their skill sets working in the backcountry also changed. After service in the U.S. Marine Corps during World War II, and stints at Seeley Lake and Missoula ranger districts, Moore returned to Powell in 1948 as acting ranger and was soon to be promoted to District Ranger.

"I came in as acting ranger when the door wasn't completely shut to people who weren't forestry school graduates," Moore recalled. "And then I was able to move up to be ranger, which didn't happen very often, because I was there, doing all the work that needed to be done."

Bud Moore breaks trail, Bob Marshall Wilderness, 1986 *Richard I. Walker*

Most of the work force had already changed. "When I went back to the bunkhouse after the war, the lumberjacks were gone," he said. The new equipment of chainsaws, bull dozers, log skidders, and haul trucks now penetrated parts of the upper Lochsa country on land deeded to railroad companies. Coming over Lolo Pass from the Montana side and into the lower elevation Clearwater country on the Idaho side, loggers made their way to the interior forests. Lumberjacks became loggers year-round and no longer spent summers with the Forest Service.

"We were in trouble: those people with the hand-skills we needed were gone, but those jobs still needed to be done," Moore said. "Those folks with those skills were gone, and the Forest Service wasn't trying to recapture them. The thrust was going the other way. The thrust was to mechanize."

Machines were brought in to solve all problems of limited labor and skills, to do it fast with minimal people, sometimes regardless of effects. After Moore took over as ranger at Powell, forest engineers presented a plan to rough-out a wider trail along the path of the old Elk Summit-Moose Creek road route. They didn't plan to make it a regular route for truck travel, because that idea was already shut down. The engineers only wanted to carve a path wide enough to take a bulldozer to Moose Creek to maintain the airstrip. "I just told them, 'Not while I'm Ranger on the Powell district are you going to take any dozers down to Moose Creek.' The Ranger still had a lot of say regarding any permanent developments in those days."

Actions of individual Rangers led to different outcomes. In the early 1950s, Bud hiked across the Bitterroots over Bear Creek Pass to go downhill on the trail along the creek on the east side of the declared primitive area. "I couldn't believe what I saw. The first few miles of the trail were reconstructed by dozer. You talk about an impact on a wild place. It was wide enough for a Jeep. They weren't letting Jeeps in there but here was something far worse than what I turned down." Today, the scars from a wide bench remain.

As the old hands retreated from the woods, Moore saw the density of people in the backcountry decline. "During the trail boom of the 20s, you had pack trains loaded with dynamite blasting trails through the country; you had lookouts going up, cabins being built, bridges being built, all these things going on. Today, you realize in many ways, the wilderness is much wilder. Now, we're intent on saving it in its natural state. We've packed out a lot of the junk that was left behind. We've rolled up the old telephone lines and packed out the can dumps. And a lot of the structures are gone."

The 1964 designation of the Selway-Bitterroot Wilderness solidified a uniform management framework and secured specific boundaries for the wilderness. In the long effort to pass wilderness legislation, the Forest Service did not take an official stance in opposition but did not offer support until late in the eight-year effort to secure Congressional approval. Along the way, many individuals in upper agency ranks, including then Forest Service Chief Richard E. McArdle, argued against getting their hands tied by special legislation, often speaking outside the public forums. From the beginning of the wilderness proposal, Moore was among a cadre of vocal supporters who he considered to be a small minority within the agency. Moore supported the wilderness declaration to preserve wild nature and to counter the rush toward mechanization.

Moore also believed wilderness could rejuvenate a backcountry work force. "While the skilled old-timers were scarce, there were plenty of new people willing to learn," he said. "They had good land ethics about wilderness and an eagerness to take care of it. These folks replaced the lumberjacks and the trail builders of the 20s, even if a lot of them pretty much had to learn from scratch."

In the early days after the Wilderness Act, there were leaders who learned and taught the skills needed in wild lands. Moore named Emil and Penny Keck, Bill Holman, the ranger at Moose Creek in the late 1960s and early 1970s, and Holman's resource assistant, Richard I. Walker, along with Jack Dolan in the Bob Marshall Wilderness of Montana. "These people valued pioneer skills and carried the torch.

They established the direction to tear out fences, clean up old fire camps and outfitter camps, haul out the half-buried garbage dumps, and do the work with pioneer tools and pack stock."

Reducing the signs of human intrusion in wild places, using pioneer skills to do it, and focusing resources in the field, all fit with Moore's views of wilderness. While these ideas were not universally embraced in the agencies, Moore recalled his boyhood hero, Bill Bell, the ranger who could pack a mule team to take on any job. "The thing that bothers me now, in wilderness the so-called professional management decisions are being made too far from the land. There ought to be a Bill Bell in charge of management in the Bob Marshall Wilderness. And he ought to have a pretty free rein. There ought to be a Bill Bell in charge of Moose Creek. Moose Creek probably comes pretty close now. They have a pretty free rein," Moore said, although our conversation was before Emil and Penny Keck left Moose Creek.

"You take these districts, particularly those that aren't all wilderness, they're run in part by computers. Data is gathered and put into computers, where it often just sits. The people in the woods are seasonal. The real professional leadership is not out there in the field, it's down at the headquarters of the National Forest."

His ideas grew from seeing Bill Bell and Ed Mackay in action. "But the first people that are laid off are those out in the woods and they're losing the people that are out there really doing the job. If I were in the service today, I'd be arguing real strong for assignment of responsibility right out there on the land, to a honcho that can take charge of the wilderness. And give him freedom to act and responsibility to take care of the country. It's split up now in a lot of ways, functionally. Fire, for example, is all run from the Supervisor's Office, the wilderness ranger has very little to do with it, it's all a specialized thing. I would like to see strong men and women out there on the land with the authority and the accountability to do the job. But it seems like we're going in the opposite direction."

Disconnects and discontent between woods-wise, independent field staff and the professional hierarchy in offices wasn't something new, just more prevalent, Moore acknowledged. His own model ranger, Bill Bell, was driven out of the Forest Service in 1928 from an ill-defined argument with the forest supervisor over horses or money or authority or cutting trees or something else.

From the initial surge to establish wilderness values, skills and creativity after the Wilderness Act of 1964, by the mid-1980s Moore was concerned. "It's a little disappointing to me today to see wilderness management deteriorating. The way I see management of wilderness, it is an important resource and I would like to see it taken care of. Management is probably the wrong word because you don't really have to manage the wilderness, you're more a custodian or a protector. If you have to manage anything it would be the people. And you shouldn't even manage them, because who the hell wants to go into the wilderness and have somebody manage him. That's the place to be free in spirit."

As Moore spoke about the way to be in wilderness, his cadence flowed and his eyes fixed on mine. "Taking care of the wilderness is a pretty complicated thing," he continued. "And you can't do it with computers. And you can't do it with people who think like computers. You've got to have people who are sensitive not only to the natural ecology but are sensitive to the interaction of people with it. And that just doesn't come quick. It takes time."

By the 1980s, the de-emphasis of field staff and the focus on the big dollar resource—timber—was not new and not limited to any one region. Beginning back in the 1950s, Moore observed the ascendancy of timber over other forest resources during his own time as district ranger at Powell.

Prior to the Wilderness Act a strange intersection of events and timing thrust Moore into a pivotal position in one of the many incidents nationwide to diminish and degrade American wilderness. The events started with a massive forest blowdown on his Powell district. A wind storm toppled trees in waves, followed by an infestation of spruce bark beetles, which led to an epidemic of beetles sweeping farther into live trees. The event was a sporadic, natural occurrence that disrupts forest uniformity. Forest Service officials decided not to stand back and allow natural decay. At the beginning of the 1950s, even at remote Powell, the agency possessed the means and the literal power to counter nature. But the outcome was unknown and proved unexpected.

The story of drastic hubris in altering natural systems by timber logging and road building is perhaps nowhere better told than by Bud Moore himself, in his book *The Lochsa Story: Land Ethics in the Bitterroot Mountains.* Almost two decades in researching and writing, Moore's book covers the Lochsa country from the days of the Nez Perce Indians to almost the end of the 20th Century. In congruent parts of history, personalized storytelling, land management analysis, and memoir, Moore weaves a cohesive story of a broad land. His analysis of Forest Service land management in his time speaks with an honesty, a base of first-hand knowledge and a personal integrity not found anywhere else.

Chapters titled "Trial by Bulldozer" and "Consequences of Logging the Beetle-Killed Spruce" explain in unflinching detail the changes wrought on the north side of the Lochsa while undisturbed wilderness held fast to the south in the Selway. Moore's original intent as District Ranger was to implement a timber management plan after a road, named, without irony, the Lewis and Clark Highway, could be completed to connect Idaho with Montana. The plan to wait for the new road and forestall harvest fell by the wayside under pressure from bugs and the opportunity for action.

Moore writes, "The pace of the race was outstripping our knowledge of the land. What would logging and road building do to the soils, water, wildlife, trout, and salmon so vital to the spirit of place in the land of the Lochsa? Our land ethic was growing but not yet mature. None of us had the wisdom to foresee the consequences of the program that we had devised. We had no [Aldo] Leopolds to give us advice. That we were moving too fast and with too little knowledge seemed obvious, but the bugs wouldn't wait and we couldn't either."

In his summation, Moore acknowledges, "During the five years from the discovery of spruce bark beetles at Bear Camp, we had destroyed a wilderness and opened much of the country to motorized vehicles." He does not skirt his own inclusion in playing a major role.

The next chapter, "Poisoning the Land and Its Waters," is equally horrific and honest. Another insect invader of the forest, the spruce budworm, attacked young trees—the future forest—and the saplings planted after the beetle logging. The scientists of the Forest Service proclaimed the options were do nothing or do massive aerial insecticide spraying with DDT. Again, neither the people closest to the land at the ranger district or the specialists who crafted the program understood the consequences.

Moore describes those consequences: dead fish, dead crayfish, and disappearing mink, elimination of all insects and eerie quiet. Rachel Carson did not publish *Silent Spring* until 1962, six years after bugs hit the Lochsa, when she drew worldwide attention to dangers of chemical poisons in the environment. Moore already learned hard lessons from drastic, unstudied actions. He writes, "In sick fish and in sandbars untraveled by mink lay for me the beginning of ecological wisdom in managing land. Everything in the ecosystem, indeed, was hooked to everything else. There was no casual attachment of creatures to water and earth, but a delivery system capable of transporting poisons from land through its water and food chains to injure or to kill all forms of life—insects, carnivores, herbivores, omnivores, and perhaps people as well."

Most of Moore's tales in *The Lochsa Story* are celebratory, even reverential. He taps the description of the Lochsa from an old woodcutter named Homer, repeatedly referring to the land as "God's country." In careful words and straight-forward photographs, both his and historical images, the struggles of human engagement in his homeland are captured with wonder and joy. Most of the last quarter of his book, however, describes the unraveling of Eden in the rush toward commercialization of the landscape.

In June 1997, a book review I wrote for *High Country News* at the time *The Lochsa Story* came out was tagged with the headline, "How the West Was Destroyed." Moore's blunt recounting of wilderness destruction by a direct participant, who was also always a great champion of wilderness, did not warrant a soft touch.

In the second to last chapter, titled "A New Look at Conservation and Multiple Use," Moore wrote an epitaph to short-sighted timber harvests. "After long reflection in my own experiences in a lifetime of work with the public's lands, I have to say I have never seen an intrusion of humankind and high-impact technology improve the productivity of multiple values in any natural place. Improvement of one or two values is often achieved but always at the expense of several other resources that had been thriving naturally before 'development' took hold of the land."

His final chapters encourage true multiple resource management and he supports the movement then budding within the Forest Service for ecosystem-based management. Moore put his considerable wisdom to proclaim balance and sustainability should be the premier directives for all management decisions. He also called for cooperation among forest users, not the endless competition and continual conflict so prevalent in the 1980s and 1990s. And he urged his successors at the Forest Service to join forces with the people willing to cooperate, to seek solutions to problems and to take actions on resource issues where there is broad support.

Moore wrote and often spoke in favor of sustainable timber harvest and careful, practical use of all forest resources. In my copy of *The Lochsa Story* I found four pages of my own scribbled notes from 1997, outlining four steps to prepare a lawsuit of a Forest Service timber project. The legal challenge took on a massive, 17 million board feet timber sale, then described by the Forest Service as ecosystem management, in the roadless forest of White Sand Creek. White Sand Creek provides the largest source of pristine waters remaining undeveloped in the Lochsa basin and borders the Selway-Bitterroot Wilderness.

In his book, Moore described White Sand as part of the core forest of greatest importance to learn from past mistakes, to balance multiple interests, to seek consensus, to find a new way to operate. And in 1997, conservationists found their interests in protecting water quality and wildlife through limited soil disturbance from harvest were ignored. Their last option was a lawsuit to a timber dominated project, lacking balance and sure to lead to degradation of other resources.

Moore wrote in support of ecosystems and encouraged multi-interest cooperation, but timber interests, conservationists, and land managers remained locked in combat through appeals and courts. Over time, conservationists succeeded in forcing change, including stopping the logging in White Sands and other roadless forests, and not only by court victories. Timber economics and land use politics played major roles in a changing time.

By dragging timber out of the driver seat for National Forest programs, using every means possible, conservationists gained a voice in a new configuration of land management. A new approach sought balance between production, protection, restoration, and recreation with engagement and compromise involving many interests. Although not fully realized, the current balance sheet for natural resources and social collaboration reflects Moore's wisdom and guidance—he was just ahead of his time.

These values of cooperation finally took hold in the new century. Representatives from multiple interests have joined together to form groups such as the Clearwater Basin Collaborative, the Payette and Boise Forest Coalitions, and the Idaho Forest Restoration Partnership. However, even after more than a decade of cooperation, conclusions on economic efficiency and ecological effectiveness of these collaborative groups remain elusive. And the big prize of additional, broadly supported wilderness for the Clearwater country, including some of Moore's beloved Lochsa, appears just out of grasp. Here lies another set of stories. Moore's book *The Lochsa Story* remains in print and sets the stage for future chapters of the forest management to be written.

Moore acted as the catalyst to launch a different major change in forest management and stewardship, to restore the natural role of fire in wilderness. Lightning-caused fires shaped the forests he knew so well, and he saw the effects of fire across the land. From the evolutionary history of all its life forms, to the structure of soils and even the contours of the land, fire forged the Northern Rockies' forests. Wilderness was designated "to preserve its natural conditions," as the Wilderness Act stated, and fires are a primary driver for natural conditions, Moore reasoned.

When Moore left Powell to move up through the Forest Service ranks, he did a stint in the Washington, D.C. headquarters on the national fire staff. After a few years In Washington, he wanted to be closer to the forest itself and to use his understanding of natural systems to guide new fire policy. And he wanted to see new fire plans put into action. He sought a transfer back to Montana. When he was appointed to a top position in the Northern Region headquarters in Missoula, as the Director of Fire Control and Operations, he knew one part of his program, and his job title, needed to change.

The purpose of his program, and much of the justification for the Forest Service itself, could not be limited to fire control, he believed. It was time to restore the ecological role of fire. It was time to let some fires burn, without human control but with human involvement. In the late 1960s, he set out to direct a careful yet quick course correction.

Moore knew from experience fires are unpredictable, as weather driven events in forests where incomplete topographical knowledge is almost always the norm. He knew people would always be fearful for life and property. To gain acceptance, he knew wilderness fires needed structured plans with management flexibility to go beyond all-out control.

Moore was not the first to recognize the historic role of natural fire and call for it to be rekindled. In his home territory, Elers Koch, a fellow Montanan with a different background including a master's degree in forestry from Yale University, was an early, prominent critic of fire

Bad Luck Lookout and fire, 1973 *Richard I. Walker*

policy. In 1935, Koch wrote a public journal article in adamant opposition to continued categorical fire suppression.

Koch earned standing in the firefighting world through direct participation in the cataclysmic 1910 Fire. His subsequent report, "History of the 1910 Forest Fires—Idaho & Western Montana," set a standard for accuracy and clarity. Koch became supervisor of the Lolo National Forest, overseeing multiple regional firefighting campaigns and then moved up to be assistant regional director for the Forest Service in Missoula.

Koch's captivating memoir, *Forty Years A Forester,* published almost 40 years after its completion, also contains a reprint of the article he wrote for the Journal of Forestry in 1935. Titled "The Passing of the Lolo Trail," the primary focus decried the desecration of the historic trail by bulldozer. Not content to only take on the road building machine, as it tore out the trail to the buffalo for the Nez Perce Indians along the route also followed by Lewis and Clark, Koch made sweeping, heretical statements against fire control.

Koch wrote, "The whole history of the Forest Service's attempt to control fire in the backcountry of the Selway and Clearwater is one of the saddest chapters in the history of a high-minded and efficient public service...Many fires have been controlled, but when the time is ripe for a conflagration, man's efforts have been puny in the face of nature's forces."

In the same vein as Moore, Koch did not excuse or diminish his own role in a misguided policy. He learned from his actions and called for change. "After years of experience I have come to the considered conclusion that control of fire in the backcountry of the Selway and the Lochsa is a practical impossibility."

Koch's call to not desecrate the Selway-Lochsa country with more roads was instrumental in the Wilderness Act including the Selway-Bitterroot. It took Bud Moore a few more years to be able to act on Koch's bold declaration of economic impracticality in fire control for the backcountry, while also recognizing the age-old force of fire as part of nature.

As director of fire programs, with the largest wilderness in the country in his region, Moore came back to Montana determined to rethink the role of fire. Orville Daniels, then a young Lolo National Forest deputy supervisor also based in Missoula, recalled Moore formulating his ideas around campfires on canoeing trips. In a phone interview in 2015, Daniels said, "Bud came out from Washington with permission to try to set up a new fire program, but he didn't have the backing of the higher-ups.".

"His boss, the national director for fire, told Bud, 'A Wilderness fire program is probably the right thing to do, but I don't think you'll be able to pull it off. Go ahead out there and try it but don't expect me to cover you if it goes bad and it probably will go bad.'"

Daniels described Moore as coming back to Montana with, "No mandate, nothing like what we call marching orders, no directive, not even support, but he had permission, and that's all he needed. Bud was ready to do it."

Never one to rely on persuasion in the abstract, Moore set to craft a plan joined by small, trusted cohort to carry it out. He found a sympathetic, strict Wilderness Act constructionist in William A. Worf, a fellow Montanan who also recently returned home from a stint in Washington to the Regional Office as the director of recreational programs in Missoula. Like Moore, Worf believed when the Wilderness Act stated these lands were to be "protected and managed so as to preserve its natural conditions," it meant lightning-ignited fires should burn in wilderness.

Worf, unlike Moore, became a wilderness supporter later in his life and career. Raised on a ranch in eastern Montana, and university trained in range management, Worf saw human manipulation of natural resources as productive and sensible. However, from his strict reading of the Wilderness Act, Worf understood the forces of nature and natural conditions should reign supreme in wilderness lands. Daniels described Worf as a wilderness convert and "like a lot of converts, he was very strong in his beliefs."

"Worf became a champion for Bud in the Regional Office, and even though they knew they wouldn't get support from the old fire horses in the organization, they would find ways to work around them to move forward on a new plan," Daniels said.

By then Daniels moved up to be supervisor of the Bitterroot National Forest, based up the valley in Hamilton. One afternoon Moore called on the telephone to suggest the next steps. "Bud said, 'I want to start a pilot project and set up a study area,'" Daniels recalled. "'I want to see if we can bring fire back into the wilderness and study its effects.' Then he paused, and said, 'Are you willing to be the guinea pig?'"

Daniels had only been supervisor for about a year but, in an effort to improve wildlife habitat, he'd already encouraged the forest staff to do more prescribed fire. In response to Moore, he said, "Absolutely, I've got a high interest in more fire on the forest."

They then hired two younger firefighters and scientists, Robert W. Mutch and Dave "Shag" Aldrich, to do field studies and draft plans. Without being encumbered by a deadline set for approval of a plan, the group moved to define a geography where fire could be observed but not controlled.

They needed an area of sufficient size and variable land types to be a practical study area. The area further needed to be surrounded by wilderness to avoid adjacent conflicting land uses. It needed a historic propensity toward the critical natural trigger: lightning. And it needed reasonable access to get observers into the project area.

At the recommendation of the field staff, they settled on the 66,000-acre White Cap Creek and Bad Luck Creek drainages in the Southeast corner of the Selway-Bitterroot Wilderness. Rising from the Selway river at just over 3,000 feet up slope to the Bitterroot divide at 9,000

Robert W. Mutch, Dave Aldrich, Bud Moore, Bill Worf at Coopers Flat. 1971
Richard I. Walker

feet, the landscape covered five ecological land units. The upper half of the project area covered the subalpine zone, including a lot of rock at the Bitterroot crest that could provide a fire break to prevent escape. Only 3 percent of the project area lay in the open savanna of mature ponderosa pine, with a frequent fire history of low severity burns in one to 30-year intervals, but it was representative of the type. And the study area was close to the road end at Paradise Guard Station along the Selway, providing ready access.

Starting in 1970, they prepared a plan to project fire behavior and outcomes using two field seasons for data collection and two winters for data analysis. One of their study steps was for key participants—Moore, Worf, Daniels, Mutch and Aldrich, joined by Hal Anderson of the Northern Forest Fire Laboratory and Richard I. Walker, resource assistant from neighboring Moose Creek—to hike the area for four days with a base camp set up at the Coopers Flat cabin about 10 miles up White Cap Creek.

They spent days looking at land and vegetation, with evenings sharing ideas around a campfire. Their conclusions provided a rationale for fire to function in wilderness: to further natural conditions and to allow the forces of nature to operate unimpeded. They acknowledged human constraints for safety and for structure protection of the few bridges and cabins in the area, but they argued for fire to run unchecked where feasible.

In a memo to the regional forester, Moore described the study scope as an "inventory [that] will include fire history, habitat types, soils, geology, fisheries and wildlife, fuels, and preattack information."

He went on to describe additional values. "Though the objective of the White Cap Study is to develop inventory and planning procedures for wilderness fire management, the ecological base under development will obviously serve nearly all, if not all, aspects of wilderness management. In addition to fire considerations this study should provide guidance and cost data useful in planning management of the total wilderness resource."

Moore's many years of solo contemplation in wild lands formed the basis for his vision and understanding. "We did talk a lot about the role of fire prior to settlement, as Bud put it together over time," Aldrich recalled in an email more than 40 years later.

"It was clear those miles of snowshoeing into the Lochsa from his early life at home along Lolo Creek were filled with keen observations and considerations of cause and effect, fire as the cause and wildlife habitat as the effect, not only for his target species but for all other animals who left tracks in the snow. These ideas were the foundation of his desire to understand those complex interactions between critters and habitat conditions. It was also clear Bud quickly isolated wildfire as a key factor in understanding the complex interactions of the ecosystems he knew. His keen mind and hundreds of miles of putting one snowshoe ahead of the other and, I am sure, cold fitful nights of sleep on his trapline gave him the opportunity to integrate a lot of things and create some working hypotheses," Aldrich explained.

While no one thought a wilderness fire plan would be accepted, much less welcomed by old guard firefighters, Moore believed in being open about the direction of their plans. Barry Hicks, who went on to be a fire management officer and then a district ranger in the Selway-Bitterroot Wilderness, tells the story of how he learned about the new fire plans.

"Bud was the director of Fire when I was a smokejumper foreman in Missoula. Along about 1970, I remember Bud coming out to the smokejumper base and telling us that he was planning to start making plans to allow some fires to burn in wilderness areas. At that time wilderness fires were our bread and butter. But Bud came out himself and stood right up in front of all of us and told us about the plans. He didn't send an assistant or try to dodge the controversy. Many jumpers thought that it was the end of the program for us."

Smokejumpers did figure in future wilderness fire plans, as fire monitors and point protection specialists, laying in fire lines around cabins and bridges, or lighting back-burns and setting up sprinkler systems. Smokejumper expertise and mobility proved to be integral in initial response to wilderness fire, even in the absence of initial attack.

Within two years the small group led by Moore defined an understanding of the fire cycles and fire effects in their study area. And they were ready to see it in action, to see fire back and burning unchecked in the wilderness.

In early August 1972, they took their fire plan to Washington, D.C. to gain approval for implementation from Forest Service Chief John R. McGuire. Only Daniels and Mutch went to Washington. "Bud did not go back with us to sell it to the Chief," Daniels recalled. "He had confidence and trust in us to do the right thing. He always demonstrated a lack of ego, he didn't seek the spotlight. But I always knew he had my back."

A small group of top staff officers joined the Chief in an evaluation of the proposed wilderness fire plan. Mutch remembers disagreement about the plan values and feasibility but McGuire, who worked in forest research before heading to the Washington Office, was supportive. He gave verbal approval to begin the program.

Written approval came quick on Aug. 17, 1972. The next day, Mutch was up White Cap Creek doing further reconnaissance, with his young daughter, Linda, on a summer break backpack trip, when a smoke was reported in Bad Luck Creek. The prescription in the shrub-field fire management zone called for observation and monitoring. They had the first approved wilderness fire on the first day of an approved plan and they took a chance in getting good results by naming it Bad Luck Fire.

As luck would have it, the sparse surrounding fuels and lack of wind were not conducive to a vigorous fire. After four days and a maximum growth perimeter of about 24 feet squared, the fire was dead out—without human intervention. So ended the first season of approved wilderness fire study.

The following August proved more favorable to fire. A lightning strike on August 10, 1973, again in Bad Luck Creek drainage, spread into grass and shrubs and became tagged the Fitz Creek Fire. Even with a plan and careful study, the fire proved unpredictable and led to unanticipated actions.

When Moore received reports of the fire moving fast toward the lookout tower on the ridge top, he projected a potential media stink bomb on a slow August news day if the Bad Luck Lookout burnt to a crisp in an approved wilderness fire plan. Moore called in retardant drops from a four-engine, B-17 aircraft to secure the lookout. The nearby outhouse was peppered in red retardant and then blew over in the backwash from a passing Huey helicopter. The incident became one of the field crews' ongoing jokes about the contents of the outhouse hitting the fan of the helicopter blades, but it did not hit the news.

Another challenge confronted them eight days into the fire. Aldrich and Mutch were stationed at the now safe Bad Luck Lookout, after the fire burned around it, to monitor the fire. Word came across the radio from other crew members that the fire jumped White Cap Creek and burned out of the study area. In an as yet unpublished book manuscript, titled *Wilderness Burning: the White Cap Story,* by Bob and Linda Mutch, they describe what the fire monitors saw:

"We each stare transfixed as the fire races up the slope towards the Snake Creek Divide ridge with 100-foot flame lengths, a crown fire spectacle for sure. The fire makes the ridge top in 30 minutes and we each contemplate that we may be witnessing two years of intensive planning all going up in smoke before our very eyes."

When Daniels learned in the evening about the fire's escape he made an unprecedented decision to suppress the flank outside the fire plan boundary and to continue to monitor the fire without control actions inside the plan lines. Daniels recalled that none of the old hands in the large Missoula-based fire operations agreed with him, except one. "Bud had my back," Daniels said in a telephone interview. "I didn't even have to call him. I just did what I thought was right and I knew he'd back me. Even when he didn't appear to pick sides, he'd let you know he was with you, even if he stayed behind the scenes."

In making tough decisions, Daniels always found support from Moore. "From the beginning, working for Bud was a partnership in trust and acceptance unlike anything I'd ever seen from someone at that level in the organization. He knew what needed to come out of it in the long run; he didn't need to control the process."

The escaping Snake Creek flank was contained and controlled. The Fitz Creek Fire burned for 43 days across a perimeter of about 1,200 acres, becoming the first significant wilderness fire for the Forest Service to watch, to study, to accept as a force of nature. Rain and snow put out the Fitz Creek Fire, as always happens in the fall within the natural process.

The next year, in 1974, when Moore told Daniels he planned to retire, to work on his homestead near Condon, Montana, the younger man was aghast. "I told him, if you leave now the wilderness fire program will fall apart," Daniels recalled. "And Bud told me, 'We all got it rolling, you don't need me anymore.'"

Daniels was surprised how quickly the wilderness fire program took off. Even before Moore left the Forest Service his ideas and methods were being applied. In August 1973, adjacent to White Cap Creek, the Management Plan for the Bear Creek Fire Management Unit was approved by the chief of the Forest Service. In taking effect on a separate Ranger District on another National Forest, the Moose Creek District in the Nez Perce National Forest plan demonstrated immediate applicability in the Selway-Bitterroot for the new concepts of fire management.

Richard I. Walker, the wilderness resource assistant at Moose Creek, who joined Moore and the others on the 1971 White Cap field trip, used the same ecological land units (ELUs) and management prescriptions defined by Mutch and Aldrich to frame the Bear Creek plan he crafted for 67,000 acres. Walker added one more category of ELU, the rolling landform, to reflect the differences in topography.

Within the next few years, the fire zone to be monitored but not suppressed expanded across the entire Selway-Bitterroot. When smokejumper Barry Hicks was hired as the fire management officer-resource assistant at Moose Creek in 1974, one of his primary tasks was to craft a new wilderness fire plan for the whole 550,000 acre district. He remembered the straightforward direction Moore presented at the jump base just a few years before and followed his lead.

When Hicks again returned to Moose Creek as district ranger in 1980, after a three-year stint in Oregon, he oversaw implementation of the plan which was already showing results. The first big fire in the wilderness occurred in 1979, with the Independence Fire. Named for its 4th of July lightning ignition, it grew to more than 16,000 acres over the course of three months, unchecked, primarily on the north side of the Bear Creek drainage of the Selway-Bitterroot. The 1973 Bear Creek plan formed the basis for the fire management. Rain and snow put it out.

Today, fire history maps in the Selway-Bitterroot show the landscape speckled with fires since the 1970s, covering most of the forested land outside the rocky Bitterroots. Fire research studies now use the Selway-Bitterroot as a baseline to understand how natural fires respond over time. Among the topics studied is how past fires can slow the spread of new fires. Fire size can be limited when new fires bump into recent fires with reduced fuels. Scattered smaller fires of 5,000 or 10,000 acres can avoid massive 100,000 acre burns where fuel buildups are dense, intertwined, and unmanageable. After more than 100 years of fire suppression that led to increased fuel loads, when weather conditions are tuned to lightning, high temperatures, and wind, one spark can lead to major fires.

These big fires, often hotter than would be expected in the mid-elevation, mixed forest types, are now prevalent across the West. Greater fuel loads combined with longer fire seasons, as climate shifts and weather events intensify, are leading to big, hot fires. The Selway-Bitterroot already began to accept fire before the warming cycle in the 1990s and the effects of climate change escalated in the 2000s. Inside the wilderness, the fire map resembles historic fire patterns and provides a base for comparative studies.

Daniels found Moore to be proven right, again, to get out of the way to let other people, often younger, take charge of new directions. Daniels remembered part of their campfire discussion at Coopers Flat, when he asked Moore, "How do people take on change."

As Daniels recalled, Moore responded by saying, "Young people can change easily because everything is new and different. Old folks, like us, have been doing things a certain way and it's been working okay, more or less. To change you have to give up something, you have to be open to risks and to opportunity, to understand that maybe it will be better with change."

As Moore described his views around the campfire, he said change requires risk, and in a risk-adverse organization such as the Forest Service, change doesn't come easy. To go in a new direction in a tradition-bound organization requires a strong, determined push.

In his book, *The Lochsa Story*, Moore did not write about the policy changes required to re-introduce wilderness fire and the process he led to make the changes. One supposes it was a chapter of his life left out because it centered in the Selway, not the Lochsa. He did write a little bit about the fire program progress and the results in the early 1980s. He wrote about in the efforts of a young wilderness ranger, Gary Oye, to monitor fires in upper tributaries of the Lochsa in the wilderness. Moore summed up the efforts of Oye and others as, "Returning natural fire to wilderness requires knowledge and guts."

The wilderness fire program expanded to other wildernesses and even to large roadless forests outside classified wilderness. Daniels was further surprised by the swiftness of its acceptance and spread across and even beyond the wilderness geography. But the challenges for fire managers to take on the difficult decisions can be daunting when risks to people and property and careers are real. In the heat of summer, especially early in the season, it can be a safer decision to put fires out than to manage a free burning force of nature.

In May 2012, the top Forest Service officials banned all unchecked fires, even in wilderness, because of budget limitations and an expected hot fire season. Bob Mutch came out of retirement to call out the ecological incongruity and political desperation of the orders. In a guest opinion printed by the *Missoulian*, Mutch summarized the economic, ecological, and even health benefits of smaller free-burning fires in wilderness. And he invoked the legacy of Bud Moore as a leader with knowledge and guts, just over a year after his death in November 2010, to look back to when he started the wilderness fire program at White Cap Creek.

Mutch wrote, "The White Cap project was the brainchild of Bud Moore who commented one day: 'The Wilderness Act says that natural processes should proceed. While in light of that, to put out a fire was almost illegal.'"

Fire Returns to Wilderness

JUNE 14, 1987 WAS LAURA MAY JACKSON'S FIRST DAY back on top of Shissler Peak as the lookout. She was in the right place at the right time to do what lookouts do: observe the path of lightning storms and look for smoke. That first day on the job, Jackson spotted a couple of strikes setting off blue-gray smokes on the west ridge above the Selway River.

The same day, thunderstorms triggered fires elsewhere across the whole expanse of forested mountains of northern Idaho. The Nez Perce National Forest radio network buzzed with activity as lookouts and work crews called in coordinates for multiple fires. Mid-June was early for a fire bust but with a dozen fires sparked in one afternoon on the forest, the summer fire season started with a bang.

It was also early in the season for all fire crews to be trained, geared up and in place, leading to a scramble to mobilize scattered troops. Airplanes took off carrying smokejumpers to catch fires when small. Fire engines and crew trucks drove along winding forest roads to put people on the ground knocking down burning trees, digging line and pumping water. Support crews set up camps with mess halls, toilets, and showers under canvas and in mobile pods.

Back in the Selway-Bitterroot Wilderness a different approach took shape. Jackson watched her first two smokes dissipate and disappear, but a strong thread of gray wafted up from the face of Bailey Mountain to the north. When she called out the coordinates over the radio, the Moose Creek fire management officer, Jim Saveland, replied with excitement in his voice, "That's good." Outside of the wilderness the full thrust of the U.S. Forest Service firefighter organization kicked into gear to combat the scourge of the forest—fire. Inside wilderness, fire was good.

When Bud Moore began the White Cap Creek fire study he faced an institutional mindset without equivocation: all forest fires are bad. Smokey the Bear became one of the greatest PR successes of all time because fire was bad and people were responsible to do good to prevent and control fires. Moore did not set out to convince people fire was good, but he declared it was necessary for ecological function. The forest and its creatures evolved with fire. Fire was necessary for the forest, whether it was good or bad for human interests. What Moore started required an exception to the orthodoxy of one-sided, always bad fire.

The new view of fire spread through the ranks of those who worked in wilderness to adapt Moore's ideas into action because it fit the ecological framework. One of Jackson and Savelund's co-workers, then a resource assistant and a veteran smokejumper, George Weldon, explained the current thinking. "In my eyes I just look at fire as natural. It's not obtrusive; it's just what occurs in nature. As foresters we are trained to manipulate vegetation but in wilderness we try to do everything we can to keep things as natural as possible. And to me suppressing fire is just manipulating vegetation."

Manipulation creates its own problems, Weldon continued. "In many cases we've done more damage by suppressing fires, with all the people and the equipment, than if we it allowed it to burn. Now we try to minimize the effects of fire control and we do it with as few people as possible."

In wilderness, fire lookouts not only look for a fire to put out, they also look at a fire to determine how and when it can burn unchecked. They fit observations into the calculations of a wilderness fire plan, formulating predictions and expectations based on prior analysis. Fire history, fuel loads, and landscape configurations are calculated to anticipate fire behavior for any given location. Final decisions to monitor and not to control a fire are then made by district rangers and forest supervisors. The first observations of a fire lookout can define options, with eyes scanning the landscape and seeing the forest beyond the trees.
Jackson watched the first fire of the season on Halfway Ridge, about four miles north of her lookout at Shissler; send up smoke for a few

Fire at Puzzle Point from Moose Creek Ranger Station, 1986 *Warren Q. Miller*

hours. When it died out in the evening, with spring conditions still green and wet, she was disappointed, not relieved. In the early days Forest Service lookouts were also firefighters, or smoke chasers as they were called. As the closest person to the smoke at Halfway Ridge, Jackson would have taken off with shovel and Pulaski to snuff it out before it grew, whether anyone expected it to grow or not. Now she was a fire monitor, not a smoke chaser.

On Jackson's second day at Shissler, another smoke from the storm the day before took hold and a spot of flames was visible through binoculars. Across North Moose Creek, on a shoulder of Bailey Mountain called Shasta Ridge, the fire flickered in heavy timber. Another afternoon storm blew in and Jackson's response was, "This wind might liven up our little fire. I hope it doesn't get much rain."

Snow accumulation remained light in the high country that year and the spring had been dry. Conditions led to speculation it would be a hot fire year and Western newspapers already ran stories of potential irrigation water shortages. Officials put out grave assessments about the threats to forests and agriculture. Meanwhile, fire staff in wilder-

Laura Mae Jackson at Shissler Peak Lookout, 1987 *John McCarthy*

ness saw favorable conditions, where fire could penetrate the mid-slope, denser and wetter forests. These choked stands could be considered stagnant with limited ground growth for wildlife browse and too crowded for vibrant tree growth.

In the new way of looking at fire, the burning tree Jackson observed on Shasta Ridge could be beneficial to open the forest. Lightning struck in the transition zone where Douglas fir and grand fir mix and then give way to crowded lodgepole pine with some Englemann spruce in the wet spots and subalpine fir farther up the slopes. The fire cycles and patterns for these mixed conifer forests are sporadic and the outcomes after fires tend to be patchy with hot and cool spots. These fire cycles can be lengthy, every 100 years or more, but when it does torch it can lead to stand replacing crown fires that consume most or all the trees and other vegetation in patches of variable sizes.

Jackson thought it might be a year when some of the dense forest and thick brush went up in smoke, then to make way for new growth. Even though she couldn't make out the exact tree species mix from her perch on the north deck of the tower, she knew from her hikes in

Fire camp resupply at Moose Creek Ranger Station, 1988 *Warren Q. Miller*

similar country that the slope was overdue for a fire. She concluded a fire on Shasta Ridge would be good.

The wilderness ideal to "let fire play its natural role" did not always match the reality of forest management and fire operations within the politics and economics of the outside world. Jackson's own experiences reflected the outside intrusions and, at times, she considered it far less than ideal.

In 1980, Jackson's first year on Shissler was slow to the point of being a non-event fire season. Only two lightning strikes on the Moose Creek Ranger District even became classified as fires and both turned out to be just a couple of burning trees. Jackson had spent three previous seasons on lookouts in the Bitterroot and she had looked forward to seeing some real fires cook and go unchecked in the middle of the wilderness. Not that year.

Her second season at Shissler, 1981, proved to be closer to her expectations. It was middling warm into August, with about a dozen fires reported. Three fires grew to respectable size of about 100 acres, burning unchecked without any suppression. But those were nothing compared to the Independence Fire of 1979, when more than 16,000 acres were included in the first major burn in the new era of fire management for the Selway-Bitterroot.

Into the fourth week of August the weather cooled, a few light rains came through, and the color tints of early fall speckled hillsides. Other lookouts came down off their perches and only Jackson remained on post at Shissler.

Late in the afternoon on August 24, 1981, a little thunderstorm blew in from the west and continued to sweep eastward toward the Bitterroots. Jackson could see active lightning, likely reaching the ground, but points of impact were blocked to her view by ridges in her sight lines. She knew conditions remained dry enough to set flames.

In addition to fire detection, Jackson also served as dispatcher and communication hub for the ranger district. Not only did she report fires, she coordinated fire actions and district communication. While the fire season in the Selway was winding down, an active fire season in other parts of the region led to a decree for all new starts to be suppressed as soon as possible to avert any new large fires. Even though the little storm was out of Jackson's vision it wasn't out of her responsibility.

It was too late in the day to order a fire patrol plane but Penny Keck was already flying in from Grangeville to Moose Creek. Jackson got Keck on the radio and asked her to swing around Wahoo Peak to check if any lightning strikes hit dry vegetation to start fires.

Keck, with veteran pilot John Moberly, did a couple turns around Wahoo and landed at Moose Creek at dusk. She reported the little storm touched off 17 fires spread over several drainages and she also reported some ignitions were in fuel types that were going to take off and burn. Keck was already in the air but without a map for the direct flight home when Jackson radioed. From her memory of the creeks and the ridges and her own experience as a lookout, she laid down the coordinates for all 17 fires and called them up to Jackson on the #9 telephone line. "Penny put everyone in the right section, maybe not the exact quarter-quarter section but close," Jackson recalled.

Keck also formed a plan on which fires to staff first and which ones were in rocks or sparse vegetation and could wait. Jackson radioed an assessment of the fires to forest headquarters in Grangeville. Although most of the fires outside the wilderness were already contained and going through the mop-up phase, the forest stayed on high alert. The fire program was ready and able to crank up to speed. Headquarters called for fire crews to gather at nearby Fenn Ranger Station along the road. Helicopters were called to ferry crews at first light. Two patrol planes were aloft at dawn. Smokejumpers suited up at Grangeville and Missoula, with more on standby in McCall.

In a full suppression fire there is little reference to the wilderness fire plan. A wilderness fire plan describes how to monitor fires, not how to put out fires. Fire suppression is the old school technique of building a fire line or barrier that stops the spread of flames and snuffs out everything inside the containment line. Even though it was late in the summer, the decision was made in Grangeville to do initial attack on as many fires as possible. A fire oversight system similar to a project fire was put into effect in town to coordinate all the separate fires.

Decisions were taken out of the ranger district's hands at Moose Creek. Some of the decisions contradicted Penny Keck's original assessment on where to move first. And some of those fires got away to grow hot and fast.

The next two weeks were chaotic. Jackson served as the liaison for aircraft and the firefighters strung out all over the east side of the wilderness leading up to the Bitterroots. At one point there were 20 smokejumpers at Wahoo. Then the call went out to drop 200 more jumpers. Later that afternoon, as the jump order was delayed because not enough jumpers could be found in the region, the crew already on the line retreated. They escaped over a ridge just before their suppression lines were overrun by flames.

Another patch of fire exploded from 50 to 1,000 acres in an afternoon when winds accelerated. Aerial observers called for crews to abandon the fire and they pulled back out of harm's way. When crews readied to resume an attempt to lay fire line, the flames reared up and they reversed direction again to safe zones.

"I was just picking up the pieces and kept going and hoping for everything to be okay," Jackson recalled. "But I had nothing to compare it to; I'd never seen anything like it before. All these people just descended on us and we had a major blow-up in the middle of the wilderness."

While most of the fires surged beyond her sight lines, massive smoke clouds billowed up and the air churned with aircraft. "I wrote an entire log book full in two weeks of non-stop radio transmissions, when I hadn't even gotten half way through the log book from the rest of the season," Jackson said.

Pilots and crews often came from out of state and didn't know the area, or even that it was all wilderness. At one point a helicopter pilot sought directions and asked Jackson, "Are you the lookout where I can see a black Volkswagen parked next to the tower." Shissler is 30 miles from the closest road. Jackson had to find the helicopter before she could direct him.

In the end, as almost always, it was September rain, not all the retardant drops and fire lines, that slowed and stopped the fires.

The crews left; the camps were cleaned up, the equipment was packed up, and the firefighting apparatus was dismantled, leaving the quiet of the wilderness. Jackson and others at Moose Creek wondered: what was the point?

"They put out a few little piddling ones, but here we had these huge fires they couldn't catch and nothing bad happened," she said. "There were no terrible consequences to the land in the final analysis. And a lot of money was spent for no real reason."

Jackson thought the lessons were obvious and would be recognized, not to repeat the same mistakes by rushing into a suppression mode. Her next three years passed without restraints. Each lightning strike that fit within the confines of the wilderness fire plan ran its course, burning unchecked. Then, in early July 1985, a series of storms set fires across the region after another hot, dry spring.

Lightning lit an erratic string of fires inside the wilderness, fitting within constraints of the fire plan and each would not be suppressed. But outside the wilderness firefighters teetered on the verge of being overwhelmed by other active and growing fires. Again, the regional fire bosses did not want any distractions. An order came down for all fires to be put out, even the fires conforming within plan constraints in wilderness. The order directed for all hands to be on deck as firefighters, not diverted as fire monitors.

"I filled-out a million jump requests for every fire there was," Jackson said, with bitterness in her voice years later. Outside conditions, politics, and economics again excluded the forces of nature in wilderness.

The next year, 1986, brought major firefighting operations to the ranger station itself at Moose Creek. A fire to the south across the Selway River on Puzzle Point threatened to jump the river and burn toward the ranger station. Dozens of firefighters were flown in to be stationed at Moose Creek, clearing fuels and digging protective line. As the fire raged, Jackson could hear 100-foot trees break and tear from roots to come crashing down with sounds carrying six miles across the canyon to her lookout. Firefighter actions proved critical to protect the ranger station buildings and the nearby bridges, while the main flanks of the fire burned unchecked. And again, the fire was snuffed out by fall rain.

Jackson's little smoke the next summer on Shasta Ridge never amounted to much. She watched it expand into the undergrowth but the upper slope remained moist in mid-June and it never reached into the trees to run hot flames. After a couple days it sputtered out to nothing. Later in the summer, another lightning strike due east from her lookout sparked flames to run across a couple thousand acres in a similar mid-elevation zone around Trout Peak, burning within the guidelines of the fire plan, unchecked as a wilderness fire and then going cold in fall rains.

Fire management in wilderness might have continued in these sporadic steps. Some years fires would burn through significant acres under the guidance of a plan; some years fire would be suppressed because of outside concerns; some years not much fire would go anywhere because of weather conditions. Fire managers anticipated many opportunities for on-the-ground learning based on experience. No one anticipated the fire year of 1988, when all hell broke loose in Yellowstone National Park.

The natural role of fire was lost in the spectacle at Yellowstone, seen worldwide on television. Multiple high elevation conflagrations in lodgepole pine thickets were driven by weather conditions of high winds and high temperatures, ideal for burning but troublesome for people. These fast-moving fires threatened historic and iconic structures in the world's first national park and made for great visuals on TV. Natural science lessons were more challenging to convey. The ecological necessity of fire did not resonate with audiences reared on Smokey the Bear and Bambi. Noble firefighters in rough, sooty uniforms of yellow shirts, green pants and hard hats told the story of the good guys fighting bad fire.

As the cost and chaos of the firefighting efforts played out on the evening news, many commentators were aghast these fires were initially allowed to burn. The intent of the management plan to include fire for ecological reasons got shorted in the story. It would be many years and many new planning constraints before fire would again be seen as a positive and necessary force of nature, not as a force of doom for people and their possessions.

Knowledge of fire behavior and the techniques needed to protect important features progressed in subsequent years, as applied to wilderness and elsewhere. Bud Moore's intention to study lands and conditions, then adapt management to include fire as a natural force within

Selway River canyon, 2017 *John McCarthy*

a plan became part of fire programs. Adaptation of the approach often depended as much on individuals' interests and commitments to science as much as geography. Soon, the unanticipated consequences of climate change, with increases in average seasonal temperatures and longer, hotter fire seasons, added to the complexities.

Fires have grown in size and intensity as temperatures rise across the West. Some mistakes in predictions and decisions in the natural fire program led to some unwanted larger fires where people and property were damaged or lost. Most of the big fires at the end of the 20th and beginning of the 21st centuries, with record breaking acreage and record setting temperatures, occurred despite the best efforts to contain and control the fire spread, often at massive expense. Knowledge has been accumulated through these experiences and studies, while harsh consequences for people, both firefighters and citizens, were not always avoided.

With or without climate change, fires will always be unpredictable and often dangerous. Taking chances with fire will always be challenging and risky. Because of its size, varied topography, and vegetation types, and because it has the longest history of unchecked fires burning within plans, the Selway-Bitterroot Wilderness provides perhaps the best laboratory in the nation to study the effects of multiple years of free-running fire. Many research projects have used the Selway-Bitterroot to examine ecological and management questions. Much more research can be done using the wilderness as a baseline. The vision of Bud Moore and other wilderness fire explorers set the course for future understandings of fire.

SETTLED LAND AND WILDERNESS

Bud Moore

RETIREMENT FROM THE FOREST SERVICE presented Bud Moore with three opportunities: to construct a homestead for his base of operations; to be in the wild places he revered since his youth; and to guide others in appreciation and understanding of wild places. He plunged into each challenge with the same determination and delight as he did on snowshoes in powder.

His early home territory around Lolo Creek was long ago absorbed into the suburbia surrounding Missoula. Private lands available in the Clearwater Valley of Idaho were distant from his old haunts in the wild country of the Lochsa, so he found a piece of rough land north of Missoula, near Condon, in the Swan Valley between the Mission Mountain and Bob Marshall wildernesses. On 80 rolling acres between the two mountain ranges, Moore and his wife Janet created a work center and home.

To gain title, the original homesteader cleared off 40 acres in the early 1900s. The land had since grown back to larch, Douglas fir, lodgepole, and alpine spruce, with wildflowers thick across the forest floor in spring. Moore took over the land soon after his retirement in 1974, naming it Coyote Forest in honor of a favorite creature whose songs enlivened the nights.

First, he put up a wall tent, harkening back to his early days at ranger stations when the crews slept under canvas. He constructed a board floor, door, porch, and side walls, and laid in log slabs to strengthen the roof to shed snow. After the first winter a young friend skied to the tent to spend a night before meeting Bud the next day. The young man woke in the middle of the night to a snorting grizzly bear pushing on the door, seeking food in spring breakup. In desperation, he grabbed a rifle and took a shot from his sleeping bag, firing through the door.

"He could tell the door wouldn't hold and he didn't have any other option but to shoot blind," Bud said. "He sat up the rest of the night with the rifle in his hands, to see if the bear came back wounded and mad. He wasn't getting any sleep anyway."

Moore found a blood trail at the tent the next morning and he followed both human and bear tracks to where his friend was skinning out the bear. Moore appreciated the quick thinking and good fortune in shooting, but he was disturbed by the fatal disruption to prized wildlife. The incident strengthened his resolve to seek balance in a home for humans and for wildlife.

He dedicated the majority of the land, more than 70 acres, to be undeveloped without structures or roads, for wildlife habitat and for sustainable timber harvest through careful selective logging. On the remaining few acres he established a residential and work headquarters, with three log cabins—each built with inscribed and notched construction. When he first built cabins in his youth, he helped old hands who could cut logs out of the forest and put up a 14 by 16-foot structure in a week, using only axe and crosscut. On his trapline, he'd built small cabins as overnight way stations, with roofs often accumulating 10 feet or more of snow. At his modern-day homestead, Moore used the same construction techniques but scored groves under the length of logs with a chainsaw to stack each log tight and then swung an axe to set notches to bind corners.

The main house was the largest structure with a 52-foot run along the purlin rafters. In the separate bath house next door, Janet once watched a black bear feed on shrubs less than 50 feet from the window as she soaked. "We were both very comfortable but maybe he didn't look in the window to see me looking at him, although I wouldn't have minded," she recalled with satisfaction.

In the combination warehouse-bunkhouse-office Bud spent several years writing his book, *The Lochsa Story*. The smaller cabin was also where we spent parts of several days talking about his life and ideas in between chores and walks through the land.

Bud Moore with sawmill at Coyote Forest, Condon, Montana, 1987
John McCarthy

Steel-jawed traps and chains hung from a nearby building, set on hooks and nails embedded in rough-cut boards, in preparation for a favored pursuit: fur trapping. When Janet went to Helena to serve as a Senator in the Montana Legislature, with the state having the good sense to govern itself with alternate year legislative sessions, Bud set day trip traplines in the Mission Mountains to be close to the home fires. In the off legislative years, Bud skied and snowshoed deep into the Bob Marshall Wilderness, setting up camps for weeks at time.

His trapping season started in the Swan Valley in early fall to catch coyotes. Bud saw no conflict in taking his homestead's namesake animal from local forests. As a practical man with an eye toward a balance point, he determined from tracks and pack howling how active and prevalent coyotes were for the year before setting his own take limits. He'd go after muskrats and otters before freeze-up in November. In the last days of the hunting season, he'd hike or snowshoe over the southern Swan Mountains east of home into the Bob Marshall Wilderness, to set up camps and to kill a deer for meat. When winter locked-in with snow, he'd travel a loop, up to 100 miles a week, stopping overnight at his line camps. The season ran until late February and some years he only came out at Christmas. When he left the wilderness, he carried a bale of furs on his back, just like the old days.

Winter was his favorite time of year, when the mountains were his alone. Being on snowshoes in the quiet of forests as snow settled on boughs gave him entry into a timeless world. At 70 years-old in 1987, he stood straight with the same square-shoulders of his youth, while his sharp angled jaw was always quick to spread into a smile in telling stories. His long stride that outpaced the old-time lumberjacks at Powell, retained its bounce and he readily laced-up snowshoes each year.

Janet told the story of waiting at the end of the road one Christmas for Bud to come out of the mountains. "The temperature dropped to 40 below in the valley and must have been 50 below zero up on the pass where Bud was coming out," she remembered. "I figured he probably had 10 miles to go on his last day, but it turned out to be closer to 14 miles. Bud told me not to wait past dark because he'd hole up somewhere if he couldn't make it out. At 9 o'clock, I couldn't wait any longer, I was freezing in the truck." She left some dry wood and some raw elk meat, soon to freeze, and left Bud to his fate.

Instead of holiday thoughts for Christmas Eve, Janet began mental preparations for a funeral. She called some family members. "Everyone said, 'Oh, Bud's been in lots worse spots, he'll be fine.' But they hadn't sat for hours with the engine running and the heater blasting and back home I was still shivering after hours next to a roaring fire. I was worried sick," she recalled, "Bud always said, 'if I've got to die, I want to die in a snowdrift or in the jaws of a grizzly.' And I thought, well, he finally pulled it off."

Bud slogged out of the mountains almost at midnight and stumbled into Janet's wood pile as he looked for running water at the creek. The fire he lit was a lifesaver.

Bud laughed at Janet's story. "That fire was real cozy. And the meat thawed out real nice."

Janet didn't laugh. "It's kind of hard living with a man like Bud Moore. It scares me to death," she concluded.

Moore's commitment to practical use of lands led to him to run a portable sawmill, powered by a four-cylinder Volkswagen engine. Using a small Kubota tractor, he skidded logs from his and his neighbor's Swan Valley woodlots. Stacks of rough-sawn one-inch boards and two-by dimensional stock were piled next to his original tent, for use in his projects or for sale.

The sawmill generated income and fit Moore's philosophy. "I feel responsible," he said, "partly because our society is willing to dedicate some of the land that I care so much about into wilderness, to do my best to provide some of the wood that America needs. I think we all have a responsibility to take care of our forests out here along with our wilderness. We can produce a lot of wood for commercial use and still preserve our wildlife and water. There's no problem there."

Moore figured he put $35,000 into the tractor, chainsaws, chokers, sawmill, pickup truck, and other tools. With a similar investment, anyone could make a living wage in good years and bad, he believed. He only thinned forest stands, improving fire resilience and providing a steady harvest. Big-time loggers with big equipment wouldn't take on the same smaller jobs. Bigger equipment also often led to bigger impacts for erosion and compaction of the soil.

Beyond philosophy and economics, Moore said his motivation was simple. "I like to make a good board."

As a logger and a trapper, Moore did not fit a typical environmentalist profile, if there is such a thing. "I'm a harvester, I love to harvest," he explained. "That's something some wilderness people can't understand: how can I support wilderness when I'm a logger? But there are many breeds of cat. And I feel good if people are a little displeased or at least confused."

On a wall in the main house at Coyote Forest hung a photograph of William Woodman, also known as Skookum or Skook. As a young boy, Bud got to know Skook during his occasional stops at the Moore homestead. Skook was a true Bitterroot mountain man, with a series of trapline cabins, the largest a 10 by 8-foot log shack with a low roof. In the photograph, Skook looked to be in his 50s, wearing two wool shirts with a full beard down to his second shirt button. Moore pointed out, "Look at his eyes, there's a man at peace with himself. In those days Skook was considered kind of a ne'er do well. Today he'd be a messiah."

Another framed photograph showed Bill Bell heading out with a loaded pack string. The picture was taken after Bell quit being ranger at Elk Summit for the Forest Service, when the bureaucracy interfered too much with his work. Moore described Bell's intense look: "He's just starting off with a mule train. It's a little like take-off of an airplane; as you get going along you check to make sure all the engines are firing, and you look back to see all the mules' ears are flapping and then you're doing OK and you're ready to go."

Bud and Janet Moore, Coyote Forest, 1987 *John McCarthy*

Moore passed on his deep commitment to working in wilderness and his knowing ways of woodcraft through writing and talks. He described a fortuitous meeting with a fresh wilderness ranger when he took a trip back to Powell Ranger Station on his last day before retirement. Once again Moore spent a night in the bunk house, finishing his career where he started, joined by a young wilderness ranger going out to begin his first season.

"This young fellow didn't have a clear sense of direction or understanding of his responsibilities. I told him to get a commitment from his immediate supervisor on what the priorities were and to be sure they were working together.

"Then the other thing you want to do is learn your country," Moore recalled saying. "If I were you, I'd spend all my time, my Saturdays and Sundays and all, for quite a while out in the backcountry."

Learn the laws of the land was Moore's next advice, because, "Most of the people in the backcountry are real good folks, but you're going to

Bud Moore and Gary Koehler at Fish Lake Guard Station, 1974 *Richard I. Walker*

run into some bastards back there. To hit them with rules and regulations is the only way to deal with some people.

"And then, above all, get your own wilderness ethic together so you can explain to people what wilderness is all about. You ought to be like the moose and show up here and there as often as you can. Be unobtrusive. Be present enough so that people in the wilderness know there's a wilderness ranger around and he's a great guy and he loves the country."

Moore had long thought about the need to get greater support and recognition for people working in wilderness. In a 1971 memo to the regional forester about the White Cap fire study following a four-day field trip, he wrote:

"Our dialogue led us beyond the scope of the White Cap Study to re-emphasize a recognized need to develop a strong corps of professional and technical wilderness managers, including perpetuation of the use of primitive skills which seem to be fast disappearing from

Forest Service ranks. This need struck both Bill [Worf] and me more forcefully than ever before. Somehow, we have to come specifically to grips with ways to develop these personnel. Considerations include factors like better tenure for Wilderness Rangers, use of the Government Employees Training act for special studies, career plans to permit personnel growth in wilderness management, and purposeful utilization of personnel like Emil Keck to train others in mountain skills. Bill Worf will follow through and I'll consider ways that fire activities can contribute to continued high quality wilderness management, including personnel development."

Recognition of the importance of wilderness to America continued to concern Moore. On a Memorial Day, several years before the collapse of the Soviet Union, Moore, an ex-Marine, talked about the meaning of freedom in light of people fighting for freedom and fighting for what they believe in. "Today the threat to our freedom is not from the communists. I don't fear that at all. The greatest threat to our freedom today is our own government. And I would hope the wilderness would be one place where our government would be understanding enough to take care of the country and leave people free."

Freedom can be found on the land, Moore explained. "People can go out there on their own and interact in a responsible way. I'm not saying we shouldn't arrest the violators. But wilderness ought to be one place where people can go to re-create ourselves, renew our spirits and renew it among sensitive supervisors who are living right on the land."

Bud continued: "There is no conflict to interact with a visitor if the representative of the government is part of the wilderness, if he really exudes a spirit of the wilderness. He understands it; he loves it; he's been there; he lives there; he's not going to town for his four days off, he's hiking up some other creek to learn more about it. If you've got that kind of thing going, these people radiate a companionship in the wilderness that has no conflict whatsoever with anybody. Even the greatest purist seeking solitude would love to be around a campfire with people like that.

"But that isn't what we're getting all the time. We need more Bill Bells, the old ranger at Elk Summit. He loved the country so much he couldn't understand why people would even want to go to town. He figured if he could keep them long enough they'd get the spell of the place. That kind of thing we still need and maybe it's too much to expect in this society, but I don't think so. There are many people that want to work at something like this in the wilderness. Given an opportunity and a little help on conception, they'll develop into Bill Bells in a hurry."

Moore continued to emulate Bill Bell in his own travels in wilderness and his land stewardship projects at Coyote Forest. He shared memories of these journeys in the Bud Moore Photographs and Sound Recordings collection at the University of Montana. His photographs from eight decades are accompanied by stories he recorded about the images as part of the Montana Memory Project at the university library and online.

Bud Moore died at home of cancer on November 26, 2010, at age 93, after a lifetime of learning and teaching the ways of the wilderness.

Wilderness Becomes Policy

William A. Worf

THE PARTY IN THE OLD NOTCHED-LOG COOKHOUSE carried on into the evening twilight of a mid-June night. People strummed guitars and sang with great enthusiasm and with varying degrees of skill. The party closed the Moose Creek Ranger Station guard school after 10 days of training sessions. There was time for a little fun before the crew of 35 men and women scattered into the surrounding wilderness for the field season. Barbecued burgers and cheap beer fueled the festivities. The cookhouse resonated with the sound and feel of an old dance hall—lamplit, full of laughter, loud voices, and music from a fiddle and a couple of guitars.

All of the administrators from outside the ranger district, the officials from town, appeared to have gone to bed. All except one. A tall bald man stood near the cookhouse door with a can of beer in hand. William A. Worf, known simply as Bill, exuded an intensity of interest in a series of conversations with the crew members half his age. He talked about wilderness philosophy and history underlying the lands that would soon envelop the young people going out on the trail. He shared insights about his long-time employer the U.S. Forest Service, offering some tips on how others might consider future careers. And he asked many questions about the young folks' backgrounds and their aspirations—both in the wilderness and in life.

The conversations were not small talk. Worf attended the training session to share his understandings about the meaning of wilderness. The evening presented another opportunity to connect informally, one-on-one, with the same purpose.

In ways not fully appreciated by most of the young crew members, Worf was one of a handful of people who determined the scope and the process of the work they set out to do. Worf played a pivotal role

William A. Worf in Bitterroot Valley, Montana, 1987 *John McCarthy*

in seeing the young crew shared a vision and a mission to protect wilderness for future generations and to provide guidance for visitors. He believed in the mission and strived to instill his beliefs in others.

It was June 1977, and Worf, soon to be 51, was then director of Recreation, Wilderness and Lands for the Forest Service Northern Region at Missoula. He'd been involved in wildland recreation throughout his life and career, active on horseback or hiking, and through administration in agency offices. The concept of wilderness did not captivate him in his early years; he was more interested in expanding recreation capacity and opportunities. The movement to craft an American legacy to preserve wilderness with limited human intrusion did not draw him in at first. He was intent on getting campgrounds built with hitch racks, corrals, pit toilets, and access roads. As time went on, his focus shifted away from recreation development. He became one of the greatest proponents and protectors of wilderness.

When President Lyndon B. Johnson signed the Wilderness Act into law, on September 3, 1964, Worf was supervisor of the Bridger National Forest in northwest Wyoming. Less than three weeks later, on September 20, 1964, Worf and three other upper-level Forest Service professionals found themselves closeted in an attic above the Department of Agriculture building in Washington, D.C., charged with figuring out what the Wilderness Act meant now that boundary lines were drawn and guidelines were set in law. They set out to establish what the agency would do in and with wilderness. They also would frame how citizen visitors were expected or encouraged to act in wilderness. The four men were shunted off to the attic to put it together.

While the Forest Service declared chunks of wild country to be wilderness or primitive areas as far back as 1924, when the Gila Wilderness was designated in New Mexico, there were no standard operating procedures or common set of regulations. What wilderness meant in those lands was largely dependent on local conditions and local decisions. Passage of the Wilderness Act required a uniform plan and policy for the National Wilderness Preservation System.

"We all went in there with the idea that we'd wrap it up in a hurry and get back home," Worf recalled in an interview almost 25 years later. "We kind of figured we'd all been involved in managing wilderness in some way, so we'd just write down how to do it and be done with it. But when we got there we found none of us looked at wilderness the same way. That was one of the reasons why the Wilderness Act was passed: to try to make coordinated sense out of the wilderness concept."

The wilderness concepts of America took root from the ideals of Henry David Thoreau, John Muir, and many others, to preserve scenic wonders and to benefit both nature and people. The inclusion of man with nature led to confusions and even conflicts. In the eight years it took the Wilderness Act to reach the president's desk—from introduction to signature—it underwent 67 revisions with many political compromises along the way. Now the four agency men set to coordinate implementation.

Worf grew up on a ranch in eastern Montana. He graduated from forestry school at the University of Montana and went to work in the wide-open National Forest lands of Wyoming and Utah. His interests in seeing new country drew him into recreation management, overseeing campgrounds, and traveling the backcountry usually on horseback. He acknowledged that he didn't develop any conscious wilderness philosophy or wilderness principles distinct from outdoor recreation until being thrust into the Washington office of all places.

The Washington office immersion led Worf to become a strict constructionist of the Wilderness Act, following its guidance to direct management decisions. But he was never a wilderness purist who imagined the land devoid of human kind. Pure wilderness without signs of human intrusion or settlements was limited to few inhospitable landscapes without indigenous people. Pure wilderness also contradicted the ideal of people appreciating the land through visitation. And pure wilderness would be difficult to explore without recreational equipment from boots to boats.

In a series of interviews over a couple days at his log house in the Bitterroot Valley just east of the Selway-Bitterroot Wilderness, Worf explained his thinking and how it evolved.

"While I believe pretty deeply in the concept of wilderness and the philosophy of wilderness, I also recognize the Wilderness Act itself doesn't call for pure wilderness. It makes some exceptions—some mandatory and some permissive—that depart from the basic pure concept. The policy we developed was to stay pure until you ran into one of the exceptions, and you went with the exception only to the degree the Wilderness Act provided. And the exceptions were pretty specific. And the instructions we wrote were pretty clear."

Those exceptions were clear to Worf but the inconsistencies could be confusing to others. A Moose Creek Ranger Station with flush toilets, hot and cold running water, propane for refrigerators and stoves, and a telephone all located at the edge of two intersecting airstrips, all in the middle of the Selway-Bitterroot Wilderness, seems far different than an area "without permanent improvements or human habitation." Even more intrusive to a pure wilderness concept was administrative exceptions to the prohibition on motor vehicles and motorized equipment, structures, and aircraft. The managing agencies for wilderness were allowed these exceptions "to meet the minimum requirements for the administration of the area," according to the Act.

What constitutes the "minimum requirements" was debated by Worf and his colleagues. To form a unified interpretation, they looked back to the purposes of the Wilderness Act. Worf used four points developed by John P. Saylor, a Republican Congressman from Pennsylvania who was the original sponsor of the bill in the U.S. House, to explain the need for an act of Congress.

First, prior to the act, the Secretary of Agriculture or Interior could declassify any wilderness with the stroke of a pen. Just as easy was changing a boundary for an existing wilderness to allow development with logging or mining or summer home construction. The simplicity to create a new wilderness by administrative action was countered by

Charlie Gindler packs trash and #9 wire at East Moose Creek, 1976
Warren Q. Miller

the ease of undoing a wilderness. No system of checks and balances existed; all designations and potential changes were done by executive orders from one of the cabinet secretaries at the recommendation of the Forest Service chief or the Park Service director. The Wilderness Act instead declared all designated wilderness permanent. An act of Congress, signed by the President, was required designate it and to change it, which in turn would require a public process.

Second, before passage of the Wilderness Act, the agency administrators lacked authority over practices for some activities such as wildlife management, mining claims, and operations, as well as adjudication and implementation of water rights. The act clarified that states retained responsibility for fish and wildlife, along with water law, but operated in wilderness under the "prohibition of certain uses" clause. Retention of a primary role for fish and wildlife management and water rights was a critical compromise to gain acceptance from state legislatures. However, in managing wildlife and water in wilderness, states could not build roads or structures, or use motorized equipment or mechanical transport, which were restrictions applied to everyone except the federal agencies. And mining also gained specific attention to set a 20-year window for filing any new mineral claims.

Third, a lack of consistency could mean an agency operated with one set of rules in one place and different rules elsewhere. Saylor recognized if some things were permitted in one place, under an expansive view of administrative exceptions, it would be next to impossible to restrict them somewhere else. The Wilderness Act established a consistent management framework.

Last, wilderness had not been considered a distinct resource or even a specific entity. Wilderness had been looked upon as a modified recreation area where wilderness-type activities occurred. The importance of a stand-alone wilderness resource and its characterization needed to be defined, leading to common standards, originating from the Wilderness Act. Specification of the wilderness resource, beyond the purposes of human control or utilization, proved to be an ongoing challenge.

"Those four points provided the foundation for most of the Forest Service wilderness policy and philosophy," Worf said. "Our manual got so thick because we felt we needed some pretty tight rules in order to keep the concept from unraveling."

The idea of wilderness may conjure up something different in many different people's minds. Wilderness is steeped in myth, romantic visions, and glorifications of sometimes dubious history. One person's view may be contrary to another's idea or even in opposition to the preservation of natural conditions. And, as Worf acknowledged, the Wilderness Act was a composite of ideas, forged in legislative compromise over the course of those eight years in Congress and many more years in formative debates. The Act borrowed from multiple guides and philosophers, including the agency leaders Aldo Leopold, Bob Marshall, and Arthur Carhart and its original author, Howard Zahniser, of the Wilderness Society.

A core issue was to clarify the idea of wilderness as a natural resource with specific values and purposes. "The lack of distinctiveness could erode the wilderness as much as anything else and I think that was one of the most difficult points to get across," Worf said.

Worf's background, understanding of land management, and his lack of previous focused attention to wilderness concepts made the work in Washington difficult. The Montana ranch boy found the idea of leaving something alone, untouched, unused, and with minimal human intrusion to be strange.

"It was tough because a lot of wilderness philosophy ran against my value system at the time. My father was a homesteader. My grandparents were immigrants from Europe. They came over here to develop this country. I looked upon development as something good and as something that should be done. You made your mark on the land and made things better. Finding new and better ways to do things, that was the way I was oriented.

"I enjoyed doing things the old ways, riding horses and packing horses. I enjoyed that. But it was almost always aimed at developing the land, not to keep it preserved in wilderness."

Worf's views were consistent with most people in the Forest Service. The emphasis on development and active management, including everything from timber harvest to campground construction, ran deep in the agency orientation and core values. But in the Washington attic, Worf soon determined if the Wilderness Act was going to carried out to meet goals of land protection and people's appreciation, some preconceived notions and established traditions needed to be altered or set aside. A new land use directive needed to be adapted to wilderness and adopted across the agency. Aldo Leopold's land ethic and wilderness ethic needed to be applied to people and places.

Worf quoted a well-known Leopold commentary from memory, written in 1925 and then used by Bob Marshall in a 1930 magazine article to draw attention to the need for wilderness. Leopold said, "The day

Dale Swee and Dick Kuhl pack trash on Moose Ridge, 1976 *Tim Rich*

is almost upon us when a pack train must wind its way up a graveled highway and turn out its bell mare into the pasture of a summer hotel. When that day comes the pack train will be dead, the diamond hitch will be merely a rope, and Kit Carson and Jim Bridger will be names in a history lesson."

Leopold's words rang true for Worf, not only to preserve a place for pack trains but also to see some lands free of summer hotels and cabins. "The cumulative effect of nonconforming occupancies and mechanization is sometimes subtle, but nonetheless real. For that reason, the fact they can sometimes be hidden from visitors may reduce their impact somewhat, but it does not make them any more compatible with wilderness," Worf wrote in a 1973 paper presented at a wilderness seminar in Arizona.

Worf came to understand that American history and the American experience laid the groundwork for the importance of wilderness preservation. "One of the things that made America great is we interacted directly with wilderness in a pretty hard way," he explained. "The Jim

Bridgers came out and lived in the wilderness. This whole continent was wilderness at one time, in the truest sense. People came from Europe and fought the wilderness, conquered most of it. At least as far as I'm concerned, one of the benefits of wilderness is to maintain some of the strengths of character that came from our interacting with wilderness."

As soon as the Wilderness Act became law, there were requests to do new things or continue to do things that butted up against the new definitions and concepts of wilderness. Government people, commercial outfitters and private individuals lined up to get their activity declared an exception and a special use or "grandfathered in" by prior, established use. Responses to each request defined and refined what wilderness was all about.

In a couple of examples, Worf sided on opposite ends of special use requests, although both ended in the same conclusion and he learned from each. Special use authorizations are issued as a permit for citizen land use or activity, including power lines or outfitter camps, on National Forests. The Forest Service Chief in the mid-1960s, Edward P. Cliff, denied a special use permit appeal to install a telephone repeater in the Mt. Hood Wilderness of Oregon. The argument in its favor was for the health and safety of people; it would have no moving parts and it could be camouflaged. But the chief determined the repeater would be an installation and a structure, both expressly prohibited by the Act. He turned it down and Worf agreed.

A few weeks later Worf suggested approval for an automated snow measuring device in the Glacier Peak Wilderness of Washington. He reasoned it was almost invisible, it was silent, it was for mountain travel safety, and it was to maintain a high-quality watershed. The chief saw it as another potential installation, prohibited by the act, and denied the exception. After further consideration, Worf changed his mind and agreed it should be rejected.

Like much of government workings, policy was established in fits and starts, by an accumulation of decisions. Unlike a lot of seemingly haphazard government directives, their effort was a concerted thrust toward uniformity and consistency, with a goal to protect the wilderness resource.

Worf recalled when he attended a Congressional hearing where representatives from the U.S Fish and Wildlife Service discussed a potential new wilderness in the Great Swamp of New Jersey. The discussion included putting in new flush toilets and boardwalks leading up to it at a comfort station in the middle of the area. The idea of flush toilets and boardwalks did not meet with favor from the committee members. While Forest Service officials were there on a separate issue, after the New Jersey testimony committee chairman Representative Wayne Aspinall, R-Colorado, questioned Chief Cliff about Forest Service policy on trails in wilderness.

Cliff said in wilderness some existing trails were too high quality, too wide, and with too many signs, which didn't fit the character of wilderness, Worf recalled. The Forest Service intention was now to blend trails into the landscape, to resemble game trails, to present visitors a challenge in finding their way, while averting erosion, Cliff explained. Aspinall agreed wilderness trails should appear part of the terrain.

On the way back to the office Worf rode in a taxi with the three top Forest Service officials. Cliff turned to Worf and said, "What I told Aspinall, that's our wilderness trail policy. See that people in the field understand it. We need to be doing things different in wilderness."

The concept of minimalist trails and limited signs was new to Worf and virtually everyone else in the Forest Service. Many existing trails were rough, obscure, and steep, but it wasn't by preference. Trails often ran the shortest distance between two points with minimal design, because of speed in construction and limited budgets, not as intention. Making trails broader with lower gradients was the current direction in planning, to make the route safer and easier. Wilderness values called for a new way of thinking, Worf said.

When Worf became the Bridger National Forest supervisor in 1960, a recent magazine article by Supreme Court Justice William O. Douglas, an ardent outdoorsman and conservationist, took the Forest Service apart on the overused conditions of the Bridger Wilderness. Worf remembered the stinging article with discomfort. While he was new to the top job, conditions on the forest were his responsibility. Douglas contended the problems reflected a lack of interest in recreation and a willful neglect of the resources. Worf responded with one idea he carried on into his wilderness policy deliberations and another idea that proved contrary to a wilderness ethic. He created a new position of wilderness ranger to contend with the influx of visitors and to provide oversight and guidance. The idea took hold and similar positions cropped up on other forests.

He also built some high-grade trails. The trails moved pack strings in and out from alpine lakes to supply drop camps. The quick trips avoided overnight stays from the pack stock at the lakes, but it also increased use on the fragile lake shores. The high grade and high-speed trails were an idea "somewhat different than what I think is appropriate today," Worf said.

He explained his personal transition: "The summer before the Wilderness Act passed, I stood on the shore of Island Lake [in the Bridger Wilderness of Wyoming] and counted 135 people around the lake, which I thought was alright. It was a recreation area, it was getting use and it was a good thing."

The wilderness concept created a new standard where trails are not for comfort and convenience of visitors or for speed and ease of use, according to Worf's new views. Trails would be an accepted part of wilderness, constructed and maintained to prevent damage from visitors to soils and watersheds while remaining unobtrusive. Trails should be the minimal width necessary to allow people and stock to travel in safety and also to protect the land. Trails should not be upgraded to increase speed.

The four men in the attic completed their initial work on wilderness policy in a couple of months and they returned to respective home forests. The recommendations went out to the Regional Foresters for review. Worf was called back to Washington to make revisions. He then prepared a general report and it proved to be of greater interest than the expected audience of a few agency people. More than 18,000 copies of the report were sent out from Washington and more than 3,000 comments came back. After more revisions, a series of regulations called the Administration and Use of National Forest Wilderness and National Forest Primitive Area was signed by the Secretary of Agriculture, Orville L. Freeman, in June of 1966.

Worf was not able to shake Washington and his career trajectory had already brought him to a full-time transfer to the office headquarters in 1965. He became the head of all wilderness programs at the national level. He stayed in Washington through 1969 to implement the administration and use regulations. "Along the way, a lot of my recommendations were accepted, and some were rejected. And the policy was molded over those four years," he recalled.

Worf returned west in 1969 to be the Director of Recreation and Lands at Missoula for the Northern Region, covering Montana and northern Idaho. There he could see how his regulations and policy worked on the ground. He took an interest in Moose Creek because it was the only all-wilderness ranger district at the time. He liked what was going on at Moose Creek.

"My first major backpacking trip was with Bill Holman [then district ranger at Moose Creek.] I was fresh out of the Washington office, as soft as they come, and about 25 pounds overweight. We hiked from Lost Horse Pass to Moose Creek. We did it in two days," going a distance of about 32 miles.

Worf also valued physical labor and its purpose in wilderness. He viewed the perpetuation and mastery of pioneer skills to be integral to the wilderness legacy. The prohibition of motorized and mechanized equipment in wilderness meant crosscut saws were recovered from neglected, deep storage, to be refurbished, de-rusted, and sharpened. Saw songs—not chainsaw whines—whistled in the woods again and

Bill Worf and Bud Moore snooze at White Cap Creek, 1971 *Richard I. Walker*

Worf was pleased. At Moose Creek, Worf saw the double diamond hitch continued to be thrown in addition to newer Decker saddle trees carrying panniers. He was gratified to see trail crews loaded with 70 pounds of tools and supplies on their backs for a 10-day, 150-mile hitch. Moose Creek was one of the places where people re-created and revived some skills taken for granted and almost lost into oblivion.

"One of the important aspects of wilderness is forcing people to do things the old ways, because people generally aren't going to do it willingly otherwise," Worf explained. "Some will, sure. But who would get a thrill out of climbing a mountain if there is a tram to the top? Who's going to want to walk to a nice mountain lake if you can hire a helicopter or ride a motorbike?"

Pressure to expand the administrative exceptions to the motor ban came early and often from both inside and outside the Forest Service. The official policy Worf promoted didn't consider cost, convenience, or speed to be determining factors in wilderness. "If you can do it by primitive means, you do it by primitive means," Worf said. Safety should be the only other consideration.

According to Worf, motorized equipment doesn't just make noise and fumes, it changes the land and the way people relate to the land. Use of chainsaws mean woodcutting may be easier, and may be even faster in some situations, but it also means more woodcutting is done. Wilderness visitors will cut more firewood than needed with a chainsaw, reducing the natural nutrient recycling and making an intrusive impact with the hand of man. The wood pile left behind will attract other people to the same campsite and concentrate use.

New trails may be cut with a chainsaw to set up a camp or for hunters to get to an elk kill when they might bushwhack otherwise. Trail crews may cut faster with a chainsaw, in some cases, but efficiency can be limited by requiring stock to carry gas, the saw, protective gear, and spare parts. Stock use means significant time must be spent tending animals and camp locations big enough for stock can require greater travel time. Livestock also show an impact on streams, meadows, and campsites. Chainsaws also do not encourage minimalist trail design as well as crosscut saws do. Each cut with a crosscut is carefully calculated for efficiency and to protect the saw teeth. Crosscuts require finesse, where chainsaws require brute force. And Worf liked seeing young people become skilled at using the tools of their ancestors in the quiet of the forest.

Worf also believed the ban on structures in wilderness carried value beyond enforced hardships. A building not only occupies the land, it makes it easier for people to impose their will and to spread their tentacles. A meadow or stream bank not only takes on a different character with a cabin or tent platform, people do more things to the surrounding land if they have a permanent base. People also concentrate at cabins and constructed camps where more traffic is funneled to settlements.

Wilderness offers people an opportunity to interact with American history, Worf said. "The people in wilderness are out there doing things, actually accomplishing work. And it's not as a show, not just as a museum piece or playacting thing. But it's an everyday kind of thing; that's the way they live; that's the way they work. And they face challenges. They have to figure out how you get this bridge stringer across the river or how you break up this rock without a motorized cobra drill?"

For years, Worf preached the use of pioneer skills and often confronted a negative, defensive reaction in the name of practicality. Speed from power tools was considered a virtue in the Forest Service. To highlight the positive outcomes from traditional skills and tools, he decided to recognize the innovative traditionalists.

Worf created the Primitive Skills Award, the Silver Axe, in 1979, for "the crew that showed the greatest initiative to do a difficult job in wilderness without resorting to motorized or mechanized equipment or aircraft." He developed the award outside official channels and funded it himself.

He started it as a regional program and then added a national award, which was later taken over by the Forest Chief. Silver Axes have gone to trail crews for major reconstruction, re-routes and bridges, using non-motorized, muscle powered, traditional tools and techniques.

Worf used the example of a trail crew in the Marble Mountain Wilderness of California as an example of what he thought was important. When trail foreman Pat Garrahan found out a wooden bridge built with local materials in his wilderness was going to be replaced with steel and off-site, treated timbers, he objected. "He said it had been done with local wood once, it can be done again," Worf said.

Garrahan recruited a high school Youth Conservation Corps crew and they rebuilt the 32-foot span bridge from scratch, skidding and fitting logs, without the imposition of modern technology. They completed the job for about $1,500, compared to the $50,000 estimated cost for steel and chemical treated timbers.

Garrahan captured Worf's ideas. "Here's a young guy, his idea of wilderness was it just wasn't right to use modern equipment in wilderness. He proved it could be done without it. And he took some kids from the city in California who had never done anything remotely close to that, and did the job with them."

Our conversations at Worf's house occurred soon after another challenge was met, when the old ways of wilderness overcame new demands. In 1985, the Environmental Protection Agency prepared to do a massive water sample study of western high mountain lakes to assess acid rain effects, and it asked for a special use permit to fly helicopters into 498 lakes in wilderness. The EPA stated the study had to be done in a narrow time frame of early summer, before lakes warmed and the water turned over in its seasonal cycle. Each sample had to get to the laboratory in a matter of hours, not days.

EPA officials expressed shock at objections from citizens and Forest Service staff when the project was intended to protect the sanctity of the environment. EPA staff reacted in disbelief that any non-motorized alternative might be suggested, which they considered would be slow, expensive, and impractical. Worf, who had retired from the Forest Service by then, followed the footsteps of EPA representatives to meetings with conservation groups, with each seeking support. The EPA argued it was our way, with helicopters, or no way and no acid rain study. Worf argued the samples could be collected without helicopters, using pack stock and backpacks for transport, and the study would be timely.

The Forest Service Chief, R. Max Peterson, backed Worf. "The job was done on time," Worf said. "There were no problems with the quality. There wasn't a lost time accident in the whole thing. And it was done cheaper than EPA would have done it with helicopters."

Visitors should experience the quiet sounds of nature and soar with their imaginations, Worf believed. "One of the nice things about wilderness is it's an adventure," he said. "There is a sense of discovery. I think the objective ought to be to manage the wilderness so that in at

Selway River rafters, 2017 *John McCarthy*

least some parts of it you feel maybe you might be the first person to set foot there. I think there ought to be a little bit of excitement around every corner, a little bit of mystery."

He recalled an argument he had with Art Seamans, the district ranger at Moose Creek in the late 1970s, over a how-to guide book for floating the Selway River. Seamans already stood up to regular pressure from outfitters and citizen boaters to expand the one group a day launch system, to get more boaters on the river. The Selway had the most restrictive launch program in the Wild and Scenic River System, which continues today. Seamans supported the wilderness opportunity engendered by the limited launch program but he thought a guide book for the steep gradient river would make it safer. Rafter deaths on the Selway were periodic, sometimes an annual occurrence, and Seamans proposed an official guidebook after a triple rafting fatality.

Worf opposed government supported guidebooks for anything in wilderness. "Everyone has a right to find a challenge. And, by gosh, when you come to the head of one of those rapids, you get up on the riverbank to scout it out and you either read the rapid right or you get dumped."

Worf won the argument with Seamans about the guide book and he carried it farther to argue against maps of the river or any maps at all. The very act of naming and mapping takes away some wildness, he said. Maps impose authority and ownership, in opposition to wilderness. He recognized maps and place names are part of human heritage, probably even human nature, but he believed people should accept nature in wild places as it is for themselves without someone else imposing a directive or direction.

"I don't think there was one single event in the history of the United States that had a greater impact on wilderness than the Lewis and Clark expedition. It was a great feat and it wasn't the fact of the crossing that had the most impact, it was the publicizing the maps and the journals that accelerated the movement of people out to the West."

Uncharted adventure in wilderness also means accepting wild nature, including wild animals, without human control, he argued. Worf didn't win the map argument with the Forest Service cartographers putting out maps for wilderness across the nation. He didn't relent on the concepts.

"Anybody that goes into Glacier Park or Yellowstone ought to accept there are grizzly bears there and if someone gets eaten, that's tough. That's the challenge of the wilderness. But society doesn't accept that, yet. If somebody gets killed by a bear, people demand it's hide, no matter who's at fault."

In a talk he gave to all employees of the Wenatchee National Forest in 1987, Worf explained his thinking. "Over the last 23 years I've developed a deep conviction that the National Wilderness Preservation System may well be one of our greatest national assets. This is not because it provides nice places to backpack or hike. We could provide those opportunities in many beautiful places where there is no wilderness left. It is not because they provide natural habitats for fish and game animals like elk and deer. We could produce more game and fish if we intensively managed the habitat for them. It is a great asset because our nation was born in wilderness and our national character was shaped by it. We must maintain some examples of this wilderness heritage to remind us—and those who come after us—of the route we traveled to get to where we are today."

When Worf retired from the Forest Service in 1981, conservation friends tried to enlist him in the struggle to get Congress to designate more wilderness. "Enough young, eager people were already doing that work," he said. "And that job was pretty well done. The system is already bigger than I ever hoped it would be. I'm concerned about the management aspects not getting enough attention from the public. The agencies are going by themselves. I think the public needs to get in there and monitor and help the agencies do a better job of wilderness management."

Worf did not limit his oversight to National Forests, and he also became a monitor for wilderness management for lands within National Parks and other agencies. His concerns focused on the principles laid out by Congressman Saylor years before.

One of the first policy issues Worf got involved in was to counter an appeal from the Idaho Outfitter and Guides Association, which was fighting a new wilderness management plan. The Central Idaho Wilderness Act of 1980 created the River of No Return Wilderness. At 2.3 million acres it was the largest in the national system at the time. Combined with the Selway-Bitterroot Wilderness, which is only separated by one dirt road known as the Magruder Corridor, it remains the largest forest wilderness complex in the Lower 48 states.

Shortly before his death in 1984 from pancreatic cancer, Idaho's wilderness champion Senator Frank Church lived long enough to see his name attached to his lasting legacy in his home state, creating the Frank Church—River of No Return Wilderness. Some people call it the Frank, others call it the Church. Some people object to wilderness named after any person and continue to call it the River of No Return.

After the wilderness was declared, some outfitters were outraged about new regulations to outlaw permanent camps, corrals, hitch-racks and winter caches. Similar regulations for all visitors existed in other wilderness management plans for more than 10 years, with no exceptions attached to outfitter special use permits. The prohibition of non-native materials for caches in wilderness was Forest Service policy for more than 20 years. Worf was concerned not only about what could be allowed in the new wilderness, he worried it could go backwards to undermine existing wilderness plans.

"Outfitters really wanted ownership, a property right to prime camp spots," Worf said. "To leave stuff in wilderness wasn't nearly as important as a right to stake a claim on an area by leaving a cache and having a built-up camp."

Outfitters wanted a privilege no one else had, in Worf's view. Outfitter camps became bigger and more elaborate, leading to greater permanence, since the 1931 declaration of the million-acre Idaho Primitive Area. With similar camps being dismantled and packed out of the Selway-Bitterroot to the north, Worf reasoned the insistence in keeping the privilege came down to money. Outfitters could charge more for the comforts and convenience of a wood floor wall tent and big, steel and iron wood stoves in a cook tent.

Worf couldn't get any national or state conservation groups to file a counter-appeal to the outfitters. The association had been supportive of the new Idaho wilderness, and outfitters were considered allies in efforts to get additional wilderness designations in other places. So, Worf intervened in the appeal as an individual and was joined by Howard Spaletta, a consulting engineer and wilderness supporter from Idaho Falls. Their intention centered on support of the Forest Service and wilderness values. They were not picking fights.

The outfitter's appeal was denied at the regional level and the association carried it to Washington for a final administrative review. After a hearing in front of the chief of the Forest Service, R. Max Peterson, he rejected the appeal. Worf traveled to both appeal steps, to Boise and to

Washington, to testify on behalf of the wilderness plan. He spent more than $1,000 out of his pocket for the effort.

The outfitters then mounted a court challenge to override the administrative process. Worf kept going as well, submitting briefs in support of the agency ruling.

As the court case moved through the system, the Forest Service administration changed. Forest Service chiefs are appointed by the Secretary of Agriculture, who are the same as any cabinet position—political appointees of the president. Toward the end of President Reagan's second term in 1987, a new chief was selected.

"My biggest worry right now is the apparent shift in the whole Forest Service philosophy that wildernesses are simply recreation areas, and that seems to be Chief [F. Dale] Robertson's idea," Worf told me in July 1989. Recreation areas promoted outdoor activities and the infrastructure to support it, contrary to the wilderness concept of limiting human intrusion, he explained. "The previous chief, Max Peterson, seemed to gain an understanding of the distinct value of wilderness as a resource. People in the agency followed, or at least didn't go against, Peterson's lead. Now the administrators shifted with the wind to change direction and follow Robertson's lead."

The shifts did not bode well for the cache issue, the court case or the untrammeled solitude found in wilderness. "My feeling is the present chief is just convinced, personally convinced, it doesn't make any sense for outfitters to haul out something they're going to use again next season. Robertson seems to think a cache is a reasonable, practical solution to the situation. But such an attitude goes beyond the practicality of a cache. I don't think he has any sense of the value and meaning of wilderness."

The concept of challenge, hardship and struggle was foreign to Robertson, Worf believed. Ease and access seemed more important than adventure. Worf talked about a friend who lost both his hands and feet to frostbite on Mount McKinley, now Denali. "The man knows he can't go back. He told me that, 'Looking for wilderness in a wheelchair is like looking for darkness with a flashlight. When you get there it's not there.'"

When it came to the Forest Service, Worf would never object to being called a company man. He understood and honored loyalty. Now he worried if the agency leadership could not find their way in the wilderness, even with a flashlight. With his intention to support the wilderness management plan crafted by local managers and the previous chief's decision to back them, Worf was cast as an interloper, an outsider off the team. "The way I'm being treated is not the way the public ought to be treated," he said.

Robertson approved a settlement agreement with the outfitters out of court to allow camp structures and equipment in the short term and to continue the caches. The settlement reversed Chief Peterson's denial of the same claims. The outfitters dropped the lawsuit. As a settlement agreement, the ruling was out of bounds to any interests except the plaintiff and the defendant—the outfitters and the Forest Service. Worf was cut out of the decisions and the conclusion.

An outfitter camp in the Frank Church-River of No Return Wilderness that morphed into a riverside resort also caught Worf's attention. In the 1960s, Norm Guth of Boise bought out a combination hunting, river floating, and jet boating operation along the Salmon River. It included a camp at Big Squaw Creek, under special use permit on Forest Service land. The camp of rough shacks was considered an eyesore and the outhouses polluted the river. Guth agreed to move the camp upstream to Smith Gulch. The informal agreement was supposed to be completed within five years of 1972, but it got postponed in the efforts to pass the Central Idaho Wilderness Bill of 1980.

Serving on the Idaho Fish and Game Commission, Guth was well respected in conservation circles as an active supporter of the wilderness bill and a fish and wildlife advocate. His construction of cabins and sheds at Smith Gulch in the 1980s did not raise eyebrows until Worf objected. The cement pilings, metal roofs, plywood floors, frame and log walls, decks, and adjacent storage sheds did not make it a camp with temporary structures, Worf contended. The use of a backhoe in construction and use of an all-terrain-vehicle to shuttle supplies around the compound further aggravated Worf.

Much of Worf's information on the site came from comparative visits by Richard I. Walker of Peck, Idaho. Walker did a historical and cultural survey under contract with the Forest Service in 1981, floating the river in a raft after the wilderness bill passed. One of his favorite places to camp along the river was at Smith Gulch. A cabin built by Blackie Foster in the 1930s, with an uncommon construction of horizontal base logs and vertical wall logs, caught his interests. Timbers and boards from a river scow used to haul ranch equipment down river were reused in the cabin, including a long ridgepole protruding beyond the front door. Walkers' findings led to a river management plan that stated, "Public access of Smith Gulch will be unaffected by the outfitter's occupation."

When Walker made another float trip in 1988, as a river guide for Northwest Dories, both the favorite place and public access were gone. Instead, Guth's construction of a resort took over the river bar. A historic fresh water clam midden from the Shoshone-Paiute ancestors was covered over with dirt by a front-end loader. The Blackie Foster cabin was converted to a storage shed with plywood nailed over the windows to conceal the junk inside. The long ridgepole was cut flush and the deer antlers over the door were gone. "Here was a historic cabin that was supposed to be available to the public and you couldn't even walk around it," Walker later said. "You sure couldn't and wouldn't even want to camp there anymore."

Worf started with administrative objections, to encourage the Forest Service to scale back or shut down the Smith Gulch operation. He wrote letters with Walker's photographs as illustrations and he held meetings with officials.

The Wilderness Act of 1964 was fraught with compromises and contained an entire section titled Special Provisions. Similar to most legislation, the authors and proponents made deals to gain acceptance of the Act, which was a primary reason it took eight years and 67 revisions to pass. The Central Idaho Wilderness Act of 1980 was also designated with numerous private inholdings including some with roads and motorized equipment, eight public airstrips, jet boats along the main Salmon River, and other exceptions to pure wilderness. Dennis Baird of Moscow, one of the key players in the Central Idaho Wilderness Act, recalled conservationists accepted some undesirable "special provisions" in the gambit to secure 2.3 million acres of wilderness.

Baird remembered a verbal commitment from conservationists to accept Guth moving his camp from Big Squaw to Smith Gulch. He also remembered Guth as an active participant in the wilderness campaign and he had no recollection of any involvement from Worf. After Worf pushed for the Forest Service to remove most or all the operation at Smith Gulch, Baird wrote personal letters in support of Guth and got the Northern Rockies Chapter of the Sierra Club to do the same.

Baird acknowledged the Guth compound at Smith Gulch may not have been to his liking and it may have been a regrettable concession to support it. But a deal was a deal, in his mind. "Conservationists cannot afford to have their word questioned by a strong supporter of wilderness of all people," Baird told me.

Worf considered the end result of Guth's compound construction to exceed any conceivable deal, unless people were duped in the first place. As someone who wasn't part of any deal, Worf wouldn't look away. After Guth sold his hunting and river floating parts of his outfitter permit to retain only the jet boat operation, Worf was even more baffled and disturbed. Jet boats can and have hauled virtually everything up Idaho rivers including milk cows, pianos, and bathtubs. "Why does he need a base camp at all?" Worf said. "He could have half a dozen spike camps up and down the river and resupply them by jet boat."

In his efforts to rid the Frank Church-River of No Return Wilderness of outfitter caches and to change the Guth operation, conservation groups ignored or rebuffed Worf, except the Montana Wilderness As-

Ralph Fireovid and Dale Swee at May Lake for acid rain survey, 1986
Warren Q. Miller

sociation and in the Idaho and Montana chapters of the Back County Horsemen of America. Montana Wilderness Association was the only group Worf knew at that time that had a separate committee on policies and management of classified wilderness. But MWA restricted its energy to Montana or issues that could affect Montana, and did not take an active role in Idaho issues.

In the winter of 1989, over coffee with two younger friends of wilderness, Jim Dayton and Bobbie Cross Guns, Worf shared his frustration at the lack of support from Idaho and national conservationists. The cache and camp issues both diminished wilderness values after designation and no one was willing to step up to defend wilderness, he said. "They said why not form a national organization that deals only with management so it's not worried about alliances with other political supporters of wilderness?" Worf recalled.

Cross Guns and Dayton came up with the name Wilderness Watch.

Worf thought it was a great idea and plopped down $20 to be the first member. Just as quick, the other two declared Worf the first president. And they agreed to join him as the original three-member board.

Worf envisioned a national group with regional chapters. While the chapter structure may not have taken off, with only three as of 2017, Wilderness Watch did become a national force focused on wilderness management. In the first year, it took on the Minnesota Air National Guard over airspace above of the Boundary Waters Canoe Area Wilderness and the U.S. Air Force itself, above the wild parts of Adirondack Park in New York. Over the years, Wilderness Watch engaged many issues in wilderness including helicopter landings, wolf killings, roads, chainsaws, air strips, camp management, communication towers, fish stocking, and many others. From the Everglades to Alaska, the group became known as a defender of wilderness.

Through National Environmental Policy Act comments, engaging in the law that requires environmental studies and public process in advance of federal actions, letters to officials and newspapers, public meetings, and lawsuits, the group stopped some things detrimental to wilderness, modified others, turned some things back for more study, and lost on some issues. The first years were a volunteer program, with Worf doing the majority of the work. Even the indefatigable Worf could not keep up with all the issues, and staff was soon hired. The current executive director, George Nickas, has been on staff since 1996.

It took eight years to resolve the cache issue. Wilderness Watch took it to court and received an unambiguous ruling for outfitters to remove all caches, water systems, and permanent camps. Worf declared victory for wilderness and Wilderness Watch. The outfitter representative claimed it was already being done anyway. The Forest Service accepted the ruling. When action to complete the court order was slow, Wilderness Watch went back to the judge to find the Forest Service in contempt for not carrying out his ruling. In 1998, the judge found the Forest Service was making a realistic effort and was in compliance. The camps were packed out, slow but sure. Caches were eliminated, or maybe hidden on the sly from anyone's view.

The camp compound conflict at Smith Gulch dragged on and did not end so well for Worf and Wilderness Watch. They won another favorable court ruling in 2000 to close and dismantle the lodge. It took yet another round in court to set a final deadline for completion of the action. Under pressure in 2003, the agency set 2005 as the end date. Guth had already sold his stake in the lodge and the new owners sought a political resolution in their favor. In one of his many efforts to undermine wilderness, in 2003, Idaho Senator Larry Craig was convinced to step in with legislation to permit Smith Gulch and two other lodges along the Salmon River to remain in existence.

At the time, I was conservation director for the Idaho Conservation League. When called by a reporter for a comment on Craig's legislation I made an off-the-cuff decision to oppose it for the organization. As Worf often complained with good reason, ICL was among the conservation groups that rarely took stands on wilderness management, our rationale being we were too busy with our focus on unprotected lands. In this case, I decided giving away the publics' access to their land and undoing part of the Frank Church-River of No Wilderness went over the line and should be opposed.

As an example of how convoluted these public land issues can be, after the newspaper article came out with ICL opposition to the camp legislation, the past president of the Idaho Outfitters and Guides Association, Doug Tims, came to see me. Tims said my predecessor as conservation director, my good friend Mike Medberry, made an agreement with him to stay out of the camp compound issue. I assumed it was benign neglect and too much other work to do, not any specific intention for ICL to stay clear of it. Tims went on to say if the legislation failed, he would follow me around wherever I spoke on any issue to tell the crowds I had gone back on a deal and could not be trusted. I told him it wasn't my deal and good luck.

While this occurred before Larry Craig pled guilty to disorderly conduct in an airport bathroom sex sting in September 2007, the willingness of Tims to align with the anti-wilderness Senator Craig demonstrated to me the character of both.

In 2004, Craig attached his bill as a legislative rider to reverse the court decision and to make the new compounds in the wilderness available only to paying guests. Wilderness Watch had no further recourse. Tims never followed me around.

My efforts as a conservationist to support the ideas and ideals advocated by Worf, to not undercut the framework of the Wilderness Act in management decisions or in new legislation, faced a bigger challenge in another legislative process. As a representative of the Idaho Conservation League, my all-consuming focus at the time was to secure wilderness for the Owyhee Canyonlands of southwest Idaho. ICL was a primary player in a complex, collaborative group called the Owyhee Initiative, which included other conservationists, ranchers, the Shoshone-Paiute Tribe, the U.S. Air Force, Idaho Outfitters and Guides Association, and Owyhee County representatives.

I was the lead conservationist on the ground to draw the boundaries for wilderness and to talk with all the local ranchers. Craig Gehrke from the Wilderness Society took the lead on shaping and drafting the legislative language for the wilderness bill. No other similar landscape in the high desert, sagebrush steppe ecosystem was represented in the national wilderness system, and the Owyhees were as wild as anyplace in the West. Our goal was to get as much public land as possible designated wilderness.

By September 2006, after five years of steady negotiations, we were convinced more than 500,000 acres of wilderness could be secured without including any of the many unprecedented special deals or new style "special provisions" proposed by the ranchers. Some long-standing special provisions common to other wilderness legislation, including continued livestock grazing operations, were unavoidable. Then an open letter to the national conservation community came out from conservationists not involved in the negotiations to oppose our efforts. The first organization on the list was Wilderness Watch, signed by George Nickas.

According to a paper Nickas co-authored in 2005, *Wilderness Watch* did not directly lobby for designation of new wilderness but in general supported designation of additional wilderness. The group letter with 98 signatories, often obscure operations with just one person who set up shop with a computer and a letterhead far from Idaho, contained five points of concern with potential to undermine wilderness principles. The letter claimed wilderness designation would be traded for public land sales and giveaways to private and state interests, water pipelines for ranchers, new local oversight groups usurping national laws, and also allow military maneuvers, stream poisoning, and motor vehicle use in wilderness.

For us Owyhee wilderness proponents, all the issues were based on rejected proposals, misinformation, fear, animosity toward ranchers and us, or ignorance of the negotiation process. Only one of the 98 people who signed the letter, Jon Marvel of Western Watersheds Project, ever called me and we'd spent hours and hours haggling over his worries and his anger about ranchers. None of the claimed giveaways and special deals were in the bill we got through the juggernaut of Congress signed by President Obama in March 2009. The Owyhee River Wilderness designated 517,000 acres of new wilderness, the first wilderness in Idaho in the 29 years since Frank Church left the U.S. Senate.

My only response to the opposition letter was to make a phone call I dreaded. I called Bill Worf to tell him I could no longer associate with Wilderness Watch. I explained it was okay for his organization to be a critic, even an opponent of our wilderness bill. It was okay to get some of the facts wrong. It was not okay for Nickas never to give me a call and to operate on misinformation and innuendo. For a person I considered a partner in conservation, even a friend, never to call to find out what was going on was beyond my tolerance. Some of our other harshest critics and tough overseers rode us hard, through many phone calls and emails, and the result was better legislation and continued friendships with no personal or public attacks.

Worf listened as I explained in some detail the dynamic of the legislation and the outcome we expected to not undercut but instead to expand wilderness. He thanked me for calling and said he understood my position. He said it was unfortunate there was a misunderstanding between Nickas and me. He did not apologize for Nickas or defend him. He accepted what I said and appreciated the call. He also backed his people. He didn't suggest he would try to fix anything. If there was something to be fixed he would have called me back. We all worked on tough, heated issues.

Worf not only stood up for wilderness values, he valued the wilderness experience. Soon after his retirement in the spring of 1982, he hiked downstream along the Selway from Paradise Guard Station to Moose Creek. His eyesight was vastly diminished with his central vision gone, leaving only peripheral and night vision somewhat intact at the time. His brother-in-law was his hiking partner and guide.

At Moose Creek, he stayed with old friends Emil and Penny Keck. He enjoyed the personal quest of being in the wilderness, free from government business. He also played with and showed around a 3 year-old girl, little Megan, my daughter, who also happened to be visiting Emil and Penny with her mother. Even though he was legally blind, Worf went for walks along the trails, sometimes alone and sometimes with others.

With the help of the cane Worf could stay on the trail and he intended to continue to hike and ride horseback with friends. "They describe what we're seeing. I've had enough experiences that my mind fills in the details," he said with a knowing smile of someone who could picture bear grass in bloom from catching the warm smell, or imagine thick lodgepole stands from hearing the wind in swaying trees. He never accepted being an invalid. He also kept up with technology when useful, using computers for writing and other electronic devices to enlarge print for reading.

To say he was active at Wilderness Watch underestimates the concept. Well into his eighth decade he was full of ideas and energy to follow up. In 2002, on the 30th anniversary of the first approved wilderness fire at White Cap Creek, Worf joined the rest of "the White Cap Five,"

Bud Moore, Orville Daniels, Bob Mutch, and Dave Aldrich, to hike back into Coopers Flat Cabin. It was, "the old and infirm leading the blind," as Daniels joked, with Bud then 86 and Bill 76. They camped at the cabin again, same as 30 years before, told stories and recounted their efforts to see the wilderness wild.

Almost 10 years later in July 2011, at the rendezvous memorial for Bud Moore, held at his old ranger station at Powell on the Lochsa, Bill Worf was there to remember his old friend and compatriot in wilderness. Bill wore a wool cap and big, ink-black sunglasses, using a combination walker and seat to get around with a little assistance. I was among the speakers, drawing from some of the great stories Bud shared with me years before.

Afterwards, I went up to Bill, who I hadn't spoken to in the years since our difficult phone call. Knowing his eyesight was almost gone, I told him who I was and he said, "Of course it's you, John. It's really good to see you and it was real good to hear you and everyone talk about Bud." We talked some more about our friend Bud, about getting out into the wilderness, and about the beautiful summer day along the Lochsa. When I left, Bill said, "It's really good to see you." And coming from a blind man, from Bill Worf, it meant a lot. I told Bill it was really good to see him.

Bill Worf died at home in Missoula in December later that year, at age 85.

In one of our evening conversations years before, Bill said, "I think the idea of wilderness was a unique experiment. And I'm not sure yet that it can work. But I think it's worth a try."

Specialist, Revivalist and Wilderness Physicist

Warren Q. Miller

WARREN Q. MILLER GOT HIS START in wilderness picking up trash, 4,800 pounds of it. The dubious beginning led to more than 40 years of practicing and teaching the skills to be in, understand, and preserve wilderness. Miller learned from the old and taught the young. He refurbished and created the tool kit for wilderness work and then wrote the instruction manual. He became the leading crosscut saw filer and filing teacher in the world. And along the way, he savored, examined, and pondered the details of the journey.

Miller joined a Sierra Club clean-up crew in 1970 at age 25, in the Isaac Lake country of the Selway-Bitterroot Wilderness. Isaac Lake is boggy, a little over 6,000 feet elevation, often with a moose standing in it slurping the underwater vegetation. It is a favorite camp spot for backpackers and hunters. The lake feeds Isaac Creek, an upper basin tributary to North Moose Creek. Much of the country spreading across from the lake to West Moose Meadows is trail-less, wild, rough, wet, dense, and home to elk, moose, and black bears.

In the course of seven days, the crew collected 4,800 pounds of junk scattered across the basin, left behind by hunters, outfitters, and from an early, later abandoned, Forest Service Guard Station. Garbage accumulated over decades. Forest Service staff directed the clean-up and packed out the crap. One of the volunteer crew had to be packed out on a horse because of exhaustion and several of the group left early in mid-week. But the wilderness resource assistant for the Moose Creek Ranger District, Richard I.Walker, noticed the capable hands and probing mind of young Miller. He stood out among the crew.

Miller was the last to leave, staying behind to help load horses and mules. Walker commented in his field notes, "Everybody but Warren Miller departed. He was a tremendous asset to help get things packed up, especially the Kimble stoves filled with glass and the old cast iron stoves (in fact we couldn't have done it otherwise)."

Among the groups' activities were evening campfire gatherings, where Walker shared stories on wilderness history and the concept of a wilderness resource. "At the time, I had no idea what classified wilderness was," Miller said years later. "Well, I probably had some idea, but I couldn't have described it to you. I had no idea there was such a thing as the Wilderness Act."

While the ideas behind wilderness were new to Miller, his motivation was basic and simple. "I'd been hanging around southern California for a while and I felt like going out into the backcountry to do some good, hard work," he said.

After getting to know one another, Walker suggested to Miller if a job came up he'd be a good addition to the paid, district crew. Walker called Miller up back home in California several times over the winter to engage him as a trail crew foreman, starting a step above the entry level. As Miller considered the possibility to return to Idaho working on trails, another opportunity came up to be a wilderness ranger. Walker was the first wilderness ranger on the district and he'd gone on to a full-time job as the wilderness resource assistant. Walker encouraged Miller to join the expanded cadre of wilderness rangers for the district.

"I didn't have any idea what the hell a wilderness ranger was but what he told me sounded pretty good. So, I said, 'You bet.'"

When Miller became a wilderness ranger on the Moose Creek Ranger District it was the only all-wilderness district in the Forest Service. With Walker as his immediate supervisor, Emil Keck as fire control officer, both Emil and Penny Keck running the trail maintenance crews, and Bill Holman as district ranger, they all set out to establish a field-based wilderness management program.

Penny and Emil Keck, Warren Q. Miller at Bearwallow, 1971 *Richard I. Walker*

"The first few years we didn't even worry about contacting people," Miller said. "Our main thrust was resource inventory. Find out where the trails were and what shape the trails were in. Find out where the outfitter camps were, where the garbage dumps were—just go out and explore for things, go everywhere you could."

Miller hiked alone the first year and his only radio contact was an occasional relay through one of the nine lookout towers in operation in and around the district, often through Gardner Lookout. "It was really quiet that first year, without any radio. It was nice."

"The first summer I was on the district I probably hiked a thousand miles and I was in the field all the time. The only paperwork was indexing the photographs I took and keeping a log."

Full-bearded all his adult life until wispy at the end, rail thin, angular and 6-foot-4, Miller defined Lincolnesque in physique and in his stern, clear-eyed visage. His long legs served him well on the trail in his new job. His analytical mind led him to seek into deeper layers of meaning and order for the work.

"What good was a bunch of photos in a box if you couldn't do something with it?" became one of his first questions on the direction of his work. Miller began to organize data, to evaluate visitor use patterns, and to track changes. He applied the procedures and purposes crafted by Walker in his 1968 master's thesis from Colorado State University titled, "Photography As an Aid to Wilderness Resource Inventory and Analysis." The box of photographs became geographic records and were filed as reference points through numbering systems Miller and Walker devised.

After the preliminary inventory of trails, camps and impacts got underway his first year, Miller engaged more in intentional visitor contact his second year. "Wilderness itself requires no management," he said. "Wilderness left to itself takes care of itself just fine. What needs to be managed is people, so essentially what we're managing is people."

Visitor contacts on the trails and at ranger stations started as a way to determine where people came from, where they were going, and what they were doing. Then came the challenges of changing how some people acted when they were in the wilderness. "Our job was to sensitize people to what wilderness stands for and what it is. Through being sensitive to wilderness, people would then take care of it."

Draconian behavior modification was not the goal. "You don't give people a lot of rules, like you have to camp a certain way in some specific place, but you sensitize them to what we want it to look like when they leave," Miller explained. "Give them the basic guidelines of how a wilderness should look, without a lot of human sign, then the small pieces fall in place by themselves."

Early in his travels, Miller found stepping over trees fallen in the trail as a backpacker did not lead to productive interactions with stock users who had to dodge around windfalls. To demonstrate direct connection to the human infrastructure and to provide a service, wilderness rangers started to cut out trails in their travels. The skills and the equipment needed to cut windfalls in wilderness led Miller to his life's work—all things crosscut saw—that utilized a blend of his technical skills and personal interests.

Miller grew up in Salt Lake City and Phoenix, Arizona. Camping trips, with canvas tents and flannel sleeping bags of the 1950s, were the favorite Miller family activities. His appreciation of nature and interests in understanding how the natural world ticked were nurtured in those trips to mountains and deserts. When he was 13, his father died in a National Guard airplane crash after it failed to clear power lines at take-off. His father worked for Motorola and was on board testing a new communication system designed for the military services. Miller's world shrank with the loss of his father's guidance and oversight. As a teenager, he focused on school, excelling in science and math, the same as his father.

In the 1960s, Miller went north to Oregon to attend Reed College, where, in a time of cultural and political transitions, smart, out of the mainstream people congregated. He graduated in 1969. "Things changed in the world quite a bit while I was going to Reed," Miller said in his typical understatement.

One of the changes was that many young men like Miller did not seek standard career paths. His curiosity led to trips to Europe, hitch-hiking and taking trains for a couple years. He continued travels back in the U.S., doing odd jobs along the way. He was driving from Idaho to Montana when he diverted his VW bus up the dirt road to Elk Summit, to join the Sierra Club on the Isaac Lake clean-up crew. The side trip led to him to where he really wanted to be and to a lifetime of working in and for wilderness.

A similar set of unexpected but fortuitous circumstances got Miller deeply involved in the crosscut saw. When Miller took an old, dull saw to remove trees laying across trails he knew there had to be a better way than scrapping and bouncing saw teeth across wood fibers. To get the saw to dig down into the logs, he plunged into a historic world critical to contemporary needs.

He learned the basic techniques of pulling a saw from Emil Keck and from experience but soon became dissatisfied by the old saw's performance. The reputation of crosscuts as misery whips stemmed from the difficulties in getting the teeth to bite into a log without binding and achieving steady cuts into the fibers. Digging out flat files and a few strange gauges from the tool shed, Miller attempted to tune up saws. The complexities of cutting teeth and cleaning-out rakers with correct configurations and alignments for each, both side-to-side and in length, captured his fascination but the variables stumped him in getting the results he sought.

"One of the things I learned pretty quick was that saw filers were few and far between. So, I figured I better learn how to do it, especially being the picky bastard that I am about tools."

Miller didn't seek approval from the permanent Forest Service staff to gather information and equipment related to saws. He didn't start an official process to get funding and authority to renew a government program. He took action on his own, starting again with Emil Keck as a connection to the glory days of crosscut saws.

Keck looked up an old friend who worked out of Olympia, Washington, Martin Winters, who he considered to be the best saw filer in the Northwest. Winters began filing saws in 1927, setting up his saw vise at logging camps through the 1930s and 1940s when crosscuts were still king. Winter's reputation as an efficient and sure filer spread throughout the Northwest and periodically a rival camp would offer him a pay raise to switch camps. When Winters left one camp, some of the lumberjacks would go with him to continue to pull the smoothest, fastest saws.

Even when chainsaws took over in the woods after World War II, Winters continued to sharpen crosscuts used in competitions at log-

Warren Q. Miller sets cutter teeth, 1977 *USFS*

ging fairs. His capacity to transfer a sawyers' strength, agility, and balance into maximum downward movement through closely aligned teeth and rakers expanded his reputation across the West.

After Miller's second field season as a wilderness ranger concluded in late 1972, he traveled toward the coast to see Winters. The young student sought the old master, who was almost in his fifth decade filing saws. Over a few weeks, the arcane knowledge of a disappearing craft and the intricacies of specialized tools were revealed.

The tight tolerances of setting, shaping, and pointing up teeth, fitting rakers, and jointing tips of both the cutters and the peelers to conform to an even curvature of the saw, all at the same arc, with teeth all at the exact same length and the raker depth evenly set lower to peel the kerf—there lay the mysteries and challenges. Knowledge of the qualities of steel, brands and shapes of saws, options for handles, the ways to repair kinks in saws, and an understanding of when a saw was too damaged to be fixed was passed on, as a swordsmith would teach an apprentice. Their intense interaction and the complexities of a seemingly simple tool launched Miller on his life course.

As the use of crosscut saws declined and then almost disappeared, the manufacture of saws and tools followed the same path. Winters filed and set old saws with old tools, all fabricated at the height of practical application with attention to the latest technological manufacture at the time. When he told Miller, "They aren't making them like they used to," he wasn't being nostalgic.

Winters explained he had to repair and refurbish both the saws and the filing tools. He also replicated parts of the setting gauges and recast some new pieces. Worn out files could be replaced with new ones of similar shapes and patterns. Everything else had to be reconfigured or reconditioned to the old specifications.

While there continued to be a few new saws manufactured, Winters dismissed the quality and designs of new in comparison to the best saws of old. Three saw-makers stood out and met the standards of Winters: Disston of Philadelphia, Atkins of Indianapolis, and Simonds of Fitchburg, Massachusetts . By the time Miller sought out the best saws, none of the companies continued to make crosscut saws and only Simonds continued to even exist as a company.

At one time there was tremendous company pride in the creation of crosscut saws. The Disston Lumberman Handbook of 1907 includes the proclamation: "No expense or care is spared in our effort to produce the best saws in the World and we guarantee the Disston Saws, under the same conditions, will last longer, cut faster, and run easier than any other brand of saw on the market."

Not to be upstaged, an undated but likely 1940s catalog for Simonds crosscut saws, handles, and tools states: "Every step in the manufacture of Simonds Crescent Ground Cross-cut Saws from steel to the final filing is carefully checked by expert saw makers. This extra care enables us to guarantee that Simonds Crescent Ground Cross-Cut Saws will cut more timber with less effort and will stay sharp longer between filings than any other saw on the market."

Simonds saw steel was poured from "a cold melt, electric furnace process, recognized by metallurgists as the most dependable high-quality steel." Adaptation of the process occurred in the American steel industry during and after World War I, to replace German steel and to shift the industry focus from quantity, also to achieve high quality products. The hardening and tempering processes were also refined during the war effort to craft the finest saws of the forest.

Winters not only told Miller what brands to look for in searching out old saws, they talked over the purposes of different designs.

Bucking saws were rigid and heavy, often used by a single sawyer who cut a log to length when it was on the ground. The extra weight and the stiffness reduced shimmies and transferred downward pressure on both the push and the pull strokes of vertical cuts with either single or double bucking. These same characteristics limited versatility in the wilderness, where extra weight and stiffness were detrimental.

When felling timber with horizontal cuts felling, or falling saws required flex to follow the slight upward pull of two sawyers' regular movements at the end of their strokes. The same flexibility would be useful when cutting logs out of trails where both the sawyer's positioning and cut angles would be limited by topography. The flex of a felling saw also allowed it to be bent over a backpack or a pack animal. The felling saw width tapered from the teeth to the back to allow wedges to be driven into the saw kerf to guide the trajectory of tree falling and to prevent binds. The same wedge advantage would relieve the bind of logs in trails to keep saw kerfs open.

Winters described the Pacific Coast lines of saws to be well suited for wilderness work, especially in the shorter lengths of 5 1/2 or 6 feet to save weight and be easier to pack. Four teeth, with alternating angles of sets to widen the kerf, were configured to one raker. Pacific Coast saws cut fast in the fir, spruce, pine, cedar, and hemlock of the Northwest, including the Selway country. The teeth extended to the end of the saw, allowing one sawyer to work the tip to finish a cut in a single bucking position and limit the exposure to pinch or to hit the dirt. The width of the backs were four gauge thinner from the teeth which allowed space at the top of the kerf to take a wedge. Deep and wide gullets for the rakers limited choking or binding, tossing out stringers of chips. Unfortunately, a 5 1/2 foot-long and 5 7/8-pound Pacific Coast saw could no longer be ordered sharp and ready to go from Disston for $13.49 like back in 1940.

Once he learned what brands and models of saws were best, Miller began learning how to repair and file them. He learned about jointers to file teeth to a uniform height along the whole arc of the saw. Then came the raker gauge to make the raker depth slightly lower than the cutter teeth so the rakers act as a chisel. Each tooth was sharpened to a point with a flat saw, again requiring uniformity in the bevel and in the shape. Hand-held anvils or tooth-set tools were then used to determine the angle or set of each tooth. To get the right set in a uniform pattern the adjustable spider gauge was used to measure the angle of the set. Each tool and step required expertise only to be gained through practice.

Miller applied the techniques he learned from Winters and collected more tools to get more saws ready for a growing, renewed need in wilderness.

Traveling back to Idaho, Miller dug into what became another of his lifelong pursuits: scouring secondhand stores and pawn shops for tools, especially crosscut saws and saw tools. "I spent the rest of that winter poking around secondhand stores and looking for saws, having a good time, living out of my bus." The search and the training were productive.

"The next summer when I came back, I ended up filing all the district's saws and I've been filing them ever since," Miller said in an interview in 1985, from his saw shack at Moose Creek. "It was really frustrating at first, not being able to get saws the way Martin did. Ever since I've been trying to achieve his standards."

Miller's interests ran the spectrum from the metallurgy of saw steels to the cut attributes of saws in the fibers of different tree species. He studied wood science and he practiced filing. In a curious way, in filing saws he applied his college education and tapped into his major in physics. "The reason I ended up studying physics is I was always interested in physical science. I figured physics would give me the best basis to go anywhere I wanted to go. It's kind of ironical I jumped in here," he said from the middle of the wilderness.

By the mid-1970s, there were three wilderness rangers at Moose Creek carrying saws in the early season to cut out trails. Three traveling trail crews and one re-route crew used one or more saws all season, with the early trail crew starting on the main river trail in May. There were additional saws for fire packs at the ranger station. Smokejumpers in Grangeville needed saws in good shape when they dropped on wilderness fires. As soon as Miller took on refurbishing and fine-tuning saws, word got out and demand increased for his skills.

He'd start early in May before his field season, and return to the ranger station late in the fall, to spend long days out in the saw shack making

Warren's saw filing shed and hay equipment at Moose Creek Ranger Station
Warren Q. Miller

precise strokes with files and sure taps with hammers. Spring and fall are always wet in the Selway country. The ranger station offered a snug base of operations. "A nice time to file is when the weather is really shitty. I'd crank up the little stove and it's nice and toasty in here," he said from the shack.

Miller designed and built a 16 by 8-foot shed for the sole purpose of filing and storing saws. Drawing from Winter's operation, he constructed an eight-foot bench and wooden vise to secure his longest saws. Dozens of saws hung on racks, marked by a system of notches and imprints keyed to a catalog. The log book tracked filing dates and repair actions for each saw, noting if it was checked out to someone. A set of north facing windows on the long side provided flat light without glare or reflections. The walls and ceiling, tall for plenty of head clearance, were painted off-white. A battery powered transistor radio sprouted a long, #9 wire antenna out the roof, with the dial frozen on the National Public Radio station in Pullman, Washington. A small box stove to burn wood scraps kept it cozy.

Soon, saw filing threatened to overwhelm Miller's own field season. People in other ranger districts of the Selway-Bitterroot and in other wildernesses wanted to use, maintain, and sharpen saws. The wilderness ranger role caught on throughout the wilderness system and they wanted to set an example for adaptation of old skills in new circumstances. Smokejumper bases all favored independence in the capacity to maintain all equipment and jumpers wanted to meet wilderness standards for appropriate tools and skills. Getting rid of chainsaws in wilderness required the capability to maintain and operate crosscuts.

Miller's depth of knowledge about crosscuts and his clear thinking with careful descriptions combined to create the Crosscut Saw Manual. Miller wrote the 32-page guide in early 1977 while on a three month paid detail at the Forest Service Equipment Development Center in Missoula. It updated and replaced the 22-page Forest Service manual on Sharpening Crosscut Saw, published in 1922 but long out of print. Miller's introduction states: "The manual provides a basic description of how and why a crosscut saw works and provides some experience-tested methods as a guide for achieving a well-running saw."

The manual is illustrated with drawings and photographs to demonstrate techniques, tools, and saw types. It begins with a glossary for terminology, a description of saw types, and how a saw functions. A schematic and description of the saw vise is presented for replication. The meat of it covers saw filing and setting techniques. There are sections on choosing, using, testing, cleaning, storing, and finding saws. The uses and purposes of setting stakes, pin gages, hand-held set anvils, spiders, setting hammers, jointers, and raker gages are defined and demonstrated. The manual is simple yet comprehensive.

The manual has always remained in print, and free, single copies are available from what is now called the Missoula Technology Development Center. It was revised in 2003, dropping the section on finding saws and tools. Today the manual is also available online as a PDF.

The newer edition also dropped the original fold-out cover with a Darius Kinsey photograph from the great Northwest forests of the

1920s. Two lumberjacks sat in the notch they'd saw cut and chopped into a giant, 12-foot diameter cedar, with a ten-foot felling saw between them. Two other lumberjacks stood at the sides on springboards with long-handled, double-bit axes. All wore caulked boots. Miller's face was superimposed over the head of the skinny guy at the right. He fit right in.

Miller also fit in at Moose Creek, where everyone worked out of the ranger station in the middle of the wilderness. "To me, those first two years were my glory days at Moose Creek. In those early days you came in when you ran out of food. A lot of the trail crews wouldn't come in at all. They got resupplied by the packer and just stayed out there. People would be out in the woods for months, exploring the country."

At the end of the field season he remembered the grand Thanksgiving feasts they cooked up when all the crew would gather before scattering for winter. The windows steamed up inside the old cookhouse, as vegetables simmered and a turkey roasted in the oven. The wood stoves cranked up the heat. Outside, the wind blew across the first of the low elevation snows, too moist to drift. Rangy, shaggy, wiry people shared stories of the year and laughter of the night, along with mugs of coffee, glasses of jug wine, and cans of cheap beer.

In those days, during the winter months, the district ranger kept a desk at the main Nez Perce National Forest office in Grangeville. For the rest of the year, all the staff operated out of Moose Creek Ranger Station, in the heart of the wilderness. "At that time when everybody was working out of here, there was a cohesiveness and a camaraderie that was lost when we split up into three portals."

When ranger Bill Holman and his wife Jane left Moose Creek in 1972, the operations and the character changed. The next ranger, Al Defler, moved the office into town and plugged into the Forest Service administrative system outside the wilderness. Defler mostly stayed in town, to be near the offices and the many meetings. He reorganized the field program into three portals: to the west at Selway Falls, Moose Creek as a supply base in the center, and to the east at Lost Horse. A trail crew and a wilderness ranger with an assistant worked out of each portal. According to Miller, the gains in efficiency by being close to roads and in reductions of air flights to Moose Creek were offset by a loss of the crew no longer living and working together as a rag-tag family. To his mind, the best thing Defler did in his three years as ranger was to bring a treadle sewing machine into the Moose Creek cookhouse where it remains today.

Miller was given the Lost Horse assignment, where a fine log cabin sits almost at the end of a long road blasted through rock slides up from the Bitterroot valley. While the cabin is in Montana, it's only a couple miles from three mountain passes that drop west over the crest into Idaho, at the source of steep creek drainages running all the way down to the Selway River. With an assistant assigned to hold down the cabin chores and visitor contacts, Miller was free to roam the country along the west side of the mountains, deep into the forests.

Accompanied by a Malamute named Shy—reflecting her quiet, reticent nature—Miller started every field hitch climbing up and dropping over one of the passes. Each trail took off from the springs at the origins of creeks and fell from there. He'd spend a week or more on the long descent of East Moose Creek, 35 miles to the confluence with North Moose, before the last few miles to the ranger station. From bare rocks to beargrass, and whitebark pine down to one of the largest old growth cedar groves left in the Northwest, the trail traversed every ecological zone of the wilderness. He'd check hunter and permitted outfitter campsites at Moose Lake and side stream confluences, as he paced his days to look for the marks of man and sense the pulse of nature.

In summer, he rarely encountered people, often only making contact with fellow Forest Service people on trails, at lookouts, or on fires. In the fall, hunters returned to their favorite locations to set up camps for weeks of elk stalking. Hunters who pulled out in a hurry or acted without care left tell-tale marks with axe scarred trees, dirt pounded bare or rutted, rough camp structures, and meat racks lashed with baling twine; equipment or garbage was often left behind.

Sometimes Miller would just clean up a mess. Other times he'd do some detective work to determine who left the scars and then plan to revisit later in hunting season, or the next year, in case they came back. Most of the offenses weren't considered crimes but were violations of the code of conduct expected in wilderness. Miller made it clear to everyone who he spoke to that being in wilderness demanded skill and care, not disregard for civility in an uncivilized land.

After resupplying at Moose Creek, he'd climb back eastward over Freeman Peak and maybe pause to look over Horsefly Meadows, stop and check out Indian Lake, or go on to the ridge toward Wahoo Peak. The cool breezes at higher elevations were welcomed in summer months. Wahoo stands in the center of the Selway-Bitterroot and the vast views show no lights at night in any direction, other than an incomprehensible number of stars. Wahoo was always a preferred camp spot.

Miller would hike out one of the connector trails to Battle Creek or Big Creek and check on other lakes, not to fish but to see if people and stock trampled lake shores. His lodgepole thin stature did not encourage heavy loads piled into the aluminum frame Kelty pack on his back, and he relinquished carrying a short saw after a couple early hitches of a week or 10 days. His first years as a wilderness ranger were all backpacking as light as possible with a radio, log books, camera, and an axe as standard equipment. Then the program was modified to use stock in the fall, both to connect with the hunters who were often mounted and to be able to carry more gear for warmth. Wilderness rangers usually led one pack animal and alternated between riding their saddle horse and walking to keep warm and to keep their own legs strong. Miller liked the challenge of becoming proficient with horses and mules and appreciated extra layers of wool and heartier food carried by the pack stock, but he never became a stockman.

When fire history needed to be studied and fuels inventoried to prepare the Bear Creek Fire Management Plan in 1973, incorporating Bud Moore's White Cap plan, Miller did the ground work. Teaming up with another young wilderness ranger, Gary Koehler, they hiked

Warren Q. Miller at Lost Horse Ranger Station, 1979 *Tim Rich*

with full packs up and down ridges, into and out of creek bottoms, on and off trail, gathering and plotting information on vegetation and topography, fuel loading, and fire history. Wherever an old trail could be found, even with intermittent overgrown blazes or rare cut logs, their location became more certain and the journey more agreeable. Miller's many exploratory side trips provided a guide to where trails might be found or had become mythical and lost.

Much of Miller's time and travels centered on tracking the hunting outfitters. The Wilderness Act changed the operational requirements of many outfitters, putting a structure and standards on a collection of independent, often feral, characters. Outfitters had been on their own without much oversight beyond a license from the state and a special use permit from the Forest Service, both used largely to define territories. Outfitter camps displayed varying levels of woodcraft skill in the logs and poles notched, nailed, lashed, or wired together to make corrals, hitch racks, outhouses, tent platforms, and camp furniture. Some constructions were clever, and a lot were rough at best. The extensive camps were permanent, built in place to last many years, and in violation of the Wilderness Act's prohibition of permanent structures. The Kecks did some early day camp obliterations mostly with a torch. Then the wilderness rangers took steps beyond cleanup to alter the extensive camp footprints.

Miller credited Bill Worf, the director for Recreation, Wilderness and Lands in the Regional Office at Missoula, for the strength of Forest Service commitment to eliminate the permanent structures. "Worf started it and supported people who were ready to do something. Holman grabbed on to it, getting rid not only of the big garbage dumps but also the big camps," Miller said. Holman started a seven-year phase-out of structures in outfitter camps and the wilderness rangers carried out regular visits to make it happen.

"The Forest Service and the outfitters were diametrically opposed at first. That's changed a lot to where we're working with the outfitters a lot more than working against them," he said in 1985.

"A lot of outfitters got out of the business because they saw the Forest Service changing. There's a lot more rules and regulations now. I think the type of outfitter has changed too. The tough old-timers, who were going to do what they wanted to do, those who were very independent, strong individuals with a pioneer connection, some of them got out."

Camp structures were dismantled and packed out or burned. The equipment for camp kitchens and sleeping tents had to be packed in and out every year, leading to downsizing and simplifying operations. Tent poles and temporary wood frames could be left behind for the next year's use, leaned up against a tree to shed rain after nails were pulled out. Everything else had to be, or was supposed to be, hauled out.

Miller told a couple of stories about how the changes played out. As trackers of wild game and readers of wildlife sign, outfitters can be adept at hiding their own sign. One year, fellow wilderness ranger Dick Kuhl hiked to inspect an outfitters camp near Chain Meadows on the north edge of the district and found a cache of camp equipment stashed in the woods nearby. He hiked back to the ranger station and got on the radio telephone to the outfitter in town. He said, "I'm hitching up stock right now to go get your stuff. If we have to ship it out on an airplane we're going to confiscate it as evidence and charge you for the flight. Or, if you get there first, you can pack it the hell out of here and you can keep it." The outfitter beat him back to the camp.

Another time Miller found a cache hidden under a wood pile in late summer, left behind before the permit for fall camp set up. Miller was traveling with stock and he packed up the load to haul it out. He met the suspected outfitter going in, now within the time period he was permitted to start to set up his camp. Miller already made sure the gear he loaded on his mule was recognizable sticking out of the panniers. The outfitter rode past him without acknowledging his stoves and cook kits. Miller figured the outfitter carried in, and paid for, two sets of camp equipment that year. And the outfitter hauled out all his gear at the end of the season.

In the mid-1980s, Miller was well-aware of Worf's continued efforts, now as a private citizen, to eliminate special privileges for outfitters' structures and caches to the south in the adjoining Frank Church-River of No Return Wilderness. Miller supported the efforts to get consistent operations and to take down the large camps. He also recognized Worf faced an even tougher circumstance. "When we did away with outfitter camps at Moose Creek, outfitters weren't as organized as a group and didn't raise as much hell as now."

While elimination of outfitter and private party hunting camps brought results, it also required more record keeping and informational contacts. "I think the district has become much more PR related," Miller said. "Of course the consequences of that is answering letters, talking to people on the phone, spending less time on the ground. But that does not necessarily mean being less productive. We've just become a lot more service oriented.

"Myself, I'm a person who likes to do work that I can see. Whether it's working on a trail, picking up garbage or, whatever. It's different than talking to somebody. I started off very much a field person, spending as little time in the office as possible. The idea of paperwork was contrary to the very concept of a wilderness ranger.

"But all systems evolve, be it a bureaucracy or a natural ecosystem. We come into a situation and somehow, we expect it to stay the same. And when it changes, that bothers us. But whether that's good or bad depends on a value judgement. Change is always going on, it really doesn't have any particular value, except in people's minds.

"I don't think the basic resource has changed. From my point of view the wilderness resource is in better shape than when I first came on the district. It's a little bit closer to being wild."

In an example often heard from wilderness rangers, Miller explained the land being closer to wild meant the clean-up rangers picked up cigarette butts and a few cans, not garbage bags full of litter. Camps were smaller and less obtrusive. Trash was more often incidental droppings, not intentional dumping. Fewer trees were beaten down at the base in a donut ring pounded by stock left tied up for hours.

At the same time, Miller and other wilderness rangers were disturbed by constant pressure from visitors to make it easier to be in wilderness. "What really bothers me is people coming in here thinking they have the right to experience the land on their terms rather than the terms of the land," he said.

"Fewer and fewer people seem to be willing to come into a place where you take your life in your hands to live on nature's terms. I'm concerned about the fate of wilderness, what people are willing to accept in wilderness, the quality of pristine-ness."

When I first did an in-depth interview with Miller in summer of 1985, as a reporter for the Lewiston Morning Tribune, the assignment also included covering a wilderness management meeting held at Moose Creek Ranger Station. The Forest Service brought together about 50 people to examine ongoing concerns about visitor needs and public support for wilderness. In the course of two days, the group, from inside and outside the agency, came up with a list of new steps to coordinate management across the Selway-Bitterroot. Many of the agency steps for coordination occured within the organization in the next few years. Some core issues about reaching and involving a broader slice of the public faltered as time went on.

The Tribune ran my two stories on July 1, 1985, on page 1A, one on the meeting and one on saw filer and wilderness ranger Warren Q. Miller. Coordinating wilderness management and engaging public support continues, as expected, to be a never-ending story and an eternal struggle. In a surprise move, the next year Miller stopped hiking the trails as a wilderness ranger and became the stationary station guard at Moose Creek.

Changes in field operations foretold his personal moves. In 1985 he told me, "It seems like the more you know about the field the more valuable you are in the office to write about it. I'm in the field less and less each year. I don't how many miles I hiked last year all season, but it wasn't very many."

Sometimes it seemed they studied the studies, redid inventories with new data systems but with no new purpose or expected outcomes and then spent money to track where the money was spent, Miller explained. "I think the district has evolved into a paper machine. I don't really know where the paperwork comes from; I don't really know what the paperwork is for."

In a curious twist, Miller spent a few weeks at the end of the previous field season in front of a computer to devise a program to track visitor information. Miller set up a searchable program to systematize visitor use data and allow reviews of activities over time or to highlight a specific location or use patterns.

"The compilation of visitor use is tedious, grinding out of data—not at all interesting," Miller said. "The idea is to reduce the tedious work

Cookhouse at Moose Creek Ranger Station, 1974 *Warren Q. Miller*

we've got to do to the absolute minimum and at the same time give us access to the data so we can use it to understand what's going on out there.

"People like Penny and Emil [Keck] say bullshit on the computer with a vengeance. As far as I'm concerned, if we can reduce our workload, the computer is no different than tracking visitor use data any other way. I kind of even enjoy it on an occasional basis. It's similar to chess. Setting up a system is challenging but using it can be a bore."

The office and paperwork trap seemed to be consuming him, when an opening as station guard—the facilities maintenance person and warehouser—came up at Moose Creek. The opportunities to do physical maintenance tasks on old log buildings not only attracted Miller, the ingenuity required to craft efficient systems and make repairs challenged his mind. The job also continued to be for a long season, with enough time for saw filing in the early spring and late fall. Miller came in off the trail.

In his 15 years in and out of Moose Creek, he already knew most of the operations—from radio transmitters to plumbing lines to propane hook-ups. At a remote wilderness ranger station few things are standard issue and everything is done by hand. The only electricity lines, after the gas-powered generator was flown to town decades before, ran from solar panels to recharge radio telephone batteries. Miller had already crafted the solar system to be efficient, clean, and quiet.

The station guard's wall tent was nestled in trees away from the main compound on the north side of the garden at the edge of a field across from the weather station. Miller took up residency in the quiet tent spot but continued to eat meals and to socialize in the cookhouse used by all the crews. His new role running the ranger station also required him to direct some of the group dynamics.

Ice cream, of all things, at the ranger station presented an early clash between social desires and physical limitations. Ice cream had become a virtual staple as a treat for the crews when they came off field hitches. One of the propane refrigerators, outside the back door with a shed roof over it, could be chilled to freezing and ice cream was its most tantalizing content. Miller wanted to reduce propane use and decided to eliminate the freezer, with ice cream and frozen meat deemed excessive and not necessary. Into early summer, as temperatures reached into the 90s, Miller didn't turn the freezer on at all. When crews returned to the station after hot 10-day hitches the grumbling about no ice cream became audible and universal. Miller relented in July to fire up a freezer. And the next aircraft carried in a cooler of ice cream.

Miller preferred to replace propane tanks with additional photovoltaic solar panels and convert to electric refrigerators. He would have gone with no refrigeration himself, relying on the root cellar to keep things cool and forgoing anything frozen. But he got no support for the no-freezer approach. Some comforts were expected and very much appreciated at the ranger station. Meanwhile, the district ranger, Dennis Dailey, opposed any more solar panels. Dailey didn't want to expand the highly visible, small arrays out at the edge of the airstrip or in the yard next to the cookhouse, where no trees blocked the sun. Dailey didn't like seeing new technology. Solar panels didn't fit in his vision of the ranger station and he rejected Miller's request to expand the solar profile. Flying in propane tanks continued to fuel the cookhouse stoves and the freezer.

In 1989, Dailey eliminated regular air flights for station supplies and instead went with regular pack trips up the river. Smaller propane tanks could still be packed in for refrigeration, but ice cream didn't pack well on the 25-mile trip. In the end, the crew didn't get much ice cream and Miller didn't get any more solar panels.

Another great comfort of the ranger station was provided by a wood fired hot water system in the tight log bathhouse. Few things were better after 10 days in the field digging in dirt than a long hot shower. Stoking the fire was a ritual on days off that went from scrubbing bodies in the shower stalls to attempting to scrub clothes in the two deep sinks. People often pre-soaked clothes in a bucket for days, in an attempt to loosen dirt before flailing away with a plunger like contraption or rubbing on a washboard.

When the use of the tractor for haying the airstrip was curtailed and then eliminated, in another of Dailey's efforts to limit technology, the wood hauling vehicle was also lost. While wood supplies were extensive around the ranger station, using horses and backpacks to haul fire wood became a different and daunting energy exchange. Conversion to gas was being considered when Miller set to retrofit the bathhouse wood system.

Miller improved heat retention of the hot water tank through double fiber-glass insulation and then wrapped it in sheet metal. He replaced the barrel stove with an airtight box stove built at a local welding shop in Orofino, called The Stove That Jack Built. He reconfigured the stove coils to increase heat exchange surfaces and to sequence flows. And he installed temperature gauges to track outputs, allowing users to slow or stop feeding the fire when it reached optimal temperatures. Miller took old metal and wood from the ranger station boneyard along with new gauges and pipe. "I used bits and pieces of scrap and some new stuff and cobbled it together," he said. The end result combined high and low tech. It decreased fire wood consumption by two-thirds.

One time, Miller started to say, "I enjoy technology." Re-starting to add a clarification, he said. "I enjoy certain aspects of technology, especially when it comes to renewable and alternative energy systems."

After Emil and Penny Keck left Moose Creek in 1987, "appropriate technology" took some strange turns. The ranger determined the warehouse the Kecks converted into a residence needed to be remodeled for new staff. Another opening was cut into the logs originally peeled and notched in 1930, for a window in the bathroom. A fiberglass bathtub was flown in to replace an old, salvaged, metal shower stall. A new bathroom vanity with a plastic top replaced an old metal sink. A new stainless steel, double kitchen sink set at the apex of the counter corner replaced a chipped enamel sink, also salvaged from another camp. New plastic countertops took the place of plywood. Varnished knotty pine cabinets were flown in to replace old scavenged board shelving. Parts of the ceiling and walls were painted white.

Flying in an off-district carpenter to do the work instead of keeping someone on the district for a longer season and cultivating his or her skills, bothered Miller. The $8,800 spent on the remodel could have been better used elsewhere, or not at all, he said. A bigger concern aggravated him. No one lived there. The resource assistant might spend a few weeks of the summer at Moose Creek in the remodeled cabin. Most of his time was spent in town and the cabin was empty.

Miller's own lodging came under scrutiny when ranger Dailey reacted to a comment from the Forest Supervisor, Tom Kovalicky, about beat-up, old tents being out of character at a wilderness ranger station. What had recently been the packer's tent, set close to the corral, barn, and tack shed, was the first to go. Originally set up for the resource assistant and his family of four in 1969, for five years as their primary residence, was almost 20 years later considered an eyesore. The pole steps, railing, and ridgepole almost blended into the forest, but the white canvas stood out when visitors arrived from the near-by airstrip.

By then the district packer was no longer based at Moose Creek. He only stayed overnight in between supply runs up and down the river. So, the old packer's tent was obliterated and was not replaced.

At the other end of the compound, out of sight from almost all vantage points, was the station guard's tent. In the late 1960s, a packer named Youderin built the tent frame out of plywood flooring, and two by fours for rafters and shoulder-high, framed walls. He used wooden aviation fuel boxes for shelves and cupboards and framed in a wooden door with a window. Another plastic window was cut out of the canvas in back. A buried plastic pipe fed cold water from a spring to a sink which drained into a pebbled leach bed off into the woods. In the 16 by 12-foot tent, there was room for a metal frame double bed, a wood heat stove, a table with four chairs, and a small propane cook stove with oven.

On frosty spring and fall mornings, inside temperatures equaled the outside because the drafty old stove couldn't carry a fire overnight. As soon as the thin walled, tin stove was lit, it cranked out the heat. The small space warmed fast and soon was toasty. Everyone who lived in the tent appreciated the simplicity and functionality of the self-contained unit, ignoring a little moldy canvas and crumbling plywood here and there.

It was suggested Miller should move upstairs into the cookhouse attic, where mouse proof cages were constructed in the 1970s, for crew members to store gear. "It would be hard to get any peace and quiet upstairs with the kitchen and common room down below, so I said 'fuck no.' I live here, I'm not here part-time. I'll go put up my own tent out in the pasture."

For a man not known for cursing, unlike many of his friends and co-workers, his anger, dismay, and disdain over arbitrary decisions got the best of him. But he did not follow his heart. Instead, at the ranger's orders, the Youderin tent was torn down.

He put up a new, bright white canvas tent in the spring and then it was taken down in the fall, at the same location. The tent frame skeleton stood empty during the winter. This was prohibited for outfitters who were required to remove all framework from their camps. Miller objected to tearing down useable equipment and buying new material, but he did the replacement job. Miller also noted a photograph of the Moose Creek cookhouse from 1932 showed two wall tents thrown up in the side yard for extra crews. Both tents showed signs of hard wear over some years but did not appear to detract from the ambiance.

Another project to maintain and retain older buildings also did not go Miller's way. The sill logs and joists of the Shake Shed that housed the tools and hardware to maintain the ranger station, showed signs of rot. Miller developed a plan to jack up the building, replace the rotten sills and joists with poles cut from the forest, and improve the footings with cement piers. "It would be a neat building to rebuild, it would be a fun project using the skills I've learned with hand tools," he said.

The forest engineers in town would not fund the project based on Miller's reconstruction plans. Architectural and engineering plans were required to include a full concrete foundation. The ranger did not intend to seek additional funding. He already thought the pole framed construction with split shake walls did not fit in with the desired look of the other notched log buildings at the ranger station. "I thought, fuck the engineers; I'll get a few bags of cement and just do it.But then I thought better of it," Miller said.

Ranger Dailey planned to tear down the building and move the tools to the hay loft at the back of the barn, which was not being used because the airstrip was no longer cut for hay. Or, he would send most of the tools to town.

Miller saw the purposes of the ranger station as a supply and training center being diminished. After Penny Keck left the district as the trail crew boss, the trail program oversight was divided among wilderness rangers, the resource assistant, and the fire management officer. Each crew leader made equipment requisitions. "They made it hell on wheels on the supply person, which is me," Miller said. "There's no

"Motley crew" at Lost Horse Ranger Station, Labor Day 1974 *Warren Q. Miller*

accountability now for the equipment. They don't have any idea what we have, what we've done in the past, and what we should be ordering for new gear. It's a whole new ball game."

"As long as one person oversaw the whole trail program, like Penny, she knew what her needs were and did the ordering. I kept track of it when it came in and checked it out to people. Trail crews gave us feedback on what was needed. It was pretty workable. Now different crews are competing for gear. It's everyone for themselves."

Making do with available materials and patching up equipment served as operative ways to be in the wilderness. New equipment was purchased when major improvements became available, like synthetic sleeping bags well-suited to the wet weather of the Selway. Or purchases were made when things wore out. Even long after expiration date, anything with any conceivable continued value was saved and stored. The intention to repurpose, reuse, and repair got short shrift when the ranger announced the boneyard was history and not part of his vision for an historic ranger station.

The boneyard was not a dump. It contained metal or serviceable plastic and wood, without any garbage. Set off behind the station compound, past the dynamite vault with material for rock blasting, hidden by trees and brush, the boneyard was only known to the few people who worked at the ranger station. The station guard kept mental inventory of the #9 wire, steel posts, sheet metal, 55-gallon drums, buckets, pipe, bed frames, wire mesh, treated timbers, roofing, and other busted stuff that wouldn't rot and couldn't be burned. Much of it would be considered junk, except if a piece of sheet metal was useful to secure the corner of a mouse proof storage cage or a piece of pipe could shore up a refrigerator base.

The boneyard contained material scavenged from old camps and cabins, from Moose Creek itself and other long gone ranger stations, from closed lookouts and the rolled up telephone wires that connected them, all accumulated since the first ranger stations in the 1920s. The best stuff was stored out of the rain above the hayloft and in the hardware bins of the Shake Shed. The other stuff you just might need some day was put in deep storage in the boneyard, off in the woods. The closest hardware store was 65 miles away in Kooskia, 25 of those miles by trail.

Maybe some pilot flying over the ranger station caught a glimpse of metal and questioned a junk yard being in the wilderness, seeing it from above and objecting to the aesthetics, although anyone would be hard pressed to see it on a flight pattern. Maybe it was ranger Dailey's preoccupation with neatness. Maybe the mysteries of broken and rusting stuff disturbed him. Maybe he didn't know how to build anything without directions anyway.

Miller could not conceive of a reason to fly the material out and take it to a dump in town. The most useful, free and available material, the stuff of possibility could be or might be found in the boneyard. The metal he used to reconstruct the chimney clean-out in the ranger's cabin came from an old bed frame. The log dogs he forged to pin logs when bucking firewood came from metal rods of unknown origin in the metal piles. The retrofit of the wood heater in the bathhouse drew from multiple piles of pipe, flat steel, sheeting, and wood scraps. The massive piles of #9 wire and other excess or redundant materials were diminished and added to light-load out-flights from the airstrip. But flying out useable stuff and taking it to the dump made no sense.

"It's so much harder to get stuff in here than it is in town. Once it goes out we'll never see it again. It's so contrary to what it used to be here; they've pretty well peeled it down to nothing," Miller said.

In the fall of 1988, a year after the Kecks departure, the new fire management officer, Mark Woods, laid out a new protocol for kitchen use at the cookhouse. "He said we should put names of people on the kitchen drawers, so you knew where you could put your food," Miller said. "Then he said that some people go out there and they're uncomfortable; it's like they're entering someone's home. And I said, you're right. It is home. What's wrong with that? I wanted to tell him, if you came out here more often maybe you'd feel more at home."

Another time Woods talked to Miller about the situation at Moose Creek being challenging for new people, including himself. "He left saying there's a culture out there, as if it was something to overcome.

"The more I thought about it, the more it pissed me off. Of course, you get a group of people in an isolated place together and they develop a culture. In the past, they maybe didn't always agree on everything but there were certain things that were understood by everyone. There were certain ways you went about doing things. And you always helped each other out."

Miller said the culture of Moose Creek did change. "There's a whole new environment out here in the last two years. No longer does anyone say: 'We've only got an hour's work left here; so what if it's 6 o'clock; let's get it done now, so we won't have to come back.' Now, it's all 8 to 5."

In 1989, Miller left the wilderness for an extended time for the first time in 19 years during summer months. He traveled to Canada, Mon-

Warren's water heater system at bathhouse Moose Creek Ranger Station, 2015
John McCarthy

tana, and other parts of Idaho, touring as always in a VW bus. He thought taking a break would put things in perspective.

He'd opened the ranger station in April and got things fully operational going into May. Before he left the ranger station he wanted to pass on information to his replacement for the critical mechanics of the plumbing and irrigating systems, the radios, the warehouses and the fuels. The office staff agreed to send in someone to learn the ropes. They couldn't seem to schedule it in advance, so they decided to have the new guy come in on the plane that would take Miller out. "They fiddle-fucked around and fiddle-fucked around until the day I left Moose Creek," Miller said. "I met the new guy at the airfield in Grangeville and we talked for a couple hours. He went out to Moose Creek on his own."

When Miller returned to Moose Creek in the fall he spent hours looking for tools and equipment not in the usual places and redoing jury-rigged systems. His absence also appeared to stall many regular maintenance tasks and he rushed to catch up before the end of season, working long hours every day.

Miller spent part of his summer out of the wilderness teaching crosscut saw filing and use at the Ninemile Ranger Station northwest of Missoula, at what would later become the Ninemile Wildlands Training Center. Miller shared his expertise in tuning saws to maximum effectiveness and he excelled as teacher by thinking of all the variables to describe how saws and sawyers work. When students asked questions about saw configurations or measurements or filing techniques, most often he'd already discovered the answer, having examined the issue himself. His explanations relied on understandable terms for definitive answers. On the rare occasions he was stumped, he'd say, "Well, I'm not sure, let me get back to you." And he would ponder, study, and return with an explanation. The initial saw course Miller developed led to more than 20 years of his annual classes at Ninemile.

As Miller's years of experience were tapped to train a nationwide group of wilderness sawyers, back at Moose Creek the ranger dismissed the saw program. Dailey decided to move Miller's saw shack out of Moose Creek to decrease the number of buildings and to eliminate another building not fitting his log aesthetic. The idea of moving saws and saw filing off the district into town was absurd to Miller. The idea of moving him off the district was collateral damage he wouldn't tolerate.

"When Dailey said he was moving my saw operation to town, I knew it was time to go and I told him so. He said, that's too bad and I said what's too bad is him tearing apart a functioning ranger station and making it into a show-me place."

Miller left Moose Creek after 20 years, before the saw shack was dismantled. He took most of the saw filing tools and many of the saws with him as all were his personal property, discovered on his time and paid for with his dime. The saws and equipment purchased with Forest Service funds were known only to Miller but no one questioned his memory or delineation of what would be left behind, even if it was only a remnant. Of course, again, it was Miller's leadership, expertise, and capacity to teach that could never be replaced.

Dailey had only used a crosscut saw at guard school, to show the crews he could do it. He never filed a saw. He rarely carried or used a saw on the trail. As a horseman bent on speed, he preferred stepping over or around logs to let trail crews and wilderness rangers do the work. In his attempt to manipulate a proven system to do complicated work he couldn't do, he lost the best crosscut saw filer in the national wilderness system and, therefore, the best saw filer in the world.

Warren Q. Miller always made careful calculations. He knew exactly what he was going to do next. He had been crafting Plan B outside Moose Creek for some time.

In 1978, Miller purchased 40 acres of rough timberland in a side canyon off the Clearwater River. An occasional bumper sticker seen in the area read, "Where the Heck Is Peck?—in Beautiful Idaho." Peck, Idaho is where Miller landed. The place where he chose to build a homestead lay at the end of a dirt road nine miles from the highway and six

Warren's saw filing shed at Peck, Idaho, 2015 *John McCarthy*

miles up Little Canyon from Peck. The population of Peck peaked at 238 in 1970 and declined to 160 people by 1990, when he prepared to make it his full-time home.

The county road stopped more than a mile from his land. An old logging road leading to his place required a ford across the creek for loaded trucks, and four logs spanned by planks made a passable bridge for lighter vehicles. The land had no amenities, only wind through Douglas fir, grand fir, a few ponderosa pines, mountain maples, brush, and some patches of meadow, covering two steep pitches with a bit of a flat ground in between. No neighbors could be seen.

He bought the land as part of a package with friends from the wilderness: his old Moose Creek boss Dick Walker and his wife Sarah. The Walkers selected some more open land to build on across the creek and some forested land adjacent to Miller. In time, a few other friends and relatives bought nearby plots. Miller's place sat on a bench on the south side of the creek, opposite from the other settlers, beyond anyone else.

For the first couple years the wilderness ranger who camped out all summer, set up a wall tent to camp all winter, and began building his homestead. From the surrounding forest he felled and peeled two Douglas fir timbers for sill logs to set up his small, tall house. He hauled in plywood, two by fours, sixes and tens, boards, bags of cement, tin roofing, and hardware to frame up and sheath his personalized construction.

The floor dimensions were the same as a wall tent, 12 by 16 feet. He raised one half of the shed roof higher for a sleeping loft and library. With two small wood stoves, one to provide heat and the other salvaged from a lookout tower for cooking options, including an oven, he was warm and self-sufficient. A sink was set on a high countertop. He carried water from a nearby spring. At the edge of the long slope to the creek, he built a triangular, single-seat outhouse with one side open without a door for a view of the canyon.

After cutting down and peeling a 75-foot Douglas fir, he raised the log upright with come-alongs and secured it on an old truck wheel anchored in cement. Tied down with grounded guy wires, the pole featured bent lengths of re-bar up two sides, staggered at 18-inch intervals to make a ladder. Near the top he constructed a crow's nest platform with railing. He mounted two photovoltaic solar panels and called it the Tower of Power.

With electricity secured from the sun for lights and power tools, his only additional absolute need was a saw filing shack. Following his model at Moose Creek, he built another 8 by 16-foot structure out of plywood, boards, two by fours and two by sixes, with a peaked tin roof and north facing windows. After parting it out, he set an ancient VW bus on blocks to provide additional storage outside the building. Inside he mounted his 94-inch-long saw vise, set high, put a small box stove at one end with racks of saws hanging behind it and shelves running along the back wall for tools. Some modifications, including electricity for lights from the solar panels, improved the original design. He continued to listen to NPR on the radio.

The whole operation was designed to be buttoned up and left without need for any ongoing expenses. Miller maintained his independence, while joining the neighbors at community events, again enjoying large Thanksgiving gatherings. He provided technical expertise to his neighbors, all off-the-grid pioneers, sometimes in trade and often gratis, to pursue puzzle solving.

Hanging a water line from his side of the canyon over the creek to the Walker's homesite to fill a 20,000-gallon cistern using gravity flow, posed a conundrum. Walker determined potential flows from a small spring, almost a seep, could accumulate in a slow but steady volume of water a couple thousand feet away. Once he determined the flows could surmount the distance, he configured the pipeline course at a gentle descent and then set to span the canyon, turning to Miller.

With 17 pages of mathematical projections, the wilderness physicist calculated the curve geometry to hang a pipeline and support cables in the air across the canyon.

In the same spirit as Bill Bell and Ed MacKay crossing and bridging White Sand Creek, Miller and Walker ran a cable to span the canyon. They pre-cut drop cables at lengths calibrated to carry the pipeline along the proper trajectory. Securing one end, they hoisted it all through winches and then anchored both cable ends into the ground with cement to bear the weight. Walker hooked up the pipe along the drop cables and plunged the pipe end into the spring. Soon, over on the other side, water dripped from the pipe, slow and steady, filling the cistern.

Miller's bridge washed out in a spring flood in 1986, leaving the ford in worse shape. Spanning the creek with an extended semi-truck trailer bed, he designed the bridge replacement with a rock-filled gabion at each end for the approaches. The bridge deck was more even but continued to lack railings and required a steady hand at the steering wheel to cross.

Much of the core homestead, including the house and saw shed, was completed by the time Miller pulled out of Moose Creek for good. For the confirmed bachelor, his solitary life full of projects, visits with neighbors, occasional forays to town, and periodic travels seemed to fill his days and encompass his goals. Then, soon after leaving the wilderness, something unexpected happened. He met a woman who would change the depth and the course of his life.

Unbeknownst to his wilderness friends, Miller liked to dance during his college years in a variety of styles with international and folk groups. When he moved closer to civilization in Peck, he joined a contra dancing group with the Palouse Folklore Society at Moscow. One time the group held a dance in Lewiston and Miller joined the Walkers going down river to the confluence with the Snake River. As luck would have it, at the dance he met Sandra Lilligren, a graduate student in geology at Washington State University in nearby Pullman. They enjoyed dancing and each other's company.

When it appeared mutual interests might lead somewhere, Miller explained he lived at the end of the road, nine miles from the highway, and it might be too much. Lilligren said, "No big deal." She'd grown up at a ranger station on the Umpqua National Forest in southwestern Oregon where her father was district ranger for 12 years. She knew all about remote living in the forest and even though she now lived in town to go to school, she still had the forest in her heart. Their first date was going up to Coolwater Lookout to hike along the ridge between the Selway and the Lochsa rivers. A lightning storm blew in from the west and they sought shelter off the ridge in the trees, huddled together.

To the surprise of his friends, Miller entered into a serious relationship with Sandy. They became regulars at the contra dances. Miller, the gangly reed of a man shockingly nimble, and Sandy, his new-found partner diminutive in comparison with a ready smile, became a couple happily swinging through dance steps. They traveled on boating trips from the upper Missouri in Montana to remote rivers in Alaska and down into the depths of the Grand Canyon. They ventured out on camping trips throughout the mountains of the West and into the deserts of Mexico, with Miller finding an able companion for his journeys. They spent time at each other's houses, out at the end of the road with birds and wind in the trees, and in town with musical and social gatherings.

Among the many unexpected aspects of the new relationship was Lilligren's daughter, Sarah, at the time a self-described "extremely angry 12 year-old child." In response to the man with the audacity to date her mother, who was also too hairy, she set upon making his life miserable. Never satisfied, questioning everything, feigning chronic boredom, and raising incessant objections typified her behavior.

Being familiar with ornery mules and being wary by nature, Miller kept his distance and avoided being kicked. In time, he determined staying out of the way was not meeting objectives to be close and involved. The tall man with a beard told the young girl to knock it off, he wasn't a monster and she should get used to him being around; he wasn't going away and she couldn't drive him away. In time, Sarah took Warren at his word, on all counts. His looming presence didn't overpower her. She saw he meant what he said, always, and he wasn't going away. More important, beyond being true to his word, he was trustworthy, even with her mother, even if he dressed like he was from another century. And the teenage girl realized the grizzly tall guy not only loved her mother, he loved her too.

While his road-end homestead kept him busy, the interests in Miller's skills with saws could not be confined to his saw shack. The saw filing trainings he began at Ninemile in the late 1980s led to three, week-long sessions every year. The sessions started first thing Monday morning and ended late Friday afternoon. The classes drew people from all four federal agencies that manage wilderness and from backcountry organizations and NGOs, along with private individuals from all over the world. Everyone was welcome and classes were always full.

Miller's approach to teaching was systematic, succinct, clear, and exact, the same as his Crosscut Saw Manual. "They're not making these saws anymore," he'd explain, quoting from Martin Winters. "So, you want

Warren Q. Miller sets cutter teeth, Ninemile Ranger Station, Montana, 2010
Robert Beckley

to extend the life of the saw as much as possible. Normally, I don't take more than about ten thousandths of an inch of metal off a saw each time I joint it, so I'm not filing off too much."

Filing away even thousandths of an inch on cutter teeth tips presented a difficult commitment for new saw filers. People hesitated to file away metal tips to joint a saw into an even arc along an imaginary circle, striving to make all teeth the exact same length. Miller showed how jointer tools defined the arc and with a file inserted along the edge of the saw it became possible to achieve uniformity within tight tolerances and with surety.

Each step in reconditioning saws required control and patience. "Cleaning a rusted saw is best accomplished with a round axe stone, using some solvent to prevent the stone pores from clogging up and then using a lot of elbow grease along the length of the saw. Power tools like belt sanders or circular grinders tend to take off too much metal, and cut grooves into the metal when you want a smooth surface without any extra friction."

Taking a hammer, ideally a saw makers cross peen hammer or a three-and-a-half pound single jack if available, and a flat bench anvil, Miller showed how to flatten out bends and bumps in old saws. "Let the hammer do the work, just bring it down flat and steady. Keep measuring along and across the saw with the straightedges to check your progress. It's a process that may take 3, 4, 5, 6 times to get the saw straight.

"Taking the time to straighten a saw is well worth it. If you don't have a straight saw it's hell on wheels when you're single bucking."

He'd start at the bottom of each cutter tooth and file with even strokes toward a slight arc along the cutting edge to set a pointed tip. The curved tooth edge presented a little more cutting surface and provided an extra hint of strength in its width. A sharp point cut into hardwood better, but the arc tooth dug into softwood faster.

He'd then go through each raker, which act like a plane to peel the cut fibers and carry shavings out of the cut groove. He'd bend the raker to be shorter than the cutter by "about" twelve thousandths shorter for felling saws and "about" sixteen thousandths for bucking saws. Using a pin gauge, he'd show how to measure the raker distance, and using a raker gauge, including ones he made himself, he'd show how to tap each raker into the correct shape.

After setting and filing, Miller took a finished saw outside to test its operational capability. First, a sawyer always cleans the log surface, usually removing bark along with any dirt by chopping it away with an axe. "It takes quite a while to sharpen one of these things up and you want to make sure you don't have any dirt in there that can dull them," he'd advise.

He'd team up with one of the students, who were usually experienced trail crew or wilderness rangers, and set the saw to singing. "It looks like it's throwing some pretty good shavings. You can tell an awful lot about how a saw is cutting by the nature of these shavings. If they're long and don't have many whiskers on the sides then your saw is cutting pretty well."

Examining the width, thickness, edges, and length of the shavings, Miller explained how to diagnose deficiencies. Long noodles without whiskers were the ideal, and the typical results from Miller's saws. The students needed several tries to get it right and they only had a week with a master to make it happen.

By the early 1990s, as the old masters of crosscuts and axes faded away, the limited training capacity at the ranger district level became more stark across the wilderness system. Expansion of the traditional skills programs and training at Ninemile struggled to fill the gaps. Regional and forest level training sessions were conducted to bring in trainers. Miller and a handful of other experienced teachers traveled to Alaska, Oregon, Minnesota, Washington, Kentucky, Florida, and elsewhere, demonstrating traditional tool repair, maintenance, and use.

After Jim Bradley, a former resource assistant overseeing wilderness rangers at Moose Creek, moved to the Eagle Cap Wilderness in Oregon in 1978, he became acutely aware of the skills gap. In the mid-1980s, Bradley tapped staff from Moose Creek to conduct a crosscut saw training session, bringing in Emil and Penny Keck, the trail program leaders, and Dale Swee, a trail crew foreman. Swee later said, "When we got there we found out no one knows anything about even an axe, and Emil says to Bradley, 'You've got us over here teaching about the crosscut, which is a pretty sophisticated piece of equipment, when your people don't even know what a goddamned axe is.' It didn't start out too good."

Swee had been at Moose Creek for almost 20 years at that point and he understood the level of training the senior staff conducted was unavailable elsewhere. "Each district doesn't want to admit they don't have the necessary skills to work in wilderness, I mean simple things like how to sharpen and use an axe," Swee said after going to Oregon.

Bradley went on to Washington, DC on a detail where the Forest Service places a staff member in another arm of the government for mutual benefit. Bradley joined the office of Congressman Bruce Vento, a wilderness champion from Minnesota, to focus on wilderness designation and stewardship.

Bradley was a true believer in the public being engaged in and inspired by wilderness, using many educational techniques to reach a broad audience. At Moose Creek, he created the 90-page, pocket sized "Selway Bitterroot Wilderness Primer: A Handbook with Drawings, Checklists, Field Guides, Stories, Manuals, Glossaries, and Other Handy Information." Some people scoffed at its elementary and catch-all approach, while others decried it going against the ideal of self-discovery promoted by Bill Worf and others. The primer underwent multiple editions and many hundreds were distributed in the days before copy machines. Starting in the 1970s, Bradley was also instrumental in getting wilderness rangers into public schools, usually with sixth graders, to do programs on wildlife, hiking, and wilderness heritage.

While never expert with tools himself, Bradley understood the need for detailed training in skills and tools to sustain agency expertise. He saw it continue at Moose Creek and a few other places within the wilderness system, but in many wildernesses people struggled to carry on the skills needed to maintain trails and to guide people on the land.

Always an idea man, Bradley envisioned a base for wilderness training and education programs, with courses offered on-site and at other locations to draw in people with similar needs from different regions. By then he'd left the Forest Service to take a full-time congressional staff position with Congressman Vento, recognizing that power lay in Congress with budget and policy capacity. Vento introduced legislation to develop a wilderness training program and it spurred the agencies into direct action before the program became law. Bradley's idea was realized in 1993, with the creation of the Arthur Carhart National Wilderness Training Center.

Building on the existing program at Ninemile to broaden its scope, the center exported trainings and expanded from a fieldwork focus with tools to visitor and resource management techniques specific to wilderness. Named after Arthur Carhart, who in 1919 became the first person in the land management agencies to advocate for undeveloped wilderness on public land, the center connected the history of wilderness with the current needs. The center opened its doors, websites, and regional offerings to all agencies, to the public, and to the world, to provide a basis for wilderness stewardship to anyone.

Miller's crosscut saw filing sessions continued as part of the foundation of the center offered at Ninemile and sometimes in other locations. Without crosscut saws, trails could not be opened in the wilderness. Without Warren Q. Miller, the value of crosscut saws as fine-tuned tools might have been lost. In learning everything related to crosscuts and in teaching it to others, Miller carried the lore of crosscuts into the 21st century.

A young trail crew leader and wilderness ranger of the next generation, Eric Melson, attended one of Miller's week-long sessions at Ninemile in 2010, when he was 24. He was captivated by the legacy and practicality of crosscuts, connecting him to the previous century. Melson later said, "Warren went deep into saws, we got into it at the molecular level and we learned how to do everything you needed to do."

In the mid-1990s, Miller co-led a training session in the Gospel-Hump Wilderness of central Idaho. Around the campfire one evening, Miller had an epiphany on what they were doing, as one of the other leaders, Bob Beckley of the Forest Service Technology and Development Program, described it.

Miller said, "These really aren't primitive skills and tools—that would go back to the stone age. We're not using stone axes. We're using metal axes and saws with high quality steel and following the traditions of highly skilled people. These are traditional skills." From then on, work in wilderness was described as perpetuating traditional skills.

Throwing more wood on the fire, they talked about how they learned these skills. "We learned from our father's and grandfather's generation," Beckley said. "Only a generation before ours, these were just your everyday work skills. The farther we get away from it being how everyone worked in the woods, we lose a little more of the knowledge all the time. We didn't learn everything our grandfathers and fathers knew. We didn't get everything. But we have to figure out how to pass on as much as we can, working with as much as we've got and teaching others what we still know."

Years later, Beckley said, "Warren was probably the best saw filer in the U.S. if not the world, for filing a working crosscut; others might be better on competition saws. Warren was also the best at capturing stuff and teaching stuff because he learned from the best: Martin Winters."

Beckley continued, "Warren said Martin was gracious in teaching. His message was: show me you have skills and commitment and I'll take you to the top level you can be. Warren became an incredibly gifted teacher and he taught with passion like Martin did with him. Martin had a lot of pride in Warren as his student."

The consideration of how to pass on knowledge to the next generation led to a series of training manuals, including a revision of Miller's "Crosscut Saw Manual" in 2003, and publication of "Saws That Sing: A Guide to Using Crosscut Saws," by David E. Michael in 2004, and "New Tools for Old Saws: Crosscut Saw Tools," with Beckley as the leader in 2005. "An Ax to Grind: A Practical Ax Manual" by Bernie Weisgerber from 1999 also stayed in print.

Miller and Beckley also worked together to produce a DVD of "The Crosscut Saw Filer," released in 2011. Unscripted but systematic, precise and clear, Miller explained and demonstrated all the steps to fix and sharpen crosscut saws. The detail of information does not bog down but presents a knowable and doable approach to achieve a fine-tuned tool. Miller is shown standing next to a saw vise, wearing another of his brownish, plaid, wool shirts and tan Carhartt jeans, speaking in an even tone free of jargon and devoid of jokes. Close-ups of his hands manipulating tools and gauges showed dirt under rough fingernails. No makeup.

There was some urgency to get Miller on video, to reach a broader audience. In the spring of 2002, Miller was diagnosed with prostate cancer. He underwent surgery in the fall, recovering and doing fine until his PSA, Prostate-Specific Antigen, levels came up again five years later. He underwent radiation therapy, then hormone therapy. By the time they filmed the video in 2009, Miller was on a treatment quest with no certain destination much less a known outcome.

His operation and treatments never curtailed his teaching, saw filing, and other activities, only requiring some pauses. He also branched into new territory. Teaming up with his neighbor, Dick Walker, Miller joined in his company called Alpha 1 Photography that combined aerial photography, geographical information systems, and cartography focused on resource issues of the region. A regular client was their neighbor, the Nez Perce Tribe, who contracted many stream channel studies for logging road restoration on the Tribal reservation in the Clearwater basin.

Walker guided his 1952 Cessna 170 along creek bottoms and across canyon sides, floating like a raven and following the contours. Miller established the flight lines, selected the appropriate lens, gauged the average Above Ground Level altitude to be flown, and the ground speed needed to assure the desired percent of overlap for later stereo viewing. Miller hung out the window with a camera, a throat microphone, headphones, a beeping timer, and followed his mental sequencing for image captures. At the end of 36 exposures, he'd holler to Walker to circle 360 degrees, reload film, calculate where to be on the same line at the same elevation, and holler again as he'd start shooting. When computers and digital imagery supplanted film, they readily made the switch. With Walker's lifelong involvement in photography and flying, and with Miller's interest in computers dating back to room sized IBMs, the two end-of-the-roaders from Peck entered the digital world of GIS with a blend of seat-of-the-pants ingenuity and technical expertise.

Miller again scoured odd places for equipment, this time computer parts and freeware programs, usually online instead of dusty old second-hand stores. He powered big screen monitors and used a collection of programs to avert the expensive standard GIS programs. With the same exactitude he applied to saw filing, Miller focused on accurate imagery of landscapes. He would thread together photographs, spooled in a seamless computer array to reveal the character of the land. The flight track and photo points would be defined by latitude and longitude, time and date, mapped to delineate the aerial routes.

Their photographs taken in 2003 in the Selkirk Mountains of north Idaho documented extensive illegal intrusions by snowmobilers into high elevation lands set aside as refuges for the last of the endangered woodland caribou in the United States. Miller and Walker's plotting of the renegade snowmobiler tracks, using GPS and photo sequencing to show exact locations, provided conservation groups the necessary data to successfully push for expanded protection zones and to a establish a migration corridor. The irrefutable data also set up the conservationists to win court cases to enforce the extended protection for caribou.

At the other pole of the technological spectrum, an opportunity to explain the values of traditional skills came in 2005 in Washington D.C. The 39th Annual Smithsonian Folklife Festival included the 100th anniversary of the Forest Service as one of four featured programs, with displays on the National Mall. A lookout tower was reconstructed, and Miller was among the demonstrators of the traditional skills used in the forests.

Miller set up a saw vise and showed people how to file and fix saws. Ian Barlow, a former Moose Creek packer who carried on from Emil Keck's early days of specialized trail and bridge maintenance, demonstrated how to use a crosscut, cutting rounds of wood from a log with a volunteer partner from the crowd and handing out the slabs as souvenirs. Among the estimated 1.2 million visitors over two weeks in late June and early July, Miller and Barlow were steady draws for attention. Visitors could see how the Forest Service got its start and how it continued to work in the wilderness of today.

A cultural excursion to Lewiston, of all places, led Miller to reconnect with Bud Moore. Moore presented the Wallace Stegner Lecture at Lewis-Clark State College a couple years after his book, *The Lochsa Story*, came out in 1996. Afterwards, many old and new friends congregated around Moore, asking questions and sharing stories. When Miller told Moore about his ongoing, annual saw training sessions at Ninemile, Moore invited him to come over to visit sometime at his nearby Coyote Forest. While Miller hesitated at first, never being one to intrude, their first visit led to a dozen years of shared experiences.

After completion of his book, Moore began another multi-year project to draft the Coyote Forest Ecosystem Management Plan. The plan defines and directs a holistic approach to the working forest, to sustain all resources and organisms. The 39-page main plan was augmented by appendices of maps, a fire plan, references, and a "List of Power Places," indicating a different perspective from standard Forest Service documents.

Miller came in to help with some mapping and application of comput-

Warren Q. Miller and Bud Moore at McFarland Place, Montana, 2009 *Sandra Lilligren*

er technology, including GIS. The Coyote Forest plan was completed in 2006. Miller got in on the ground floor on Moore's next big project: the restoration of old mining claims on land surrounded by the Lolo National Forest.

Located a few miles from the Idaho-Montana border on a tributary to the Clark Fork River, the McFarland Place offered Moore another opportunity to pursue his vision of land stewardship. Moore got title to the 210 acres in 2008. He was 90. He knew he'd need some help, and Miller, then 63, was one of the younger people to join in the restoration project. The land was pock-marked by hard rock diggings and cut over to provide timbers for the mining operations and fund it with logs. A series of 20, ten-acre claims ran along both sides of the steep canyon walls leading to the creek. Most of the corner points were obscure or gone. Surveying the land and its components was step one.

"Bud needed Warren's legs and his smarts and his eyes," is how Suzanne Vernon from Condon, Montana described their connection. Vernon worked with Moore for six years to catalog his historical and personal archives, observing how he utilized Miller's expertise. "Warren would report back to Bud on what he found, and they'd talk about what to do next. A lot of the time Warren knew what to do and he would just keep going, keeping Bud informed. They had an extraordinary way to communicate, they thought a lot alike and they were often intuitive about each other's thoughts."

Miller's partner, Sandy Lilligren, described Warren as "the great measurer." Miller hiked all over the land, plotting way points, making photographs for references, setting up permanent camera points and mapping the results. He glued a Velcro strip onto his hard hat to hold a GPS receiver to free his hands for searching in the dirt or grabbing hand holds and then snatch a quick reference point. He'd spend a couple weeks at the McFarland Place in between or after his early spring crosscut saw filing trainings at Ninemile. Miller never wanted payment for his fieldwork or his technical expertise, but Moore insisted on getting him some sporadic payment without any argument or refusal allowed. The fascination of discovery and the potential to delineate restoration actions was ample pay for Miller.

When Moore was diagnosed with cancer himself in the winter of 2010, Miller stepped up his fieldwork. Then, in the late summer and into fall, he stayed for months with Moore as his health was failing. Miller continued to draft maps and restoration plans, looking toward a future neither man was likely to see. He did chores around both Coyote Forest and the McFarland Place and did household things like getting groceries and driving Moore to doctors. The two men also talked about living and dying, how to live a significant life and then die at peace. "Bud was Warren's idol," Lilligren said. "They both knew they were coming to the end. When Warren was facing his own illness and all the hard questions about what to do, he'd often ask, in his own way of thinking about things, 'What would Bud do?'"

After his death in November 2010, Moore left instructions on what to do with the McFarland Place with a lot of details mapped out by Miller.

In the fall of 2013, a collection of people who'd worked at Moose Creek in the 1970s and 1980s gathered at Johnson Bar along the Selway River. About 60 people showed up for the reunion over the course of a long weekend, camping out, sharing stories, food, and drink. Warren's poor health made his appearance tentative. He made it accompanied by Sandy, staying two nights and talking in excellent spirits the whole time with people who'd been with him across two decades in the wilderness. An informal survey confirmed Warren was at Moose Creek longer than anyone except Emil Keck.

Moose Creek was consolidated with the neighboring Selway Ranger District in 1995, retaining the name Moose Creek but losing its status as the last all-wilderness ranger district. The combined headquarters was located at Fenn Ranger Station along the Selway River road upstream from Johnson Bar. Most of the files from Moose Creek were sent to Fenn, but the context for photographs and records did not accompany the material.

When Warren left the district in 1991, no one who'd been there for more than a half dozen years remained. Continuity was soon lost. At the reunion, some of the current staff from Fenn came down to meet people, partly in the hope of gathering some historical context. Warren, for his long time spent at Moose Creek and his categoric memory, was singled out as the motherlode for answers to questions.

The morning after the reunion when everyone scattered, I drove upstream toward the end of the road beyond Selway Falls to go for a wilderness hike in fine September weather. As I drove past Fenn, Warren and Sandy were going into the main office building. Sandy told me later what she thought would be looking at a few photographs turned into more than three hours of pouring over pictures. Warren was in his element, in another form of data analysis, identifying people and places over the years.

It would be the last time I saw Warren, who was volunteering, again, sharing his knowledge about wilderness. They'd only scratched the surface of what he knew, and they could have stayed much longer, but his energy level was taxed.

Warren Q. Miller died February 10, 2014, at home in Clarkston, Washington, with Sandy and other friends and family with him, a few days short of his 69th birthday. The cancer caught him after a 12-year chase.

Sandy asked me to speak at his memorial, held at the end of May across from the home they shared along the Snake River. I closed with a favorite line of Warren's, which can be applied either to looking at historical photographs or meticulously filing saws or picking up trash. "As Emil says, 'What the fuck's your hurry in the wilderness?'" Warren would repeat that line with absolute certainty, for many occasions. And then, ending, I reminded people, when we pull a crosscut, or remember pulling a crosscut, we honor Warren, a man of the wilderness, a man who made the wilderness real today.

Following the Trail

Epilogue

WILDERNESS SYMBOLIZES A NATIONAL COMMITMENT to honor our original continent. As a system to preserve wild nature, more can be done to stock our ecological bank to preserve all land types. More can be done to represent the full geography of America, perhaps requiring restoration then preservation. What we have set aside as wilderness is vast, varied, and under-appreciated.

More people can be enriched by the resources of wilderness. More people can learn about themselves, the human condition, the wonders of nature and the mysteries of life, by being in wilderness. Reverence for wilderness is not only about the land. Appreciation of wilderness is about people, active and inspired people.

Deep into the heart of the Frank Church-River of No Return Wilderness, Laura Nichols, then 21 years-old, spoke with the truth of youth. A recent graduate from the College of Idaho, Laura told me, "When I'm in the wilderness, I feel more connected to the person I really want to be. What better way to be here than to help maintain the trails and make the wilderness more accessible for everyone."

When I think back about the young men and women I got to know when we were trail crew, fire lookouts, wilderness rangers, and packers, and consider what we did with our lives, it's no stretch to say all of us carried wilderness values into the rest of our lives. We went on to be teachers of art, science, and history, a surgeon, a veterinarian, a fire scientist, firefighters, fire managers, pilots, journalists, conservationists, librarians, carpenters, artists, Congressional staff, local and state government staff, business operators, and more. Only a few continued their entire careers with the Forest Service. All of us continued as teachers and students of wilderness, with our kids, our friends, our communities, our lives.

Allison Zehner leads guard school crew, Moose Creek Ranger Station, 1987
John McCarthy

The point isn't we were special. We were typical of the times. In the 1970s and 1980s, we were the generation that came into the wilderness after the people before us accomplished the complicated efforts to designate the new National Wilderness Preservation System and then set up management for it. Many of my contemporaries remember the good old days at remote ranger stations across the West and out in the wilderness. We had elders, masters, old-timers, to emulate and to be our teachers, our guides. We were in over our heads at first. We got good at being in wilderness, accomplishing tasks, learning skills and learning from the land. We belonged there.

Some people who revere wilderness may never see it. Some people may find that a single exposure or rare experience in wilderness contributes to their worldview, endearing them to the land. Most people want a deeper, more involved connection inside the wilderness. To know wilderness—to interact with nature unfettered, undiluted, and untamed—people need to see it. To assure strong support for wilderness, many individuals must go into wilderness, often, in all seasons and in all kinds of weather. Then they may engage to keep wilderness wild.

Jenny Estes and Dani Mazzotta, Cecil D. Andrus-White Clouds Wilderness, 2016 *John McCarthy*

The people who took wilderness from a philosophical ideal to a political designation of a landscape with a distinct value shared two things in common: They championed the wildest land, seeing its timeless values,. and they wanted to help others to be in the wilderness, to learn from the wonders of the land.

People who then established how to work in wilderness and how to be in wilderness after the political designation, shared both those original values. They cared about the wild land and they guided visitors.

Bud Moore often talked about people who go into wilderness on a personal quest, calling them "pilgrims." As seekers of beauty, challenge, insights, and meaning, these pilgrims gained Bud's respect. Bud also talked about harvesters, both the old-time trappers and lumberjacks and the present day trappers, hunters, and loggers. He demonstrated some harvesting could be compatible with wilderness. He was adamant some intrusions, such as roads and logging, were incompatible with wilderness. Bud believed all the land must be treated with respect and we should strike a balance between use and protection. Bud also

Seth Bader and Peter Lund pack tools and bear-proof box to camp, Frank Church-River of No Return Wilderness, 2013 *John McCarthy*

cautioned visitors in wilderness to travel with careful footsteps.

Visitors to wilderness may be hunters, boaters, climbers, hikers, horse riders, birders, anglers, star gazers, photographers, painters, botanists, or pilgrims. It doesn't matter much what anyone does. It does matter for people to see wilderness for themselves. People can appreciate the beauty of wilderness through a photograph or a video, but it isn't enough. For society to sustain wilderness, significant numbers of people need to know the wonders of the land firsthand. From there a commitment can grow to pass it on.

Leaving the land alone, allowing nature to be supreme and undisturbed, would be fine for pure wilderness, a land unencumbered by people. Even in the quest to know oneself through a connection with the land, one's presence can disturb wilderness and diminish its wildness. To appreciate and to protect pristine waters, wildlife running free, the full cycle of forests, and the quiet of emptiness, people must be involved, aware, careful, and artful.

As the last remaining wild lands shrink into defined boundaries of designated wilderness and parks, vulnerability from human intrusion intensifies. Modern people make trouble in the natural world everywhere they go, even if they go with good intentions. To know how to step with care, people need to be shown the way. Guides, in their broadest sense, are part of the tradition of wilderness and wilderness preservation.

When the Owyhee Initiative negotiations to designate wilderness were underway, for most of the first decade in the 21st century, Grant Simonds, the representative for the Idaho Outfitters and Guides Association, often said, "What good is wilderness if people can't get there." As one of the conservation representatives in the group, I didn't argue with Grant. While an argument can be made that wilderness stands as a natural resource unto itself, whether anyone goes there or not, his point was and is a practical reality.

If people can't see the wild land, our society will not commit to its preservation. If people don't experience wilderness in significant numbers, we will not have sufficient numbers of wilderness protectors. If we don't have enough wilderness protectors, the forces to dilute, diminish, develop, and eventually destroy wilderness will prevail, whether it's insidious and chipped away over time or overpowering with a dam, an oil rig, or a road.

Simonds, from the outfitter association, was concerned about his group of professional guides being able to take paying clients into wilderness. He wanted reasonable access points. While the number of people who can afford a guided trip is limited by economic status, guides for rivers and lands provide an introduction to wilderness for the uninitiated. Professional guides can assist people with interest and enthusiasm but limited skills and abilities. The general public needs similar access routes to go out on their own, to find their own way to see the wilderness.

In the open sage savannah of the Owyhees, people and animals can travel without roads and without trails across the sparsely vegetated lands. For centuries, people walked and rode horses along canyon rims, down into canyons and along creek banks in the places where the rock can be navigated, following the unmarked routes of the first peoples, the Shoshone-Paiutes and their ancestors.

A few historic roads leading to empty lands without trails were appropriate in the Owyhees. While wilderness doesn't need access roads, providing access was critical for public support. We secured the Owyhee River Wilderness through a collaborative group with multiple, broad interests. Definition of a few access points allowed us to stop indiscriminate off-road, cross country motorized travel and close many miles of redundant roads.

The group found a balance point between untracked wild land and appropriate human access. Wilderness boundaries define the limits of motor powered and mechanized reach. Very few defined trails cross this high desert landscape and very few additional trails are likely to ever be built to improve travel routes. People can always go their own way on horse or on foot, across the rocks and between the sagebrush.

In forested and mountainous wilderness, trails are critical for extended travel. People can scramble off trail, step over windfalls to penetrate and explore deep into forests. Hunters can stalk their quarry on rough game trails and search uncharted slopes for movement. Trails open the way for everyone to get around, to set up a camp, to get back to camp, to get an animal out, to get many miles into wilderness.

Trails are a historic inheritance in our American wilderness. Sweat and skill, traditional equipment, and steadfast commitment were required to build trail systems. Commitment to trail system maintenance is proving to be a challenge today.

Forest trails are beset by age-old forces of wind and erosion. Windfalls are scattered across trails as live and dead trees blow over. Washouts and landslides occur in spring run-off and in storm events through summer and fall. Today windfalls and washouts are exacerbated by increased fire, where both the scale of fires and the intensity of burns are greater than past decades. Warming trends have led to longer and hotter fire seasons. Big, hot fire years occur with regularity and cover hundreds of thousands of acres leaving thousands of dead trees in the wake, all coming down at some point. All manner of bugs and blight, natural and introduced, are also advancing in forests at rates and locations not seen in the past, again linked to a warming climate. Mudslides, debris flows, and avalanches are all part of the mountain West landscape. With greater prevalence after fires, the earth is washing downhill at increasing rates due to more and bigger fires.

How the landscape will contend with increased fire size and intensity is an experiment society did not set up to study, but people did set it in motion. Over the course of the last century, people conducted a valiant effort to stop fires and keep fires as small as possible. An unanticipated consequence was the build-up of dense trees and brush in fire-dynamic forests that concentrated more fuels. Late in the 20th Century, carbon pollution-caused climate change began to lengthen fire seasons and raise temperatures. In the last 20 years, increased forest fuels and warmer weather, combined with lightning or careless human ignition, resulted in more big, hot fires seen all over the West.

At the same time, we are not seeing more trail crews. There are fewer, with shorter seasons. The increased challenges of clearing more windfalls and washouts in wilderness trails are not being met. The only thing to do is to get more people running saws, crosscut saws, and more hand tools, getting in the dirt and the brush.

Historic maps of any wilderness plotted the full trail system, dating back to the early firefighter era. The legend for the Selway-Bitterroot Wilderness map of 1970 delineated the main trails, marked in red, and secondary trails described as "Manways—Use at your own risk," in black. The legend of the Selway-Bitterroot map of 1980 defined three trail categories: "Mainline Trail (frequent maintenance); Secondary Trail (infrequent maintenance); Primitive Trail (generally not maintained.)" By 1999, the Selway-Bitterroot map did away with euphemism to define one category: trails, marked in red and without any description of maintenance levels, whether hopeful or imaginary, or periodic.

By the 21st century what were called primitive trails or "manways" are now difficult to distinguish from the hillside. Only rare lengths of benched tread, maybe a few remnant cut logs or double axe blazes chopped into trees, remain visible. Most are long gone from any functionality for a hiker much less a horse. Secondary trails are found but present major challenges to step over dozens of windfalls per mile, plow through brush, and even find tread. Many red-marked trails on the 1999 map are like "manways," archaic and lost.

Today, cutting out the main trails over ridges and along canyons is a major challenge. Frequent maintenance is limited to the Selway River trail and a few connectors, a familiar story told in other large wildernesses. Infrequent maintenance is a hopeful and laudatory goal, infrequently achieved though not from a lack of concern but from a lack of resources.

The short-term fix proposed by some people to fire up chainsaws for a limited time to rip through burned area windfalls won't repair tread, cut brush, or move rock. A horde of chainsaws could cut out downed trees but would not fix trails much less maintain them. Only trail crews, with two or more skilled people, can move rock and big wood, shore up slides, engineer re-routes, re-establish tread, replace puncheon, set rip-rap, open alder thickets, beat back brush, and more.

Debates over what kind of saw is fastest are pointless in the end. Only crosscut saws fit the spirit of the wilderness. Only trail crews with crosscut saws can do all the tasks for trail work in wilderness.

For more than 10 years, I've done one or two, week long volunteer trail projects every summer with Idaho Trails Association or the Selway-Bitterroot Frank Church Foundation, non-profit organizations focused on trails and wilderness stewardship. I've also done one day field projects, from trails to collecting sagebrush seeds to rolling up old fence wire. Sometimes I'm the nominal leader for volunteers, with experienced agency or organizational staff running the program. Often, I'm the actual leader, doing field training, setting the pace, and directing the tasks.

My overriding truism for volunteers is: it always works. Trail work gets the spirit of the wilderness ingrained in hearts, heads, and backs in ways not achieved by recreational visits. Getting gritty doing direct labor connects people to the land. Being out in the wilderness for days doing difficult tasks with a crew, coalesces in a unity of purpose. Becoming intimate with a place through labor brings understanding, appreciation, and knowledge.

The value of these volunteer projects is best understood when we appreciate that it goes beyond the tasks completed. The greatest value in volunteer projects is to build a base of support, then to support well-protected and well-run wildernesses. The real accomplishment of these projects is shared intense involvement with wilderness, leading to a recognition it takes effort and commitment to maintain its trail system and to retain its wildness.

A common refrain among people out in the field from the old days in wilderness—back in the 1970s and 80s—was: volunteers could never do justice to our jobs. An accurate statement today would be: volunteers can't do what we did or do all of what is needed now but we've got to have them. There aren't enough paid jobs for seasonal employees to do the fieldwork of trails or visitor contact, and volunteers are needed to pick up some of the slack. Getting people to commit time from their busy lives to volunteer is a tough proposition, especially when projects are in remote locations requiring a day's journey by vehicle and foot at both ends.

The best projects have some strong young people with energy and some experienced oldsters with knowledge, whether they are packers, ex-trail crew, rangers, firefighters, river guides, or all around wilderness travelers.

Young people teamed up with folks who have decades of wilderness experience, who may be moving a little slower in their later years, is where the ferment of ideas and actions bubble. When the crew mix has depth and variety, is well equipped and prepared, with a solid project design, everyone thrives and wants to do it again.

The challenges in fielding volunteer projects goes beyond logistics and costs. The whole purpose of volunteers in relation to the land management agencies is variable, often not clear, and often limited in scope. Arguments can be made volunteers are peripheral, a feel-good add-on, a make-work vacation, and maybe diverting scarce dollars from paid crews. My experience with volunteer crews has shown me otherwise, but my experiences have also been variable.

A big part of the problem with getting more paid seasonal staff working in wilderness goes back to fire. A report released by the Forest Service in August 2015 called "The Rising Cost of Wildfire Operations: Effects on the Forest Service's Non-Fire Work," stated:
"In 1995, fire made up 16 percent of the Forest Service's annual appropriated budget—this year, for the first time, more than 50 percent of the Forest Service's annual budget will be dedicated to wildfire. Along with this shift in resources, there has also been a corresponding shift in staff, with a 39 percent reduction in all non-fire personnel."

Many young people go where the money is: fire. Challenges in putting together remote wilderness crews are exacerbated by the draw of youth toward the extra money made on fire crews, with hazard pay a major bonus at all pay grades. Career ladders also go higher and faster with more opportunities in fire.

It took some years, but Congress took a significant step to separate wildfire management from the regular Forest Service budget with the Wildfire Disaster Funding Act passed in spring 2018. The legislation provides up to $2 billion a year for active firefighting and management, as well as money for fire prevention. The fund is separate from the operating budget. The dollar amount is realistic to the annual costs of fire today. The new approach won't start until 2020 and its effectiveness will be critical to restore budgets to manage wilderness and all public lands.

Getting sensible and adequate funding for public lands is problematic. The political idea to turn public lands over to states or private interests for management or ownership, with or without wilderness, diverts people from the real issues of getting more effective and more productive land stewardship.

If we are going to have good trails to get around in wilderness we're going to have to have more people pulling crosscut saws and swinging Pulaskis. More people with saws requires more support—technical, financial, political, and personal commitments. More support for wilderness can not achieved in isolation.

All four of the agencies charged to maintain wilderness—Forest Service, Park Service, Fish and Wildlife Service and Bureau of Land Management—also oversee lands once utilized by settlers. Wilderness advocates are wise to respect and support care of both the pristine lands and the production lands, whether active or historical. As we rebuild support for all aspects of public lands, we can also secure greater support for the wildest lands in wilderness.

Efficient, even-handed, and well-balanced land management by the federal agencies may seem to be contradictions or impossible goals. Experience tells me it can and does happen. In the seven years I directed a forest management program in Idaho for the Wilderness Society it was clear many communities are ready to cooperate with the Forest Service to craft broadly beneficial projects. The projects focus on ecological restoration, contend with the historic road boom from logging, speed fuels treatments, improve recreation, and design selective timber harvest from existing roads.

Staff scientists from the Nez Perce Tribe, both tribal members and non-tribal staff, and practical can-do loggers and foresters from the local timber industry stood out among participants. These men and women are local experts. They care for the land as people and in their jobs. They are either active supporters and appreciators of wilderness or they respect other people's interests in wilderness. There is the key to cooperative conservation efforts with local communities: respect for each other's interests and a commitment to making those interests compatible for the community and for the land.

Shake shed at Moose Creek Ranger Station, 1963 *Richard I. Walker*

Many staff people in the Forest Service—from District Rangers to the array of ecologists and specialists with excellent science backgrounds—are also attuned to cooperative land management. A cross section of people in the communities, from county commissioners to small business operators and outdoor recreation club members, are also involved and creative participants.

The cooperative process is tedious but does bring results, sometimes slow or limited but better than alternatives. When conservationists step in with local organizers like me, along with ecological scientists and Washington, D.C. analysts of the agencies, our expertise is welcomed and we all become more effective. People in communities of the West are practical, skilled, and able to get things done. When conservationists strive to bring in and practice the same attributes, we are taken at our word and by our actions as contributors toward efficiency and balance on the public land.

Cooperative management efforts continue in many communities for many forests and grasslands in Idaho and elsewhere, with many conservation-minded individuals and groups involved. These coalitions and partnerships secure significant improvements in habitats for fish and wildlife, along with recreation amenities.

As conservationists practiced community cooperation, Idaho moved up to number three in the national list of states with wilderness acreage in 2015, behind only much larger Alaska and California. When Idaho secured its first new wilderness designation in 29 years with the Owyhee River Wilderness, signed into law by President Barack Obama in March 2009, we moved up to number four for wilderness acres. Idaho conservationists, ranchers, recreationists, local government officials, and Shoshone-Paiute tribal representatives worked together to craft legislation for Senator Michael Crapo, R-Idaho, to carry. It succeeded because of broad support and it addressed many interests, not only wilderness.

Then the first forest wilderness in Idaho in 35 years was passed by Congress and signed by President Obama in August 2015. With the Boulder-White Clouds Wilderness, Idaho moved up to the number three position for states with wilderness. Representative Mike Simpson, R-Idaho, pushed a more traditional leadship role, acting as the hub to direct multiple interests for more than 15 years and then move fast at an opportune moment to pass a bill. Simpson's efforts succeeded because he opened a dialog with key players, both staunch wilderness supporters and opponents, to shape legislation none of them opposed in the end because it was better than the alternatives.

In both cases, members of Congress from Idaho, who are practical people and serve their constituents to get things done, listened to a broad range of ideas and interests to craft bills that met the spirit and law of wilderness. Even in the polarized political climate of today, coalitions and compromises can be fashioned to deliver big conservation victories. Even without a wilderness champion like the great Senator Frank Church of Idaho, efforts to protect the wild lands can succeed.

Many people wrangle with the politics to designate the last remnant wild lands as wilderness. Untamed lands with ecological continuity and wild character remain at risk in large areas of Idaho, Utah, Montana, Wyoming, Oregon, Alaska, and in smaller but no less important land units all over the country. These struggles will play out, as always, based on people being organized and persistent, to get their collective voices heard and to force action.

A lesser understood risk, with a less active citizenry to address it, is in losing the reverence for the already declared wilderness. Care of wilderness and involvement in the field has expanded in some newer organizations and as part of a few groups' tradition. More non-profit groups engage members in service projects. These efforts are admirable but not sufficient to the challenges.

The National Forest System Trails Stewardship Act was passed in 2015 to double the number of volunteers working on trails. The implementation strategy developed by the Forest Service highlights 15 priority areas including the Selway-Bitterroot, Frank Church-River of No Return, and Bob Marshall Wilderness in Montana. But no new money was allocated to supplement volunteer budgets or increase Forest Service budgets for coordination and logistics, leaving in doubt the potential effectiveness.

An estimated $300 million backlog of trail work is closing out Forest Service lands. Other agencies face similar trail and infrastructure needs. More funding for professional trail crews is required. Even with tens of thousands of hours of work from dedicated volunteers, citizen efforts won't get all the work done. Public support to fund trail crews is the ground game. The need to protect the legacy of wilderness is the bigger picture.

Going back to the simpler times when I worked in wilderness is impossible. Going forward with intention to nourish new generations of young people steeped in wilderness is possible, and critical.

When budgets are increased to meet the needs in the agencies and pri-

Tools of the trade, Frank Church-River of No Return Wilderness, 2014
John McCarthy

vate contributions are focused on action, there will be young people ready to go out into the wilds. While some of their backgrounds will be different, there will be as many young women as young men ready to go.

A critical factor to recreate a wilderness culture will be to assure it reflects the current social fabric of the nation. Broadening crews to get more people of color and different ethnic backgrounds to capture the reality of America today will require deliberate recruiting. All the techniques teachers know about inclusivity and appreciation of differences can be applied to expand the reach for wilderness participants. Getting new people involved in wilderness from sports, fitness, education, arts, adventure, and health spheres proved enriching in the past and can be in the future.

If fielding more young people to care for wilderness is a matter of straightforward steps limited by money, resuscitating a wilderness culture is another necessity and perhaps a more difficult undertaking. Inside the Forest Service, the consolidation of ranger districts and combination of national forests—forced by budgets—resulted in centralized management that eliminated or diminished the value of the decentralized, often remote ranger stations.

Many of my contemporaries recall the vibrancy of life-changing experiences at ranger stations like Magruder, Avery, Chamberlain Basin, Big Creek, and Yankee Fork, all in Idaho, and over in Montana at Big Prairie and Spotted Bear. The same was true all over the West. Many of the bunk houses now sit empty or are even shuttered much of the season. The cook houses and warehouses may retain temporary functions but have slipped into disorganization through disuse. The ongoing pulse of these outpost staging grounds appears weak and sporadic and may be slipping away.

When I hiked into Moose Creek in mid-May 2015 for the first time in 21 years, I found a ghost ranger station. One 80 year-old caretaker, the very pleasant and engaging Captain Harry B. Harden, was the only person there. The buildings were locked up, except what used to be called the cookhouse and now has a sign as Office. Back when Moose Creek was a work center, in mid-May there would be a dozen or more people at the ranger station. The station guard and the saw filer, Warren Q. Miller, might be the only staffer working there every day. An early trail crew and a wilderness ranger would be in and out. Emil and Penny Keck would be on the go, stopping in to resupply and to line-out crews. There was often one or more people on special projects, either at the ranger station or elsewhere on the district. The packer would be getting stock and tack ready for the season. Even the ranger, or assistant ranger, or fire management officer, would make a beginning of the season appearance.

The last district ranger to have a crew at Moose Creek was Dennis Dailey. After he left in 1995, the all-wilderness district was combined with the Selway district, retaining the name Moose Creek but moving primary operations to Fenn Ranger Station downstream along the Selway road.

Dailey didn't destroy Moose Creek, only the connectivity of the culture, and he only put the work center to sleep. He was instrumental in Moose Creek being listed on the National Register of Historic Places in 1995 and it can't be torn down. There are signs on all the log buildings now, with names and dates of construction, such as Office 1921 for the cookhouse, Warehouse 1931 for the fire cache, Residence 1930 for the warehouse Emil and Penny converted to their base camp, and Washhouse 1937 for the bathhouse. There isn't a sign on the fuel shack, because it's built of boards, not fitting the log aesthetic and was built to house the chlorinator in the 1970s. There isn't a Shake Shed sign marking the beautiful peeled pole and split shake tool shed, because it was torn down and all the tools were crammed into the emptied hay loft in the back of the barn.

Of all the disappointments lurking in the ranger station, nothing was more disturbing to me than seeing tools jumbled into dust and rust piles in the dark hole of the barn. Back in the day, if people didn't put a tool away in the place and shape they found it, they were berated and might be banned from stepping foot into the Shake Shed. Now, everything was jammed onto shelves, under and on top of once functional work benches without organization.

Even to operate the hand crank Champion Blower & Forge Co. drill press, manufactured in the early 20th century, someone would need a head lamp and would first need to oil and clean the gears. A fine Stanley miter box saw gathered dust on a table next to buckets of junk, a copper pipe cutter for propane lines, and an old two-burner camp stove. It would take more than an hour to clear and clean a work surface to use the saw, which always cut true at all angles.

Since Dailey wouldn't listen to Warren Miller when he was the station guard and he proposed to repair the Shake Shack sills, the tools dating back to the days when the ranger station was built were relegated to an unusable mess. As anyone who uses tools knows, especially when more than one person shares tools, tools must be organized and must be kept clean. Miller, the most meticulous of tool users, did not stay to see his saw filing shack and the Shake Shed dismantled with the tools piled into the barn.

Before Miller left Moose Creek, he foretold it's likely future. "It's becoming sterile just like so many places that end up being interpretive sites," he said. "So many interpretive sites aren't used. It's interesting to look at old stuff but it's obviously stuff that sits around and is not used. And pretty soon stuff gets lost and everything starts to slip away."

After hiking out from Moose Creek to the road end near Selway Falls, I stopped by Fenn to meet with Anna Bengston, the capable young wilderness ranger for the reconfigured Moose Creek district. As I talked about how strange I found the condition of the old Moose Creek station, she grew defensive and even irritated. She explained there can be as many as 20 people at the station in July or August, with a crew of 8 to 10 regularly working out of the station on trails and other projects. It was good to hear her chaff at my assumptions and defend her program. There are people doing the hard work in wilderness. No doubt she, and others, tire of old cranks talking about the good old days. Bengston's commitment is another demonstration of the greater opportunity. Young people today would rally to do more and go deeper into the wilderness.

A couple years later, on another trip back to Moose Creek in July of 2017, I met one of the two district packers, Mark Horner, who'd been running teams up and down the river for more than 20 years. He'd stayed after Dailey left and kept swinging rope, pulling stock, and delivering supplies to ranger stations and lookouts. I also met Val Armichardy, whose husband Pete is the other district packer and was out in the field at the time. Their two boys grew up at Moose Creek with a good chunk of their summers every year spent at the station.

When I walked onto the airstrip at the ranger station on that warm mid-July morning and looked out to the east, toward Freeman Peak, a column of smoke rose from the trees. Lightning struck the day before and the new ranger, Jenni Blake, made the call to monitor and not suppress the fire. The fire continued to burn under the wilderness fire management plan until the rains hit in September. The fire burned over more than 3,000 acres, disrupted a lot of summer plans, and was left unchecked, which playing out on the land the concepts framed by Bud Moore 40 years before.

And at the ranger station I also noticed the tools and equipment in the back of the hay barn were a lot more orderly, the benches and floor were swept clean. The miter box saw was accessible even if the work bench was covered with paint cans. It was still dark and not very conducive to craftsmanship. While the light in the barn may be dim, it was clear people who are committed to wilderness and stewardship are still out there.

The following year, the exposed hillside from the 2017 fire set off two landslides that covered the trail north of the ranger station. The lead wilderness technician, Brad Bence, traveled with stock to blast out the slides and rebuild the trails. At the same time, the main Selway trail was closed after a micro-burst wind storm. Dozens of big ponderosa pine and Douglas fir windfalls, both green trees and snags, made the trail impassable. Bence said they never considered using chainsaws. Trail crews were dispatched to the scene with crosscuts, knocking out three-foot in diameter trees, and rolling out massive root wads. In a reflection of what can and is being accomplished today, Bence told me over the phone, "Nothing is too tough for them, they are as good any crew I've seen in my 35 years of doing wilderness work."

Outside the wilderness, around a few bends of the Selway River downstream from Fenn, what had been the Kecks' house continues to appear to be unoccupied. Penny Keck completed her career with the Forest Service in 2002, with the final 15 years as the Fire Management Officer at the renamed Moose Creek district. Her charge was the west half of the district, out of the wilderness and away from what many people consider the real Moose Creek. She continued to train and to lead many young people to work in the forest. After she left the Forest Service, she moved farther downstream, off the main Clearwater River, upstream from Kooskia.

Penny sold the house along the Selway and bought a little acreage where there is more sun and more space for a garden. When I stopped by in May of 2015, Penny showed me her raised beds for strawberries, raspberries, gooseberries, and all kinds of vegetables, surrounded by a high fence to keep out the deer. She put a small manufactured house on the land, barely visible from the highway, with a wrap-around driveway that also acts as fire protection. The house came with electric baseboard heat, but she'd never used it. She stoked an efficient airtight stove and the racks of firewood she'd split, stacked, and covered with tin next to the house would keep her warm for years to come. She planned to keep cutting wood from her property, but at age 73, she tired of bucking and hauling wood for neighbors who were unable to do it themselves. "I'd like to maybe take a break from cutting wood all summer," she said.

She continues to be an active EMT for the upper Clearwater, going on an average of 25 calls a year. She also serves as the auctioneer at the annual fundraiser for the volunteer ambulance service. In a crowd where she knows everyone, she has no trouble pushing for generosity and people are more than a little reluctant to argue with Penny Keck.

I talked to Penny about my hike up to the old ranger station at Moose Creek. Neither my descriptions of the main Selway trail being in good shape or the ranger station being a shadow of its former activity drew a response. She didn't engage in nostalgia or criticism. In recent years she's done an oral history interview for the Selway-Bitterroot Wilderness History Project, talking about bridge construction and winter life in the wilderness. And she's talked to the young people of the Selway-Bitterroot Frank Church Foundation about the old days when she ran multiple crews in the wilderness.

The following year, when I stopped by on my way to another spring Selway River hike, Penny recounted the previous fire year's intensity. At 10:30 on an August night she got a call from a neighbor saying one of more than a dozen fires along the Clearwater River was burning on their ridge-top, lighting up the sky. Penny turned on all her sprinklers and waited to see if flames moved to the forested hill on her land above the house. She'd already reduced fuels on the hill and she expected the fire to stay low on the ground and not climb into the tree crowns.

At 1 a.m. a young deputy sheriff pulled into her driveway to tell her the area was declared a Level 3 Evacuation, which is translated as: Go,

Leave Immediately. She told him thanks for the notice, she had it under control and was not leaving. She didn't tell him that she was an old fire pro, that she had fusee flares in her back pockets and was ready to do a back-burn on the hillside.

The fire never reached her land and the next day she surveyed the effects on surrounding lands to consider her next preventative actions. More than 150,000 acres burned along the Selway and Clearwater rivers in 2015, mostly on state and private lands. It may have been luck that the flames didn't reach Penny's place. She was ready.

Penny continues see old friends from the wilderness years and is always happy to have friends stop by. She sometimes meets Joyce Seamans—one of the older generation of Forest Service women who carried the title of "the ranger's wife" with pride—for lunch on her periodic big shopping trips to Costco in Lewiston. Penny stays busy, as always.

As connections from people in the early days of wilderness fade and drop away, it gets more challenging to retain a vibrant linkage with the past. For a symbolic gesture to reconnect with the old ways, and to operate a ranger station, a good step would be to rebuild the Moose Creek Shake Shack. Former trail crew foreman and station guard Dale Swee, who became a Forest Service staff specialist at rebuilding and restoring historic cabins, could likely be called back into action, at a price, to train and to lead a reconstruction crew.

Swee could teach some young people how to frame and sheath a building to the exact specs as before, peeling red fir poles and splitting cedar shakes. He could also show how to clean, organize and use all the tools to maintain a working ranger station. Swee could lead the way for a young person to be the next station guard, maintaining the base of operations and outfitting a crew.

Those of us who got a taste of wilderness when we were young valued the unity of purpose, the common goals, the mutual trust and the lasting friendships. Operational ranger stations were not then, and are not now, a luxury but a necessity to manage the surrounding territory. The

Tom McKean, Susan Irizarry and Andrew Bushnell hike out, Frank Church-River of No Return Wilderness, 2014 *John McCarthy*

bonds forged among work crews in isolation were then, and could be again, an extra value and are also part of the American heritage.

Retaining some ranger stations, appropriately staffed and in working order, would serve the traditional, practical function to stage maintenance, guidance, and study of the surrounding lands. Teaching young people the skills and attitudes of the pioneers from these stations would continue the social alliances drawn from American history.

People who want convenience, comfort, speed, motors, and mechanization, whether it's chainsaws, campgrounds, mountain bikes, or ATVs, can go to the hundreds of millions of acres of public lands surrounding wilderness. Those lands and trails also need and deserve attention. Cooperative support, not concessions or conflicts, benefit everyone's appreciation of public lands.

All of us who value wilderness would be wise to understand more about the surrounding lands and the people who live nearby. The last half century has been a time of major change, even turmoil, in the rural West, with increased urbanization in Western states and a shift away from natural resource economies. The changes have not been easy or welcomed in many places. The causes are numerous: from market shifts, depleted resources, competing interests, mechanization, out migration of people and capitol, boom and bust, and environmental protections. Economic value generated from wilderness has not been realized in many communities, with gateways to National Parks perhaps the exception. These economic and social struggles in rural communities put people on edge and do not bring people together, especially with outsiders. Recognition of different ideas and interests can be difficult in all directions.

In the transition from open, untamed land to intentional designated wilderness, Americans made a commitment to keep some lands as pristine as possible. Enough people cared about wilderness to structure standards to retain its values and traditions. Vast valleys, mountain ranges, river systems, wetlands, and prairies were lost to development before enough people determined to keep some lands forever wilderness. A growing risk today is loss of social connectivity to our wilderness. The risk is forgetting how to be in wilderness.

Wilderness itself is not in crisis. Wilderness thrives with natural resilience. Wilderness holds the beauty and mystery of life, is both fragile and solid, is both timeless and in transition. The importance of wilderness is great and well worth investing in, even in the face of many other current and pending disasters in dire need of attention.

We have the opportunity to be in wilderness and to celebrate our wilderness. We carry forth from the wise ones who struggled to give us the opportunity. We pass on the wildest of our lands to future generations. It's as simple and as complicated as the wilderness itself.

Wilderness stands as its own value. People do not control wilderness. People learn from wilderness, taking away knowledge of nature, beauty, and self. Wilderness doesn't need people. People need wilderness.

ACKNOWLEDGEMENTS

IN THE DECADES-LONG JOURNEY to craft this book, many people provided assistance along the way. Its final completion reflects their good counsel, encouragement, and direct contributions. I hope to have proven worthy of their faith.

All the people who I interviewed, who provided words, information and ideas, photographs, and background made this work possible. To all those who are quoted and referenced in the text, I appreciate the time and insights shared, and often your hospitality at homes and camps. In crafting these stories, I hope to have done justice to all our stories.

First among the contributors is Richard I. Walker, known to his friends as Dick Walker. Dick is not only the primary photographer, he helped frame a photographic concept and visual story. Over the years, Dick also shared with me many stories about wilderness, from his times on the ground and from his historical studies. In addition to his personal photographs from more than six decades, his historical photo collection chronicles the homestead, hunting guide, and early Forest Service eras to provide context and appreciation across time. He also opened his archives of historical material on wilderness. Many of the reports, memos, letters, and journals tapped in the writing came from his extensive files, which have not yet been fully cataloged for use by other writers and researchers.

Among the advance readers, Mike Medberry dug deepest into details and ideas, Rich Rayhill pushed my assumptions and intentions, and Megan Rae gave a much appreciated contemporary review. Sarah Walker helped make the chapter on our friend Warren Miller be more accurate and real.

An earlier version of the book concept included an additional set of people who shared hours of their thoughts and provided important background on wilderness, both from their lives and in history. While these interviews did not become detailed in the final book, their ideas contributed to my learning and understanding. I thank Ian Barlow, Don Baty, Bob Oset, Paul Snyder, Larry Keown, Jim Dolan, Wendell Beardsley, and Tom Kovalicky for their time and insights.

Unfortunately, through the course of life, a number of people who figured in the book's arc are no longer with us. They are missed and I am grateful to have known: Dolly Koons, Don Easthouse, Jim Bradley, Woody Hesselbarth, Art Seamans, and Connie Saylor-Johnson were all part of the Moose Creek story.

The origins of the book grew from story assignments in the wilderness as a reporter for the *Lewiston Morning Tribune*. I approached the adventures with open mindedness and support from editors Diane Pettit, Barry Kough, and Paul Emerson. Now under the fourth generation of direction and inspiration from the Alford family, the *Lewiston Tribune* remains the best newspaper in Idaho and one of the best small papers in the nation.

For all the people who are quoted and mentioned in the book, my intention was to treat your words and ideas with care, leading to a greater understanding of wilderness and other wild places. Responsibility for any success is linked to your participation, while the inevitable mistakes are all my own.

In bringing the project to conclusion, special appreciation goes to the team at Caxton Press – publisher Scott Gipson, designer Jocelyn Robertson, and editor Steven Hatcher.

One person kept a fire under me and a light shining for guidance,: my Babette McCarthy Munting, who is always the most welcome explorer of the wilderness with me.

SELECTED BIBLIOGRAPHY

and reading list

Agee, James K. *Fire Ecology of Pacific Northwest Forests*. Island Press, 1993.

Akenson, Jim. *7003 Days: 21 years in the Frank Church River of No Return Wilderness*. Caxton Press, 2016.

Arney, Jo. *Wilderness and the Common Good: A New Ethic of Citizenship*. Fulcrum Publishing, 2015.

Barker, Rocky. "*Scorched Earth: How the Fires of Yellowstone Changed America*. Island Press, 2005.

Byl, Christine. *Dirt Work: An Education in the Woods*. Beacon Press, 2013.

Cooley, Earl. *Trimotor and Trail*. Mountain Press, 1984.

Curtis, A.B. *White Pines and Fires: Cooperative Forestry in Idaho*. University of Idaho Press, 1983.

Egan, Timothy. *The Big Burn: Teddy Roosevelt & the Fire That Saved America*. Houghton Mifflin Harcourt, 2009.

Finkin, Arnold I., *Weather and Climate of the Selway-Bitterroot Wilderness*. University of Idaho Press, 1983.

Harvey, Mark. *Wilderness Forever: Howard Zahniser and the Path to the Wilderness Act*. University of Washington Press, 2005.

Holm, Richard H. Jr. *Bound for the Backcountry: A History of Idaho's Remote Airstrips*. Cold Mountain Press, 2012.

Kinsey, Darius and Tabitha. *Kinsey, Photographer: A Half-Century of Negatives*", Black Dog & Leventhal Publishers, 1978.

Koch, Elers. *Forty Years a Forester*. Mountain Press, 1998.

—*History of the 1910 Forest Fires - Idaho & Western Montana*. U.S. Department of Agriculture, 2010 reprint.

Maclean, Norman. A River Runs Through It and Other Stories. University of Chicago Press, 1973.

Medberry, Mike. *On the Dark Side of the Moon: A Journey of Recovery*. Caxton Press, 2012.

Moore, AnneMarie, and Dennis Baird. *Wild Places Preserved: The Story of Bob Marshall in Idaho*. University of Idaho Library, 2009.

Moore, Bud "*The Lochsa Story: Land Ethics in the Bitterroot Mountains*. Mountain Press, 1996.

Nash, Roderick. *Wilderness and the American Mind*. Yale University Press, 1967.

Scott, Doug. *The Enduring Wilderness*. Fulcrum Press, 2004.

—. *Our Wilderness: America's Common Ground*. Fulcrum Press, 2009.

Snyder, Gary. *Earth House Hold*. New Directions, 1969.

—. *The Back Country*. New Directions, 1971.

—. *Turtle Island*. New Directions, 1974.

Swanson, Frederick H. *Where Roads Will Never Reach: Wilderness and Its Visionaries in the Northern Rockies*. University of Utah Press, 2015.

U.S. Department of Agriculture. *When the Mountains Roared: Stories of the 1910 Fires*. 2010 reprint.

WEBSITES

Arthur Carhart National Wilderness Training Center: http://carhart.wilderness.net/index.cfm

Bud Moore Photographs and Sound Recordings, Montana Memory Project:
http://mtmemory.org/cdm/search/collection/p16013coll58/page/3

The Selway-Bitterroot Wilderness History Project:
https://selwaybitterrootproject.wordpress.com/

WILDERNESS TRAIL & STEWARDSHIP ORGANIZATIONS

Idaho Trails Association. Idaho Trails Association, 2019. idahotrailsassociation.org.

Montana Wilderness Association. Montana Wilderness Association, 2019. wildmontana.org/discover-the-wild/volunteer-trail-crew.

Selway-Bitterroot Frank Church Foundation.Selway Bitterroot Frank Church Foundation, 2019. selwaybitterroot.org.

National Wilderness Stewardship Alliance. National Wilderness Stewardship Alliance, 2019. wildernessalliance.org.

PHOTOS

All photographs in Selway-Bitterroot Wilderness unless otherwise specified.

Cover – Warren Q. Miller at Bear Creek, 1978 *Warren Q. Miller*
Back cover – Emil Keck rebuilds foot bridge over Moose Creek, 1983 *Glenn Cruickshank*
Richard Kuhl on Moose Ridge, 1976 *Tim Rich*
John McCarthy in Hells Canyon Wilderness, 2017 *Babette Munting*

CPSIA information can be obtained
at www.ICGtesting.com
Printed in the USA
FFHW011120090519
52369550-57767FF

9 780870 046254